Later Woolen Mills
in Oregon

Clarence Morton Bishop
1878-1969
Founder
Pendleton Woolen Mills, Inc. 1909

Later Woolen Mills
in Oregon

A History of the Woolen Mills Which
Followed the Pioneer Mills

By

ALFRED L. LOMAX

Professor Emeritus of Business Administration
University of Oregon

BINFORDS & MORT, *Publishers*

Portland · Oregon · 97242

Dedicated to the memory of my good friend, Clarence Morton Bishop, whose leadership and genius as a woolen textile manufacturer built the Pendleton Woolen Mills into a company and a name known far beyond the boundaries of the Oregon Country.

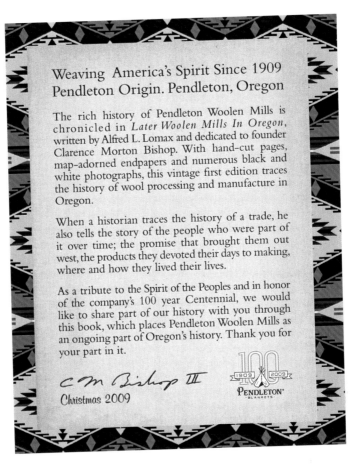

Weaving America's Spirit Since 1909
Pendleton Origin. Pendleton, Oregon

The rich history of Pendleton Woolen Mills is chronicled in *Later Woolen Mills In Oregon*, written by Alfred L. Lomax and dedicated to founder Clarence Morton Bishop. With hand-cut pages, map-adorned endpapers and numerous black and white photographs, this vintage first edition traces the history of wool processing and manufacture in Oregon.

When a historian traces the history of a trade, he also tells the story of the people who were part of it over time; the promise that brought them out west, the products they devoted their days to making, where and how they lived their lives.

As a tribute to the Spirit of the Peoples and in honor of the company's 100 year Centennial, we would like to share part of our history with you through this book, which places Pendleton Woolen Mills as an ongoing part of Oregon's history. Thank you for your part in it.

C M Bishop III

Christmas 2009

1909 100 2009
PENDLETON
BLANKETS

Contents

Part I
Willamette Valley Woolen Mills

[v]

the enterprise becomes a Koppe family business—ceases operation in 1950.

Part II
The Oregon Coast Woolen Mills

Part III
Eastern Oregon Woolen Mills
and Scouring Plants

Part IV
Southern Oregon Woolen Mills

Part V
Mill Ends

Part VI
Pendleton Woolen Mills

CHAPTER XIX—New Owners Vitalize the Woolen Mill

C.P. Bishop of Salem and T.C. Taylor of Pendleton discuss ways of saving the woolen mill—Bishop family incorporates the Pendleton Woolen Mills, February 16, 1909—Clarence and Roy Bishop become managers—concrete building erected —Rounsley hired and Jacquard looms installed—Blue and Gold label emphasized—Washougal mills acquired—Multnomah Mohair Mills becomes Oregon Worsted Company— Vancouver, Washington woolen mills started—Portland office opened—Chauncey and two sons, Charles Kay and Robert, move to Pendleton—Clarence and Harriet Broughton married —Coast Mills Wool Company—building at N.W. 9th and Flanders leased—Washougal mill fire—Clarence Morton Bishop, Jr., and Broughton Hayward Bishop born—fixed marketing and merchandising policy established—Charles C. Wintermute employed—death of Chauncey Bishop—Melvin D. Fell superintendent at Pendleton mill—J.D. Buchanan and E.W. Haggerty employed as accountants—Haggerty becomes Corporate Controller of Finances—Meier & Frank warehouse leased, purchased later—effects of Great Depression—Ernest N. Brooke, superintendent and designer at Washougal—statistical record of the company—Earl C. Rogness, accountant, added to staff—Pollock, Schultz & Boyd, Los Angeles pants firm purchased—Charles K. Bishop goes to Washougal—James C. Aitchison production manager for all three mills—national advertising campaign begun— garment business expands—Robert Bishop recommends factory in Omaha, Nebraska—Clarence M. Bishop, Jr., joins staff—Clarence and Robert Bishop contemplate womenswear market—Frank King employed—"49er" jacket an immediate success—death of Roy Bishop—Broughton H. Bishop joins staff—merger of Washougal Woolen Mills with Pendleton Woolen Mills—Portland specializes in menswear, Omaha in womenswear—Oregon Woolen Mills plant bought—men's slacks manufacture moved to Oregon City—Disneyland store proves outstanding success—garment factory built at Milwaukie, Portland suburb—Foundation Woolen Mills leased

Illustrations

Albany Woolen Mills Company factory facing the Willamette
River.   [*Author's collection*]

Thomas Kay Woolen Mill Company original building, 1889.
[*Thomas Kay—third from right*]

The millrace whose waters powered the looms and spinning frames of the Thomas Kay Woolen Mill, Salem, Oregon.   [*Author's collection*]

Introduction
and
Acknowledgments

The present volume is companion to the earlier *Pioneer Woolen Mills in Oregon*, published in 1941. It concludes the project initiated by Clarence M. Bishop, president of the Pendleton Woolen Mills, of writing and publishing the complete history of Oregon woolen mills. Mr. Bishop handed this important work to the then School of Business Administration of the University of Oregon, and the research was begun in 1921.

The book covers the histories of the woolen and scouring mills which were organized, established and in full operation during the last twenty-five years of the nineteenth century and the first two decades of the twentieth century. The Brownsville and the Oregon City mills, which were rooted in the pioneer period but operated well into the twentieth, are not included, and their later history must wait for future research and writing.*

The title of the book was chosen to indicate not only a chronological distinction between the pioneer mills and those which came later, but to show geographic differentiation. The pioneer factories were concentrated in the Willamette Valley with the

---

*Many of the chapters appeared in the Oregon Historical Quarterly with permission to reprint them, also the Lane County Historian, and local newspapers. The Pendleton Woolen Mills chapter and the Paris Woolen Mills chapter have never been previously published.

exception of the unsuccessful The Dalles mill, and the profitable southern Oregon Ashland mill. The factories which came later were widely dispersed from the Coos County seacoast to the semi-arid sheep country of Wasco and Union counties, respectively, although the Willamette Valley still claimed the largest number.

Like the predecessor mills which were established on the availability of raw wool, waterpower and markets, but with a deficiency of technicians, the later mills depended upon these factors also, but with less emphasis on waterpower as the more expensive steam-operated machinery was installed. A pool of skilled workers was available, many of them descendants of those trained earlier under the supervision of English and Scotch immigrant technicians employed by the pioneer mills. Local townspeople augmented this core of workers.

As railroads came to the Pacific Northwest in the 1880s and 1890s market contacts improved, and Oregon-made woolen goods, especially blankets, achieved a national reputation for their fine quality and steadfast colors.

Most of the mills cultivated the Indian Reservation trade through the Indian agencies and traders on the reservations. The Pendleton Company took full advantage of its proximity to the Umatilla Indian Reservation.

Financial promotions involved local investment capital augmented by local bank service which was not available to the pioneer mills. Investment of family fortunes whose members exemplified high administrative and executive talent was much in evidence.

Every important Oregon town was eager to have a payroll-producing woolen mill. If Salem can have one why can't we? was the attitude, thus giving rise to the habit of industrial imitation. The mood was like an economic fever heightened by promises of eastern woolen mill owners to move their factories to the Pacific Coast, providing bonuses were promised. Even local entrepreneurs demanded this concession, but too often these gratuities were not forth coming and enthusiasm declined. Citizens' committee reports (mouthpieces of boards of trade) approved or rejected these propositions with the result that many projects were stillborn in committee rooms.

Occasionally, eastern money was used to finance a project, as when the Pendleton Wool-Scouring and Packing Company was organized by two New England wool merchants. The most successful woolen mills were financed by family money exemplified by the Thomas Kay mills at Salem and Waterloo; Wilbur at Stayton; Koppes at Eugene; and Bishops at Pendleton and Washougal.

When close family supervision prevailed, the mills lived long and useful industrial lives, some of half a century or more. When their existence ended it was either because of family disinterest, changing competitive conditions, or unwarranted capital expenditures to modernize an old mill. Regional competition of Southern mills and the impact of synthetic fibers were other aspects of the problem.

Labor disputes scarcely marred congenial employer-employee relations. Workers for the most part had a high regard for their owner-managers and management reciprocated. That mill would be an exception where the owner or superintendent, walking through the factory between clacking looms and whirring spindles, would not call the workers by their first names. In family-owned mills this informal relationship was especially pronounced as younger members of the proprietor's family worked their respective ways through the different departments into responsible administrative positions, but they never lost contact with their former colleagues.

Formal source material, especially business records, were irritatingly unavailable. Factory fires were a common cause of record destruction; owners' indifference to record preservation when the mills closed down was another. A much-appreciated exception was the perusal of the minute books, stock certificate record and correspondence of the Thomas Kay Woolen Mill Company made available by the understanding courtesy of Thomas Kay III., great-grandson of the eminent Oregon pioneer industrialist, Thomas Kay.

The most satisfying sources of information other than those mentioned above were the local newspapers, whose editors, strong advocates of home industry with its lucrative payrolls, printed almost daily stories of such activity. Their value lay in presenting chronological sequences of events such as promotion programs, the names of subscribers to stock solicitations, dates of incorporation, arrival of machinery, fires, and other relevant news, which, when pieced together created a coordinated pattern of the mills' affairs.

Such research was facilitated by the very complete University of Oregon microfilm library of Oregon newspapers. Grateful acknowledgment is made to Frances Schoen and her staff for their courteous and helpful assistance.

Martin Schmitt, Curator of Special Collections, University of Oregon Library, and Glenda Kupper, library assistant, permitted the use of the J. K. Weatherford correspondence files in the preparation of the Waterloo mill chapter. Records of the Eugene Woolen Mills Company, deposited in the library by Carl Koppe, former president of the company, were most valuable.

Vitality and color were added to the various mills' histories by personal interviews with persons associated with the industry, especially Clarence M. Bishop, president of the Pendleton Woolen Mills; Charles M. Carter, president of the Portland Woolen Mills; Carl Koppe, of the Eugene Woolen Mill Company and later superintendent of the Paris Woolen Mills; and Melvin Fell of the Pendleton staff for his help in recalling his father's experiences with the Pendleton Wool-Scouring and Packing Company.

Sincere acknowledgment is made of the continuing interest of members of the Bishop family in their desire to complete this industrial history project initiated by Clarence M. Bishop fifty-two years ago. Without their help this book would never have been published.

Special acknowledgment is made to Mr. E. W. Haggerty who was closely associated with Mr. Clarence M. Bishop from 1929 through 1969, and as a collaborator in the history of the Pendleton Woolen Mills.

My wife Nancy deserves a bountiful share of gratitude for her unlimited patience listening to the repititious reading and corrections of the manuscript and her sometimes sharp, but always constructive criticisms.

Alfred Lewis Lomax

Eugene, Oregon

PART I

Willamette Valley Woolen Mills

Chapter I

THE ALBANY WOOLEN MILL

"There is a refreshing hum"

EARLIEST manifestations of wool fiber manufacturing in the Willamette Valley were the simple carding machines used to supplant the laborious hand-carding operations of pioneer housewives. E. L. Perham and Company had one at Albany in 1854, as did A. L. Stinson, who had the only hosiery mill in the state. In 1873 Stinson moved to Jefferson, Marion County. In 1875 the $10,000 Jefferson Hosiery Company owned by Dickinson and Jerguensery was reported at Albany.[1] Philomen Crawford had a picker and carding machine on a $2,000 investment employing one female and two children. Four months' operation on 2,500 pounds of wool produced 2,130 pounds of rolls valued at $1,650.[2]

Other evidence of a growing industrial awareness in Linn County was Jim Elkins 1873 construction of a twelve-mile canal from the South Santian River near Lebanon to Albany at a cost of $6,200. It was first used for floating loaded barges to Albany which were horsedrawn back to Lebanon, but its principal use was for power for the flour, woolen, and lumber mills clustered at the Linn County seat.

(1) *Historical Atlas Map of Marion and Linn Counties, Oregon,* Edgar Williams and Co., San Francisco, 1878
(2) Ninth U.S. Census, 1870

While these minor industrial activities were casually instrumental in stimulating local interest in wool manufacturing, the successful pioneer woolen mills at Salem, Oregon City and Brownsville set the pace.[3] The Willamette Woolen Manufacturing Company at Salem had another year to go before it would burn on May 3, 1876, a victim of mismanagement and political maneuvering. The Jacobs Brothers' successful Oregon City mill would be winning prizes for top quality blankets at the Philadelphia and Paris expositions. But Albany could point with pride to Linn County's pasturing farm flocks whose fleeces bypassed it for want of a woolen mill.

Faint evidence of industrial promotion appeared on November 16, 1875, when Thomas Monteith, J. F. Backensto, D. M. Thompson, Samuel E. Young and C. P. Burkhart incorporated the Albany Woolen Mills Company for $12,000. And the 1880 U. S. Census reported P. V. Crawford's carding machine on the Calapooia at Albany with a capital investment of $1,800, employing one skilled male at $3.00 a day. As encouragement, Stewart and Gray announced a $12,000-$15,000 gift of cash, real estate, waterpower and building materials to any company which would establish a four-set woolen mill at Albany. Two acres of land south of the Falls of the Santiam and the canal were included in the offer.[4] Stayton in Marion County boasted a carding machine, some small businesses and "two drunkard factories."

(3) Alfred L. Lomax, *Pioneer Woolen Mills in Oregon*, Binfords & Mort, Portland, 1941

(4) W.G. Steel, *Resources of Oregon and Washington*. Vol. 3, No. 2, pp. 7-8

Woolen mill gossip was rampant at this stage of Oregon's industrial growth and provided newspaper editors with wordy ammunition to boost home industries in their respective localities. News reached Eugene of proposed woolen and flour mills at Albany, evidence of that community's enterprise as compared to Eugene's lethargy. The former was The Albany Woolen Mills Company, incorporated by seventeen Albany businessmen on May 16, 1883, with a captialization of $50,000. Construction was to start in the late summer or early fall of that year. But the Portland *Oregonian's* New Year's edition of 1885 did not list an Albany woolen mill among three flour mills, two furniture factories, a sash and door factory, a wire cloth and mattress factory, and three foundries and machine shops. Apparently this was one of several stillborn projects characteristic of the industry at this time.

Compensating and eminently more stimulating were the promotional activities of Colonel T. Egenton Hogg and his Oregon Pacific Railroad, then building from Yaquina Bay on the Lincoln County coast to Albany, and planned to run thence via Santiam Pass to an eastern Oregon railroad connection. Albany businessmen had raised $12,000 to purchase a seventy-acre site on the eastern outskirts of the town for car shops, property originally owned by Abram Hackleman who contributed $2,000 toward the project. Hackleman's Addition encompassed much of the business and residential area of present day Albany. Provision for railroad rights-of-way were included in the original plats. When the first train arrived January 6, 1887, over the Albany extension there was much rejoicing. [5]

Wool continued to move north from as far south as Ashland with the Albany firm of Monteith & Seitenbach and Samuel E. Young handling much of the tonnage, which sold for 18c to 21-1/2c a pound.

On July 2, 1887, a citizens' meeting was called to hear the report of a previously appointed committee on woolen mill promotion. Committee members were C. E. Wolverton (later prominent among Oregon's judiciary), J. W. Cusick, and E. J. Lanning; J. L. Cowan was chairman. The principal topic was waterpower and the probability of obtaining a four-acre factory site in proximity to the Falls of the Santiam in which the equities of John A. Crawford and the Santiam Canal Company were involved. Crawford was willing to donate the Elkins Falls portion of seventy-five horsepower for five years and would continue to furnish the same amount of power continuously at the regularly scheduled rates.

The consensus of the meeting was that a joint stock company capitalized for $100,000 should be organized and stock sold to the public, with emphasis on reaching both eastern and local capitalists. A committee composed of George E. Chamberlain (later governor), C. E. Wolverton, and W. H. Goltra was appointed to draw up incorporation papers and arrange for further promotion. Before adjourning, the Albany Woolen Mills Company was so named, but unfortunately the stock books remained unopened.

(5) Leslie M. Scott, *History of the Oregon Country*, IV: 235 Riverside Press, Cambridge, 1924

At this point the affairs of the Brownsville mill are intertwined with the Albany woolen mill promotion. Dissolution of the old, but very profitable Brownsville Woolen Mills Company occurred in 1889, but prior to its termination the Brownsville Woolen Manufacturing Company was incorporated on December 5, 1888, with J. M. Moyer, F. F. Croft from the old company, and Joseph P. Galbraith.

The announcement that Thomas Kay had severed his connection with the old company and was looking for a mill site for his own company had a catalytic effect on industry-conscious Willamette Valley towns, especially Albany, Eugene, and Salem. All three began immediately to raise the usual $20,000 to $25,000 bonus requirement to snare the fat payroll.

Salem met the Kay $20,000 bonus deadline during the first week of March, 1889 to outdo both Albany and Eugene. While the capital city rejoiced over its industrial victory, J. M. Moyer and Fred F. Croft, erstwhile associates of Mr. Kay in the Brownsville woolen mill, were in Albany negotiating for a $25,000 bonus for a proposed woolen mill. They outlined plans for a company capitalized at $75,000 and a factory employing 75-100 "hands," which would bring a $3,500-$4,000 monthly payroll. They were successful in obtaining several $1,000 and $2,000 pledges and many smaller ones. On the strength of this showing the Brownsville Woolen Manufacturing Company bought the whole of Block 115 in Hackleman's Addition to the city of Albany, a site fronting on the Willamette River between the Red Crown Flour Mills on one side and the Farmers' Warehouse on the other, and adjacent to the bridge across the Willamette River.[6] A two story brick building was planned to be finished by September, 1889. John Crawford agreed to furnish waterpower sufficient to run the four-set mill.

New machinery valued at $10,000 began to arrive the second week in April. Construction of the $8,500 factory building was begun two months later when J. M. Moyer, F. F. Croft, John Waters, and J. P. Galbraith gave the go-ahead signal. The three-story brick building on a stone foundation was completed by the middle of September and a wing added to the main building.

Shafting turned in the new factory on December 27, 1889. By the following September sixty people were on the payroll at an average daily wage of $1.15 for skilled workers and $1.00 for unskilled. Goods produced had an annual value of $140,000. Officers of the company were J. M. Moyer, president; J. P. Galbraith, secretary-treasurer; F. F. Croft, superintendent. Capitalization was $75,000 with shares at $500 each.

On June 18, 1891, the Brownsville Woolen Manufacturing Company changed its name to the Albany Woolen Mills Company.[7] On January 12, 1893, articles of incorporation were drawn for the Albany Woolen Mills Company with $100,000 capital stock divided into shares of $500 each. Incorporators were: E. D. Moyer, L. D. Cole, W. T. Cochran, and Robert C. Cochran. Then on July 11, 1893, the

---

(6)   Plat Book 1, p. 2, Linn County Recorder, Albany, Oregon
(7)   File 538, Department of Commerce, Corporation Division, Salem

Brownsville Woolen Manufacturing Company deeded to the Albany Woolen Mills Company for $5,250, Block 115 and Lot 4 both in Hackleman's Addition.[8] The deed was signed by J. M. Moyer, president, and J. P. Galbraith, secretary of the Brownsville company.

Moyer was a very active business man, and among his interests was the Brownsville Woolen Mill Store which he operated under the name of J. M. Moyer & Company, successors to the Brownsville company. In the January 9, 1893, issue of the *Oregonian*, J. M. Moyer & Company, 140 First Street, Portland, advertised they were headquarters for the celebrated Albany Woolen Mills clothing and that "we are the manufacturers." Men's suits sold for $8.50 and up; overcoats $4.00 and up; pants $3.00. L. D. Cole was store manager.

The summer of 1893 came with successful bidding to furnish uniforms and 5,000 blankets for the Oregon National Guard, and blankets, cadet coats, and kersey cloth[9] for the United States Indian Service. Although the panic of 1893 was at its height, the Albany mill and the two Kay mills at Salem and Waterloo created a locally prosperous atmosphere which tended to ameliorate the inevitable hardships which accompany bank and factory failures during such economic reversals. Annual wool consumption of the Albany enterprise was estimated at 350,000 pounds.

(8) Deed Book 46, pp. 466, 467, 468, Linn County Recorder, Albany
(9) A lightweight, smooth surface woolen cloth named after the wool-manufacturing town of Kersey, England

An interesting sidelight on the above-mentioned contract was U. S. Representative Binger Hermann's influence in obtaining a concession from the United States Navy favoring the use of Pacific Coast-made blankets on Pacific Coast-based ships with delivery at San Francisco. New York had been the traditional delivery point. Later, a bill was introduced in Congress making regional contract allocations mandatory.

Repeat orders for blankets for the Indian Service and the United States Army were on the books, as were orders for blankets and uniform cloth for the Oregon National Guard. Other buyers of the Albany Mill's products were the Old Soldiers Home at Roseburg, the Portland Military Band, and the local District Telegraph Company. The factory was now well established and furnished employment to seventy-five people. W. J. Welch was head weaver but resigned in July 1897 and went to Pendleton.

This prosperous condition was rudely interrupted by the appointment of a receiver in bankruptcy (L. Flinn, a banker) in October 1896 upon complaint of J. M. Moyer, L. D. Cole, E. D. Moyer, and Mrs. F. F. Croft, all members of the board of directors. The action was precipitated by the J. M. Moyer Company, Lowenstein & Company of Chicago, creditors for $8,000. Total value of the factory, goods, notes, and accounts receivable was $140,000, obligations $120,000. At this late date it is difficult to explain satisfactorily the exact nature of this action. Shortly thereafter a court order was issued to permit the woolen mill to operate as the volume of orders on hand justified the action. Sometime during 1897, J. M. Moyer & Company declared bankruptcy and paid off its creditors at the rate of seventeen cents on the dollar.

In 1897 Albany declared itself an important Willamette Valley manufacturing center boasting a woolen mill, flour mill, two chair factories, a foundry, sash and door mill, tannery, cigar factory, soda works and a brewery.

On January 29, 1898, the board of directors of the Albany Woolen Mills Company empowered J. M. Moyer, president, and L. D. Cole, secretary, to deliver to L. Flinn, receiver and trustee in bankruptcy, all the real, personal and mixed property of the company for the sum of one dollar. The document was signed by J.M. Moyer, Mrs. E.M. Moyer, and Amor A. Tussing.[10] On February 10, 1898, reincorporation was made under the title of the Albany Woolen Mills, capital stock $30,000 at $100 a share.[11]

On February 8, L. Flinn and wife Cynthia S. Flinn had sold block 115 together with buildings, fixtures and machinery of the factory for $17,500 to P. A. Goodwin, the only bidder of a group composed of himself, Patrick F. McGhee and Stephen L. Riley. Next day Goodwin deeded back to the Albany Woolen Mills Company the following described property:[12]

---

(10) Flinn was president and principal stockholder in the First National Bank of Albany, which was referred to as Flinn's Bank

(11) File 5922, Department of Commerce, Salem

(12) Deed Book 59, pp. 348, 356-59, Linn County Recorder, Albany

    2 sets of Davis & Furber 48 x 48 iron frame cards
    4 sets of Johnson & Bassett self-operating jacks,
        240 spindles each
    2 Crompton 92 inch fancy looms, 27 harness, 4 x 4 boxes
    6 Crompton 115 inch cam looms, 2, 3, 4, leaf, 4 x 4 boxes
    2 Crompton 109 inch fancy looms, 4 x 4 1886 pattern
    6 Knowles 92 inch fancy looms, 30 harness, 4 x 4 box
    1 wool opener, dusting machine, picker, finishing
        machine, dryer, dye vats, wool washer and other
        machinery and a pullery.

McGhee was named superintendent of the 65-man plant which continued to manufacture cheviots, tweeds, flannels, and robes. No shoddy was used. Markets were in Portland, San Francisco, Milwaukee, and Chicago. Monthly production of goods was estimated at $10,000.

Directors at this time were E. W. Langdon, W. L. Vance, S. E. Young, D. P. Mason, P. F. McGhee. Officers elected were Young, president; Goodwin, secretary; Flinn, manager.

Sometime during the year W.A. Semple, an experienced woolen mill man from Norwalk, Connecticut, became manager. Continued output was assured with orders on the books for a full nine months ahead, or until September 1899. Partly on the strength of this prosperity, and possibly influenced by the Spanish-American War and the Alaska gold rush, plans were made for expansion. It was even suggested that the Brownsville factory be leased, but nothing came of this.

Semple's enthusiasm for the woolgrowing and woolen textile opportunities in Oregon were evidenced in a speech he made before the Manufacturers' Association of Portland (then propagandizing for a woolen mill) in January 1900. He pointed out the unsurpassed quality of both the wool and the chemical-free, pure water, important attributes in washing and dyeing. Furthermore, the moist, temperate climate of western Oregon decreased the static electricity created by the fibers as they passed through the carding and other machines.

He elaborated upon the possibilities of manufacturing Scotch cheviots and broadcloths, fine kerseys and meltons.[13] He expanded upon the quality of Oregon-made woolen goods which eastern manufacturers had long acclaimed, and wondered how such fine goods could be turned out in small factories. These same people prophecied that Oregon was destined to be one of the leading textile states of the nation, a prediction which has since been adequately fulfilled over the years. Charles Coopey, a Portland tailor and continuous booster for home industry, especially woolen mills, likewise gave vent to his feelings on the subject.

The Albany woolen mill was not alone in anticipating the benefits to accrue from exploiting the Alaska market. All of the Oregon mills featured mackinaw cloth and blankets. Wholesale houses in Portland and Seattle were the distributors. Prices for the Klondike trade were posted in the January 1, 1898 *Morning Oregonian* New Year's edition as follows:

	Portland	Tacoma	Seattle
Heavy woolen underwear—3 suits	$7.50	$9.00	$9.00
Heavy woolen overshirts—2 suits	4.50	4.50	4.50

(13) Well-fulled, heavy woolen cloth with a short nap used for overcoats. Named for Melton-Mowbray, England, famous also for its pork pies

Heavy woolen socks—6 pair	2.00	2.00	2.00
Heavy woolen mitts—6 pair	2.40	3.00	3.00
Heavy mackinaw—1	4.00	4.50	4.50
Heavy mackinaw pants—2 pair	5.00	6.50	5.50
Wool-lined overalls—2 pair	2.50	3.00	3.00
Sleeping bag mackinaw lined	10.00	15.00	16.00
Woolen sweaters—2			2.50
Wool cap—1	.50	.90	.50
Food, tools, cooking utensils, etc.	—	—	—
Total	$335.67	$381.71	$381.72

Both administrative and marketing changes were made in 1900. S.E. Young of the First National Bank of Albany was president, and P.A. Goodwin, secretary, from which it may be assumed that some sort of financial control was deemed necessary.

Offices were opened in San Francisco at 214 Pine Street; in Chicago at 164-65 Market Street; and in Louisville, Kentucky at 1498 Story Avenue. Under Semple's management the mill was producing 175,000 yards of cloth annually.

The next two years of the company's affairs are locked in obscurity. Apparently the mill was involved financially and turned to the newly-formed Bannockburn Manufacturing Company for assistance. This company was incorporated on March 14, 1903 by Portland business men, namely Charles Coopey, F.A. Bancroft, James C. Stuart, R.W. Wilbur, and Harvey W. Scott, eminent editor of the *Oregonian*. The obvious purpose of the company was to lend financial assistance to the Albany woolen mill, perhaps with an ultimate outright ownership. One senses the guiding hand of Charles Coopey in this transaction; not only would he be engaged in the manufacture of fine fabrics, but a portion of the output would be channeled into his tailoring establishment which had a reputation for excellent workmanship on custom-tailored suits and uniforms.

Evidence of the above transaction is found in the Linn County Recorder's office[14] which shows that the Albany Woolen Mills Company was bound to the Bannockburn Manufacturing Company in the sum of $35,000. Terms were that $15,000 was to be repaid in $5,000 installments on or before January 1, 1904. The balance of $20,000 was backed by a mortgage which included Block 115 in Hackleman's Addition (the factory site) and all of the furniture, fixtures, tools, machinery, etc., except the right-of-way owned by the Corvallis & Eastern Railroad and the Oregon & California Railroad. The $5,000 equal installments on the mortgage were due on July 1 and January 1, the final payment being due on January 1, 1906.

Late in July the mill was leased to the Oregon City woolen mill while repairs were made to their fire-gutted plant, an arrangement which enabled them to fill their orders on hand, and provided financial aid to the Albany company.

Frequent visits were made by the Bannockburn directors to their Albany property; Charles Coopey was especially zealous in maintaining contact. His announcement that a clothing manufacturing plant would be established in Portland upon expiration of the Oregon City lease brought optimistic comments, although some people thought that such a factory should be located in Albany.

---

(14) Deed Book 73, pp. 494-95, Linn County Recorder

The old saying that one person's bad luck is another's fortune was exemplified when shortly after the expiration of the Oregon City lease, the Portland Woolen Mill Company's two-year-old factory building at Sellwood burned to the ground on February 18, 1904. On March 14 Superintendent Charles H. Carter moved twenty employees to Albany to continue his disrupted production schedule. Enough orders were on the books to keep the mill going for a year, or at least until the new building at St. Johns, a Portland suburb, could be completed.

In the meantime, President Coopey and Secretary H.M. Grant had met with members of the Alco Club to discuss refinancing plans of the Albany mill. It was suggested that a $6,000 block of stock be allocated to Albany and sold at par value ($500 a share) instead of the 33-1/3% above par on the open market. Promises were made that as soon as the required capital was raised a knitting mill and a pants factory would be added, thus promoting the local clothing market and saving freight on such goods now imported from eastern clothing manufacturers. R.B. Montague and J.L. Tomlinson were appointed a solicitation committee.

The intermittent and fluctuating business plight of the Albany woolen mill was further aggravated by a disastrous $75,000 fire on the morning of March 29, 1905. The alarm sounded at eight o'clock, shortly after work had begun. So fierce was the heat and so rapidly did the fire spread in the grease-saturated building, that employees rushed to safety regardless of their personal belongings. Women ran through the doorways with their aprons over their heads as protection against the heat.

Typical of woolen mill fires, combustion started in the drying room annex where cotton was being processed. Efforts of the fire department were ineffective on the factory building, but the nearby flouring mill and Farmers Company warehouse were saved. While the fire was at its height, the Women's Christian Temperance Union served coffee to the fire laddies.

The loss was centered mainly in the factory structure and the machinery. Only a small stock of raw materials was on hand and no manufactured goods. In the 55 x 150-foot three-story brick building, the top floor housed the sorting department; the second floor the picking, carding, spooling, and brushing operations; while on the first floor were the looms, inspection, and finishing departments. An annex on the river bank sheltered the dyeing, cleaning, and drying divisions, and the boiler room. The mill was operated by waterpower.

Only six weeks had elapsed since the company had paid off all indebtedness. A.H. Burrell, Portland fire insurance agent, had a $20,000 policy; local Albany agents had $11,800.

The embers had scarcely cooled before the community was conjecturing whether or not the factory would be rebuilt. Hopes rose when Charles Coopey and H.M. Grant appeared in Albany to appraise the the loss and discuss the situation with the town's businessmen. The twenty-inch-thick walls of the gutted building had withstood the heat as had the iron pillars. The boiler survived as did some overhead shafting and a few looms which possibly could be rebuilt. There was talk that the directors of the Bannockburn company would rebuild with the addition of a cravennetting and knitting department.

On May 4 a meeting was held at the courthouse where President Ellis of the Albany Commercial Club and J.W. Weatherford, prominent attorney, made enthusiastic speeches emphasizing the investment opportunities in Oregon woolen mills. Weatherford as a boy and young man had worked in the Brownsville woolen mill where his lifelong friendship with Thomas Kay began.

Weatherford pointed out that the Brownsville company had been a moneymaker as were also the Jacobs Brothers Oregon City factory and the Thomas Kay mill at Salem. It was alleged that the Albany mill would have been profitable if a diversion of funds had not been made to support the clothing store in Portland. Others who spoke feelingly were Dr. W.H. Davis, mayor; officers of the First National Bank; and F.J. Miller of the Albany Iron Works. G.E. Sanders, a bank director, pledged $1,000 for the bank, Miller $500, and Weatherford $750 for two clients he represented.

Although the money-raising campaign was reasonably successful, interest lagged to such a degree that the outlook for a rebuilt woolen mill was pessimistic. A glint of optimism prevailed when a report was circulated that Jacobs Brothers at Oregon City would rebuild the factory if local capital would support the move, but nothing came of the rumor.

In May, 1907 an organization of eastern capitalists which called itself the Willamette Woolen Mills Company indicated it would bring a ten-set mill to Albany. The company was headed by G.A. Huddleston of Worcester, Massachusetts, who it was reported would distribute the products of the proposed mill through company-owned wholesale and retail branches. But nothing more is reported of this scheme or any others to make Albany a flourishing woolen mill town.

One regrets that financial and other business records are not available to give greater continuity and historical accuracy to this account of the Albany woolen mill. These and the Commercial Club minutes of meetings were either burned in the fire or in some manner destroyed. While woolen mills flourished elsewhere in Oregon at the turn of the century, the Bannockburn company in spite of its eminent incorporators, lacked the vigor to live, and Albany businessmen the promotional aggressiveness to restore the whir of spindles and the clatter of looms to make the town an important woolen mill center.

Chapter II

THOMAS KAY WOOLEN MILLS COMPANY

"Salem becomes a woolen manufacturing center again"

THE industrial history of Salem, Oregon, is traditionally associated with the establishment and operation of woolen mills, first by the pioneer promoter, Joseph Watt, and later by Thomas Kay, the foremost of the English technicians who came to Oregon in pioneer times. After the Willamette Woolen Manufacturing Company factory burned on May 3, 1876,[1] Oregon's capital city was without such a factory until the Thomas Kay Woolen Mill Company was established in 1889. The intervening years were sterile insofar as this industry and Salem were concerned.

There were feeble, perhaps well-intentioned efforts like that of the Willamette Woolen Works Company incorporated on November 17, 1879, for $100,000 by R.P. Earhart, T.W. Davenport, George Edes, Lewis Johnson, L.E. Pratt (former superintendent of the first woolen mill), W.H.H. Walters, and Colonel D.A. Reed. The company had purchased the water rights at the site of the old Willamette Woolen Mill Company on Mill Creek.

---

(1) *Oregon Weekly Statesman*, Salem, May 5, 1876

Another sporadic attempt to industrialize North Salem was that of the Salem Mills Company in 1881 which included in its plans the operation of a woolen factory. Like its paper-born predecessor above, it too, chose the old woolen mill site. Interested parties were William Reid, William Dunbar, John D. Hurst, W.J. Burns of Balfour, Guthrie & Company (an English firm with international branches), Alex P. Ankeny and Ellis G. Hughes. A. Grant was manager of the enterprise which got as far as hauling stone for the foundation, but ceased construction when the subsidy pledged by Salem citizens did not materialize.

The year 1883 brought more promotion and the announcement through the newspapers that a $60,000 mill would soon be erected in Salem financed by the citizens of that city. W.F. Boothby, Emanuel Meyer, T.B. Wait, John Hughes and Squire Farrar were a stock solicitation committee. Before they had finished, $15,000 had been pledged by 281 subscribers including $1,000 from the Capital Lumber Company, and many five and ten dollar pledges.

Five years elapsed before serious consideration was again given to the woolen mill problem, but on the evening of December 18, 1888, an enthusiastic meeting of Salem businessmen was held in the parlors of the Capital National Bank to hear Thomas Kay, recently part owner of the Brownsville woolen mill, discuss the prospects for such a project. J.H. Albert was chairman, C.B. Moores, secretary. Kay's many years' experience in the business, twenty-five of which were in Oregon, mostly with the Brownsville factory, had gained him the reputation and prestige as the most experienced woolen textile man in the state.[2] Matters of policy were not going well with this company in which he owned an interest. A decision to dissolve the corporation some time in August left him free to investigate business opportunities elsewhere, notably in Albany and Salem, both of which places were eager to harbor a woolen mill, as were also Pendleton, Eugene, and Spokane Falls, Washington.

A proposition that he would invest $55,000 in a four-set mill which would eventually employ 400 hands, providing Salem people would raise a $20,000 bonus, met with ready response. Messrs. Moores, Albert, Boothby, Squire Farrar, H.W. Cottle, and R.J. Hendricks were a committee to investigate sites and waterpower rights. Urgency was necessary as Mr. Kay was planning to visit his old home near Leeds, England, the center of woolen textile factories in which vicinity he had worked as a boy.

Interest of the committee centered on the 12th and Ferry streets site of the old tannery and oil mill property owned by the Gray brothers which could be bought for $16,000. January 15, 1889, was the final date for acceptance or rejection of the latter site. In the meantime, and immediately after Christmas the committee was busy endeavoring to raise the $20,000 bonus and working on the option on which they hoped to get an extension. "Twenty-thousand dollars

---

(2) Alfred L. Lomax, *Pioneer Woolen Mills in Oregon*, Binfords & Mort, Portland, Oregon, 1941

is no great sum for a city of our wealth and size to raise," said the editor of the *Capital Journal*. A month passed with very little progress reported on either the bonus or the power site. Kay was in and out of the city working with all interested parties. The Grays finally agreed to sell the Pioneer Oil Mill Company site and its waterpower to Thomas Kay for $15,000, the former owners to retain 150 feet for building purposes.

The big night came on February 7, 1889, when a joint meeting of the City Council, the Board of Trade, and all interested citizens was held. C.B. Moores, chairman pro tem, turned the meeting over to J.G. Wright, president of the Board of Trade, who, after a few remarks called for Albert's committee report which announced Mr. Kay's successful deal with the brothers. He continued by stating that Mr. Kay had agreed to build a mill employing fifty people the first year and one which would consume 200,000 pounds of wool annually. Eventually, it was to be the largest woolen mill in the state. Terms were that $20,000 would be raised by Salem citizens, with the first payment of $2,500 on March 1, and $5,000 on August 1, the balance on January 1, 1890, provided the mill was completed by that time. If these plans miscarried and the building was not finished on the above date, then only $5,000 would be payable on January 1 and the balance when the factory was completed. To insure his good faith, Kay stated he would permit a lien to be placed on the plant until he had fulfilled his contract in every detail.

Among those who spoke in praiseworthy terms of both Kay and his project were Squire Farrar and E.M. Waite. J.B. Stump, G. Stoltz, and a Mr. Friedman were a committee appointed to secure the names of seven others to act as a bonus soliciting team and work out the final details with Kay. These were: chairman, R.S. Wallace (president of the Capital National Bank), J.H. Albert (cashier of the same institution), Thomas Holman, Squire Farrar, C.B. Moores, R.J. Hendricks, with E.M. Waite and I.A. Manning serving in place of banker Asahel Bush and W.S. Ladue who declined appointment.

Two weeks of intensive solicitation were required to raise the $20,000. Terms of payment were twelve and one-half per cent on March 1, twenty-five per cent on July 1, and the balance on December 1. Payments were to be made to Board of Trade trustees or to any member of that body. The promotion received the whole-hearted support of the editors of both papers who urged elimination of personal objections, if any, to the subsidy and the backing of the project which would mean so much to the business life of Salem. Subscriptions in varying amounts from $10 to $700 came easily and over $6,000 were pledged the first day of the campaign.

It is significant that the names of some of the town's prominent citizens do not appear on the subscription list, whether from the awareness of the risks inherent in woolen mill investment or because of just plain conservative opposition called "mossbackism" in the vernacular of the times. Although scarcely heard of today in the Pacific Northwest, it was a condition of thinking which tended to retard the economic advancement of the state for many years. Exceptions were men like Thomas Kay who were willing to stake their reputations and their fortunes on the resources at hand.

The community financial aid just described was a common promotion pattern followed by other Pacific Northwest cities where woolen mills were concerned. In spite of increasing industrialization in the state, especially in the Willamette Valley, most young enterprises depended almost entirely upon local financing. Eastern capital had not in the pioneer period or in the post-pioneer times, flowed abundantly as far west as the waterpower sites of the Pacific Northwest, not even in public utilities; an exception was found in transportation where railroad and steamship lines were promoted by the dozens out of combinations of Eastern and Pacific Coast capital.

In the case of the Kay mill, there was a happy association of both local capital and private funds. Kay had unbounded confidence in his ability to make money from woolen textiles. He had staked his own fortune of $55,000 against the combined money-raising ability of the entire Salem community; he had not asked for gifts, but only for help and he had been willing to take the greater risk of entrepreneurship. Salem people, on their part, recognized the administrative capacity and integrity of the man, by raising the bonus.

Said the *Oregon Statesman* of January 3, 1890, in reviewing Mr. Kay's life:

> He is not only a manufacturer of great experience, but he is also a shrewd and conservative business man of unquestioned integrity, and he will, if he is spared a few years, make the Salem woolen mills a *worthy heritage for his children* (italics ours) and the pride of the capital city of the state of Oregon.*

Salem's response to the proposed mill was, in fact, much better than that of other communities which had used the same tactics. The project either never got started, or if it did, the problem of refinancing always appeared, with the smaller contributors selling out to financially stronger individuals, for example, the Dallas woolen mill, the one at Union, and others. The fact that Tom Kay was back of this project was largely responsible for the success of the bonus campaign, small though some of the contributions were.

During the course of the solicitation period, both newspapers kept daily scores of the subscriptions as they mounted. By the last week of February, 1889, there had been 264 subscribers and $16,543 pledged. On February 28, $18,910 was chalked up and by the fourth day of March, the $20,000 bonus had been fully pledged by 352 loyal residents, quite an achievement for a town the size of Salem with its approximately 13,000 population. Immediate a meeting was called to select a board of trustees to handle the collection and stewardship of funds, with the follow-

(*)   This desire has been fulfilled through his daughter, Fannie Kay Bishop and son T.B. Kay, and their children.

ing personnel: J.H. Albert, J.G. Wright, E.M. Waite, H.W. Cottle, C.B. Moores.

Soon after the completion of the subsidy contract Kay, his wife, and son, Harry, left for the East. The son remained to visit various woolen mills and machinery houses while the mother and father journeyed to Leeds, England, to visit friends and relatives in Yorkshire. Thirty years had elapsed since the family had come to the United States. In addition to renewing these friendships, he had promised his Salem backers that he would inspect the English mills to learn what improvements had been made in machines and techniques so that they might be applied in the new factory. Visitations in North Andover, Worcester, Lawrence and other New England textile towns augmented those made in England. Orders were placed with American manufacturers for the latest cards, looms, spindles and other equipment, most of which had to be manufactured according to Kay's specifications.

The Kays returned to Salem about July 1. On July 16, 1889, the Thomas Kay Woolen Mill Company was incorporated in the office of W.F. Boothby, and the articles were filed the same day with the Secretary of State showing Thomas Kay, Squire Farrar, and C.P. Bishop the incorporators. Capital stock was $50,000 divided into five hundred $100 shares. The incorporators, who held the majority stock, then proceeded to elect three directors who in turn elected officers as follows: Squire Farrar, president; E.J. Swafford, secretary; R.S. Wallace, treasurer; Thomas

Kay, general manager. Offices were taken with Judge J.J. Shaw in the Patton Block.

The following day the directors met to adopt by-laws. In August, company offices were moved to the renovated oil-mill building, Swafford resigned as secretary and R.H. Coshow was elected his successor. A ten per cent stock assessment was made, followed in November by one of forty per cent.

Late in July, workmen and teams began clearing the ground preparatory to repairing the oil-mill structure and the construction of a three-story main building. Bids were opened on August 25 as follows:

B.F. Southwick, $8,442.00; Ely & Company, $8,520.00; A. Olinger, $9,995.000; J. Benoit, $14,767.00; Jackson & Hutchins, $9,467.00; G.A. Stevens, $8,945.00; Henry Rogers, $9,642.00; J. Craven, $8,725.00; with Southwick the successful bidder. Considerable expense was eliminated by repairing the two-and-one-half story building, and to align it with the new building on the west; the old structure was raised three feet to accommodate the waterwheel and line shafting.

Stone from a Polk County quarry was dumped on the premises for the foundation. In September, the framework was up two stories and work begun on a third. The building took on a more finished appearance as window lights and the hydraulic elevator were installed and the outside walls painted. The final dimensions of the structure were 136 feet by 55 feet, three stories and an attic high, with a dye house, two woolhouses and the office.

Thomas Kay held stock certificate number one for 200 shares; Squire Farrar number two for 100 shares; and C.P. Bishop number three for 80 shares. At the December 2, 1889, meeting capitalization was increased to $75,000[3] and the following appeared as stockholders: T.B. Kay, certificate number four, 50 shares; O.P. Coshow, Jr., certificate number five, 40 shares; R.S. Wallace, certificate number seven, 10 shares; R.H. Coshow, certificate number six, 20 shares. Somewhat later number eight went to Thomas Johnson of St. Louis, 50 shares. Certificates numbered ten to eighteen inclusive dated April 12, 1892, were issued to all of the above in varying amounts to augment their original holdings, signed by Thomas Kay, president.[4]

Further perusal of the minutes book and stock book reveals the constantly increasing number of shares purchased by Kay, T.B. Kay (son), C.P. Bishop (son-in-law), and O.P. Coshow (son-in-law). This concentration of family control was manifested later as the daughters and other relatives acquired stock ownership either by purchase or by gift.

The factory was formally opened to the public on March 13, 1890, with Thomas Kay, Squire Farrar, and Harry Kay the happy hosts. As the visitors strolled through the plant they saw all the various operations involved in manufacturing woolen textiles from the sorting bench to the finishing processes. Dirty wool passed through the wool-scouring tubs and

---

(3) Supplemental articles were filed December 17, 1889, for this amount
(4) This material and much of that which follows was taken from the original book of minutes, 1889-1940, and the stock certificate book, courtesy of Thomas Kay III

came out fluffy white after drying, to be immediately colored in the steam dye vats. The doffing combs on the carding machines mysteriously collected the fibers into loose strands prior to being spooled for the spinning frames. The fascinating operation of the two mules each with 336 spindles was followed by weaving on the first floor where the dexterity of the workers in threading the heddle frames (the design control mechanism of the looms) held their attention. The twelve looms in operation would soon be turning out yardage of flannels, cassimeres, tweeds, and blankets.

Burlers picked out the lumps and loose ends, the fulling mills shrunk the cloth to width, and if it had not yet passed through the dye vats as raw wool, the fabric was colored in the piece. The tenter room on the fourth floor dried and stretched the cloth to its final width, thence to the shearing machine, or if blankets, to the napper. After the several finishing processes had been completed the cloth was bolted and labeled ready for the market.

Some of the machinery installed in this two-set mill was as follows: [5]

> 2 sets of carding machines
> 2 sets of spinkle mules each with 335 spindles
> 8 harness looms
> 30 harness frames
> 4 blanket and flannel looms (112 inches)
> 2 fulling mills and wash boxes
> 3 spoolers
> 1 winder

---

(5) Adapted from copy of order placed with Davis & Furber Machine Company, North Andover, Massachusetts, June 21, 1889; and the *Oregon Weekly Statesman*, January 3, 1890

2 twisters
1 picker and duster
1 cloth winding machine
6-8 dye kettles
1 70 horsepower steam engine
400 feet of 4 inch belting
300 feet of 2 1/2 inch belting
150 feet of 2 inch belting
    rinse boxes, scrapers, scouring boxes, shears, presses, brushes.

Against fire, the arch enemy of all woolen mills, a new force pump and three hydrants were installed. It was the most sturdily constructed and modern woolen mill on the Pacific Coast.

A foregone conclusion was, that the products of this plant like those of the other factories where Tom Kay had worked, and he had been in all of the Oregon mills except Oregon City, would continue to win prizes for quality at fairs and expositions throughout the country.

In charge of the various operations were Harry G. Kay, spinning and dyeing; James W. Hutton, weaving; George Woeful, finishing; Peter McIntyre, sorting (later promoted to wool buyer); James Denton, carding; Robert H. Coshow, bookkeeper. Peter McGee was first superintendent.[6]

Among those who worked in the mill at this time were Clarence M. Bishop, spooler; Roy Bishop, spooler; Chauncey Bishop, soapmaker, later to be owners of the Pendleton Woolen Mills. Emil Koppe was acting superintendent and later became owner of the Eugene woolen mill.

---

(6) Other superintendents at various times were: Frank McGee, son of Patrick; Cameron, and McGregor.

Within six months the mill was referred to in the newspapers as a pattern for all Oregon cities to follow if they were seeking to stimulate home industry. The Portland *Oregonian*, the metropolitan torch-bearer of this economic philosopy, gave the following data:[7]

```
Number of hands ................................50
   Skilled ......................35 (women and girls)
   Boys ......................................15
Wages, skilled (daily) .........................$2.25
Wages, unskilled (daily) .......................$1.00
Capital .....................................$75,000
Outside capital .............................$40,000
Output, 1890 ...............................$120,000
Expenditures, local .........................$20,000
Expenditures, abroad ........................$40,000
Value of Products .............$15,000 (sold at home)
Value of Products ............$105,000 (sold abroad)
Wages .......................................$25,000
```

An interview with one who worked in the mill from the beginning, revealed that boy spoolers were paid five cents an hour for a ten-hour day, and a sixty-hour week.[8] Weavers made $32.50 a month, some as low as $25. Lou Pickard, boss dyer, received $4.50 per day, the highest paid worker in the factory; if the dyes were not true color the cloth would not sell. Daily pay for pickinghouse employees was seventy cents.

As low as these wages were, even in those days, penalties were invoked for poor workmanship, especially at the looms. A standing rule in some mills was, that if a defective blanket was turned out the

---

(7) *Morning Oregonian*, Portland, September 22, 1890
(8) Interview with John Fisher, Salem. He was one of the first employees who started as a spooler at eleven years of age and was with the mill for fifty-seven years.

worker was compelled to buy it at the factory price, the Kay mill being no exception to the general policy.

Reference to an original timekeeper's book for 1893 shows daily wages by departments as follows; Wool sorting $2.00; dye house $1.50-3.50; finishing $1.00-4.00; card room $0.80-3.00; spinning $1.25-2.00; weave room $0.50-3.00; wool pulling $1.50-2.50; spooling 50 cents.

At the end of the year Kay, Bishop, and Farrar were voted a salary of $125 each per month retroactive to March 1, 1890.

At the April, 1891, meeting of the stockholders, Kay, Farrar, Bishop, O. P. Coshow, Jr., and R. S. Wallace were elected directors with Kay, president; Coshow, secretary; and Wallace, treasurer. At this meeting R. H. Coshow was voted a salary of $1,200 a year as secretary and Kay's was renewed at $1,500 as superintendent. It was moved to change the name to that of the Salem Woolen Mills Corporation and to file supplementary articles of incorporation. There is no record in the Corporation Commissioner's office of a name change, and in later annual meetings the company was always referred to by its original name.

Oregon woolen mills purchased fleeces at three different sources, namely, the wool sales held in Eastern Oregon towns like Pendleton, The Dalles, and Echo; through middlemen who maintained offices in Portland, Willamette Valley and the above-mentioned localities; and considerable quantities direct from farmers, especially in Western Oregon.

The establishment of wool-scouring plants in the first two communities and later in Echo, stimulated marketing activities in both the raw and scoured product. Buyers came from all over the United States to attend these wool sales which were held in private warehouses. Middlemen as well as mill men were purchasers. Some of the best-known wool buyers with Salem offices were Fortner, Tiffany & Company, Squire Farrar & Company, and F. Levy & Company.

Insofar as the Kay mill was concerned, all three sources were employed to supply their expanding needs. Purchases from Marion County farmers with their small flocks of long-wooled sheep has prevailed from the establishment of the factory until it closed its doors in 1959.

At the time the mill opened, blue suitings for summer wear were being made as well as scarlet and other colors for flannels, cassimeres, and tweeds. Shortly after the factory opened, a branch wholesale store in charge of C. P. Bishop, son-in-law of Thomas Kay, was opened in Portland in March, 1890, at 5 Oak Street on the northwest corner of Front. This operation was short-lived as the company did not have sufficient capital to carry the credit demanded by the retail trade. The jobbing business was thereafter given preference as these middlemen were sold cloth on a shorter term basis and paid their accounts regularly.

In spite of its temporary duration the idea was soundly conceived if for no other reason than that it brought the company closer to sources of credit. This was evidenced by Bishop being authorized almost immediately after the store's opening to negotiate a $5,000 loan at the Commercial National Bank.

The E. C. Small store, 293 Commercial Street, was agent for local distribution in Salem, but in July the company apparently discontinued this relationship and opened a store on the premises formerly occupied by J. J. Dalrymple, 299 Commercial Street, in charge of H. S. Belle.

This establishment had been in operation about nine months when the question of its disposition was debated at a meeting held in the offices of the Capital National Bank on April 16, 1891. A proposition was made to C. P. Bishop to sell to him the entire stock of clothing and other goods of "our" manufacture at seventy-five cents on the dollar, and all hats and furnishing goods at eighty-seven and one half cents, clothing of other makes, fixtures, etc. at invoice price or at cost; terms cash. Bishop accepted the offer, paid $20,000 cash and took charge of his own establishment, which was known as the Salem Woolen Mills store, on May 1, 1891. Both parties benefited from the move: Bishop became owner of the leading mens' clothing store in Salem, and the woolen mill was relieved of a severe financial strain under which it was laboring at the time.

Charles P. Bishop was born in Contra Costa County, California, September 23, 1854, and came with his parents to Portland, Oregon, in 1856. As a young man he worked as a clerk in a clothing store in Brownsville; met and married Fannie Kay, daughter of Thomas Kay, one of the owners of the woolen mill located there, on October 8, 1876. He soon thereafter bought a store in nearby Crawfordsville which he later sold to purchase a retail clothing store in

McMinnville in 1884, in which his brother-in-law, Thomas B. Kay, later became a partner. In 1891 he was attracted to Salem's opportunities in retailing in association with the Kay woolen mill as related, having previously managed the Kay's branch store in Portland.

In spite of its credit problems, the mill was responding to market demands evidenced by its annual wool consumption of 400,000 pounds and a payroll of from fifty to sixty people whose wages amounted to $30,000 a year. Orders were coming from various Pacific Coast points including Mandell Brothers for a specially made blanket called "The California," and from Hale Brothers, San Francisco, as well as from New York and Alaska. Woolen socks, knitted from the same yarn used in the manufacture of fabrics, were part of the merchandise line. The company was listed as one of the heavier taxpayers in Marion County. In September, 1891, Kay felt securely enough established to build a fine $2,000 residence with a brick foundation on the corner of Twelfth and State Streets, two blocks from the factory. The president continued to make periodical trips to San Francisco. Another try was made at wholesaling by opening a branch on Alder Street near the Holton House.

The prosperity of the mill was evidenced at the annual meeting of the stockholders on April 12, 1892, when a $15,000 stock dividend was declared, this being twenty-five per cent of the paid up capital stock, against which move Bishop cast a negative vote. The motion carried nevertheless and the secretary was ordered to issue the stock.

The oldest son's name, T. B. Kay, appears for the first time as a stockholder and director taking the place vacated by R. S. Wallace. The same officers were reelected with the substitution of J. H. Albert as treasurer.

Not much news appeared in the local papers during 1893, nor does the minute book reveal anything of importance except a listing of the stockholders at the annual meeting of April 11 as follows:

Thomas Kay	250 shares
Squire Farrar	125 "
C.P. Bishop	100 "
T.B. Kay	62-1/2 "
Thomas Johnson	62-1/2 "
S.R. Jessup	62-1/2 "
O.P. Coshow, Jr.	50 "
R.H. Coshow	25 "

or a total of 750 shares, the outstanding stock. Directors were reelected and declared a ten percent cash dividend. R. H. Coshow was elected treasurer to succeed J. H. Albert.

Like any successful manufacturing company, the business was in constant need of working capital, especially the purchase of wool and supplies, and sought sources where this accomodation could be obtained on the most favorable terms. At this meeting a committee of three composed of Kay, Farrar, and Bishop was appointed to meet with the officers of the First National Bank of Salem "to find out how much money and on what terms it could be had for the purpose of carrying on our business for the ensuing

year." The committee immediately called on the
bank's officers while the rest of the stockholders
waited patiently, and returned within the hour to
report that they had been unable to obtain the desired
information but would have an answer at the next
board meeting of the mill company.

It was then reported that the bank would carry a
$50,000 overdraft with interest at nine percent per
annum on the exact amount due each day. On
motion, these terms were accepted and the woolen
mill account was moved from the Capital National
Bank to the First National Bank.

What appears at first to be a rather odd sideline
was the operation of a tannery; but it must be
remembered that many woolen mills owned pulleries
where wool was "pulled" from sheepskins. Enlarge-
ment of this unit was planned as the result of a recent
visit by Kay to San Francisco where he had inspected
tanneries owned by mills in that area. Both sheep and
deer skins were to be tanned for the glove trade. In
addition to the usual tanning materials, chicken drop-
pings were bought from small boys who no doubt
made eager raids on the piles of this refuse usually
found not only in the suburbs of small towns, but
almost as frequently within the urban limits. The
following year (1894) the directors decided to stop
buying tannery stock and the business was closed up.

A meeting of the North Pacific Sheepbreeders' and
Woolgrowers' Association was held in Salem in
January 1894 when resolutions were passed opposing
the Wilson tariff bill which would place wool on the
free list. The venerable sheep breeder John Minto was

chairman. C.P. Bishop spoke from the viewpoint of the woolen textile manufacturer stating that the market for woolens was very dull, especially in San Francisco where the company was doing a $70,000 annual business and that Eastern buyers would place orders only at a forty per cent discount under prices of last year.

The point he was trying to make was that middlemen would curtail their buying in view of the possibility of free foreign wool, and that this would be reflected in the lower price of cloth.

The aforementioned bill finally passed the Congress, a factor which embittered all wool men against the Cleveland administration and its free trade doctrines. But the Thomas Kay Woolen Mill Company continued to prosper in spite of the poor conditions created during this political regime.

R. H. Coshow was now secretary-treasurer with Kay and Farrar in their traditional offices. T. B. Kay was employed as assistant manager at a salary of $125 per month.

The feeling of peaceful security and prosperity which the Salem mill diffused was suddenly shattered on the morning of November 18, 1895, by the agonizing shrieks of the factory whistle as William F. Brown, the nightwatchman, tried desperately to summon help. The fire had started in the dryhouse and was discovered by him at 5:15 A.M. One hour-and-a-half later the mill had burned to the ground with a $90,000 loss covered by only $20,000 of insurance. The $2,600 monthly payroll of the seventy-five employees now thrown out of work would be sorely missed in the community which had gone all out to raise a $20,000 subsidy nearly seven years before in order to establish the factory.

The loss was even a greater catastrophe for Kay who had put his personal fortune into the project. Perhaps more than the property destruction was the shattering of an ideal, for he had taken great pride in this, his own, the finest and newest woolen mill in Oregon. At all the other factories he had been an employee except for the immediate years at Brownsville, where he had been part owner. From the very beginning, he had planned it, visualized the layout of machines and ordered them to meet his particular standards for weaving fine blankets, flannels, and tweeds. Now, as he stepped off the train from Albany to be greeted by a consoling kiss from his daughter, Fannie Kay Bishop, always his confidant, a pile of smoking embers and ruined machinery lay before him. Tears streamed down his face. It was not a very happy situation at his time of life; but self-pity was not a part of his character. A day or two only elapsed when it was joyfully announced that there would be another mill in Salem.[9]

As it was reported at the time, Brown, the watchman, and Samuel Wright were on duty, the former oiling machinery in the wheelhouse which was at the north end of the dryhouse and east of the main building; Wright was asleep on a pile of blankets in the main building. Brown, when he saw the wisp of

---

(9) By coincidence, Clarence M. Bishop, his grandson, later president of the Pendleton Woolen Mills but then a student at the University of Oregon, was on his way home from Eugene and met his grandfather on the train at Albany. Mr. Bishop corroborated the events as related.

flame, immediately ran out the hose connected to the big pump, sounded the alarm from the engine room by giving five short toots on the whistle, then ran back to the wheelhouse to set the turbine wheel going and the pump, but by this time the fire had cut off his pathway to the pumphouse.

He then rushed over to the office in the northwest corner of the yard to telephone the fire department, but could make no connection with the central telephone office, so ran back to the boiler room and opened the whistle wide.

A passing postoffice clerk on his way to work, Theofil Muelhaupt, saw the fire and roused out the firemen. The department made an exceptionally quick hitch, and as they drove out of the house, the telephone in the engine room was heard to ring. Going up State Street the hose wagon and engine met Wright's little son coming down that thoroughfare on horseback at racing speed. From him they learned exactly where the fire was, and he was sent on down to turn in a general alarm by ringing the big bell.

The LaFrance engine laid out two lines of hose as it stood on the north bank of the race south of the mill. By the time the connections were made steam was up, but the dryhouse and wheelhouse had burned and the flames had reached the main building. The two streams were effectively fighting the conflagration when it was discovered that coal for the engine was exhausted. Chief Coss then sent driver John Duncan with the hose wagon back to the enginehouse for more coal, but on account of the tired condition of the horses, fully twenty-five minutes were required for the trip. Fireman Frank Welch had tried to keep steam up with wood, but that was useless. The heat at this point became so intense that the firefighting apparatus was forced to move to the railroad bridge close by.

Effort was now directed to save adjacent buildings such as the old tannery across the race where $6,000 worth of wool and pelts were stored, the nearby Salem Soap Works, houses and barns. Stacked in the yard were 1,200 to 1,500 cords of firewood valued at two dollars a cord of which only 100 cords were lost. A north wind and a November fog helped prevent the spread of the conflagration.

The origin of the fire remained a mystery. Gossip at the time attributed it to incendiarism, the work of a revengeful, recently discharged employee of the Waterloo factory who vowed to get even. The mill closed down between 4:30 P.M. Saturdays and 7:30 A.M. Mondays with no fire in the boiler until ten o'clock Sunday evenings.

The factory was covered by policies written by George M. Beeler, agent for the Sun of London, $5,750; Lyon of London, $3,000; the Hamburg-Bremen of Germany, $7,500; and the Firemens Fund Insurance Company of San Francisco, $3,750, John G. Wright, agent.

Salem citizens were sharp in the criticism of their fire department, and since some good comes from bad, the need for a fire alarm system was emphasized, a matter which received but little attention although it had been discussed five years before when a manufacturer of such a system had made overtures for installation.

The loss of the woolen mill was bad enough, but the failure of the State Insurance Company and the Williams & England bank, one of five in the town, added to the business troubles of the growing city. Moreover, the fire insurance company had deposits in the defunct bank. But in spite of these discouragements, Salem citizens eagerly voiced their enthusiastic approval of rebuilding the woolen factory just as soon as the board of directors could meet and announce plans. In the meantime, some of the mill employees offered to clean up the premises.

The directors met the next day on November 19 and voted to put the proposition of rebuilding up to the people of Salem. It was agreed that the capital stock should be increased to $100,000 providing the town would agree to make up the $25,000 difference between the original $75,000 and the new figure. A three-set mill would be built and eventually it would be increased to four sets of cards. This started the citizens of Salem buzzing with enthusiasm again and such prominent men as Jefferson Myers, A. Klein, O. E. Krause, F. B. Southwick, F. C. Baker, John Q. Wilson, and J. J. Dalrymple, came out openly for the project, stating that Salem could not afford to be without such a factory. In the meantime, contractors had been invited to bid on the proposed building.

A Board of Trade meeting was called to discuss a program for refinancing the woolen mill. The mill company had received flattering offers from other cities in the Pacific Northwest, such was its regional reputation.

The quickest way to sound out opinion would be to have a big public gathering at Reed's Opera House, to which end a committee consisting of E. P. McCornack, I. L. Patterson, Ernest Hoffer, Anthony Klein, and E. C. Cross was appointed.

In spite of a stormy December night, E. P. McCornack, president of the First National Bank presided over a filled theatre. So many people spoke in favor of the project, of Kay's capacity as a manufacturer and as a respected citizen of the community, that the gathering had all the earmarks of a testimonial meeting.

The highlight of the evening came when Kay, called upon to speak, held the audience spellbound for twenty minutes by "native eloquence not thought of." His talk was an avalanche of convincing facts, as Kay traced his successful career as a woolen mill man, pointing out that he had made $250,000 in his fourteen years with the Brownsville company in contrast to the two failures of that organization prior to his taking over. Moveover, his Salem mill had operated continuously in spite of hard times, and that at the time of the fire he had orders on the books from New York, Chicago, and Pacific Coast cities. In conclusion he stated that the mill had paid fifty-five per cent dividends in its nearly six years of operation. It was the consensus of opinion that the mill would be a good investment.

J. J. Dalrymple was the first to sign the subscription list, with several others equally as enthusiastic in their financial support. Among those who made substantial pledges were: J. K. Weatherford (Albany) $5,000; J. J. Dalrymple $1,500; Thomas Johnson $1,500; J. M. Wallace (trustee) $1,250; A. Bush $1,000; Phil Metschan $1,000.

The rest of the subscriptions ranged downward from $500 to $100. It is significant that most of the subsidy was raised during the meeting and little if any solicitation was necessary. Furthermore, there were no five and ten dollar pledges as in the first promotion project.

Architect W. D. Pugh was hired to draw plans for the new building which was to be patterned after Kay's mill at Waterloo. Ground was broken about December 20, 1895, scarcely a month since the fire, on the site of the original mill. Fifteen bids on the new structure were opened on Saturday, December 28, and two days later at a meeting of the board of directors they were rejected on account of a change in the fireproofing specifications which the company made at the last minute. Bids were ordered re-advertised to be opened at Pugh's office in Salem on Thursday, January 2, 1896, at two o'clock. The successful bid was by John Gray and Henry Lukers.

Details of the construction were made public. The three-story $80,000 brick and stone factory fronting Twelfth Street would have a 58-foot width and extend 150 feet east along the north bank of the millrace. Rock from the old mill was used in making the two-feet thick stone and concrete foundation walls nine feet high. The brick walls above the first floor were seventeen inches thick and above the second floor twelve inches. A special feature was the immense floor timbers, seventeen in all, sixty feet long with 12" x 16" faces. Three inch planks were then laid and 1-1/4" flooring on top of these. A full cement basement was a feature.

A one-story structure for the dye room, dry room, picking, and mixing was separated from the main building on the east by a forty-foot corridor. A boiler room, pump and dynamo house stood south of the latter building again separated by several feet of space as a fire precaution. A fire alarm system was installed. A temporary office was immediately opened to interview and to rehire former employees and others who wanted work. Supplemental articles of incorporation were filed for $100,000 on February 12, 1896.

In light of present day highly developed personnel departments, one looks in vain for any provision for employees' comfort or safety. No well-appointed washrooms or lavatories were a part of this modern factory. Outhouses on the premises served as toilets and a convenient faucet of cold water was the place of wash-up.

In the meantime, Kay and his son, T. B. Kay, left for the East to purchase new machinery, with some emphasis on worsteds as there were now enough trained hands to make this kind of cloth.

Secretary R. H. Coshow was empowered to settle all fire insurance claims and in doing so made the following brief report:

Net resources $84,435.53
Loss by fire $69,332.27
Insurance $20,000.00
Sale of ruins 248.00
20,248.00
Net loss $49,084.27

A fifty percent stock assessment was made on the new subscribers and ordered to be paid at the company office or at the First National Bank, and in March the remaining part of the obligation was called. T. B. Kay was elected assistant manager and salesman at the March 23, 1896, meeting and C. P. Bishop a director on February 29.

By April, all of the separate smaller buildings were completed and the truss work on the sturdy main building was more than half done. Announcement that the factory would open about June 1 came with the appointment of a housewarming committee composed of Dr. J. N. Smith, Frank Davey, and Charles A. Gray. Decorations were the responsibility of prominent society women of Salem.

On the afternoon of May 15, 1896, the doors of the fine, new mill building were opened to the public to the strains of music from the Second Regiment band under W. B. McElroy's leadership. Although there was a formal program of speeches, some of the 2,000 visitors toured the grounds and buildings and were awed by the vastness of the floor space, soon to be the scene of rattling looms and other machinery, but now gayly decorated and devoted to the festivities of the day.

On the semi-circular stage were Mr. and Mrs. Kay; the Rev. J. P. Farmer, pastor of the First Baptist Church, and Miss Farmer; the Hon. Claud Gatch, Mayor of Salem; Frank Davey; the Hon. J. K. Weatherford of Albany; the Hon. C. B. Montague and his son, J. D. Montague, of Lebanon, the youngest mayor in Oregon. Mayor Gatch's welcoming address was followed by an appropriate poem written by Miss Emma Babcock and read by Frank Davey.

The occasion was an opportunity for Kay to again express his grateful appreciation for the financial assistance he had now twice received from Salem citizens, and pledged his word "that no contributor should ever lose an iota so long as his hand guided the destinies of the plant." He feelingly reviewed the losses of the recent fire and the depth of his emotions as he stepped off the train literally into the ashes of the burned factory; paid loving tribute to his wife and spoke brightly of the future and the continuing part which the mill would play in Salem's business life and that of the people. C.B. Montague was the final speaker and concluded his talk by leading three cheers for the woolen mill.

In the evening McElroy's orchestra furnished the music for the dance whose grand march was led by Charles A. Gray and Miss Augusta Lownsdale (Mrs. R.B. Sinnott of Portland). It was reported in somewhat ecstatic language and detail that the great room took on new beauty in the glow of electricity and the whirling mass of lovely tints and warm colors of the ladies' gowns and decorations. It was not only an outstanding social event; it was an open, heartfelt expression of company and family gratitude for a community's assistance in time of stress.

Ten carloads of machinery rolled onto the railroad spur from the Southern Pacific's main line which ran past the site, and were immediately placed in position on the factory floors. In addition, a large elevator was discharged from the steamer *Ruth* and installed. Two large pumps for firefighting purposes were connected so as to be controlled from outside the building. An Edison dynamo supplied electricity for the 325 lights used to illuminate the factory and grounds. A well was dug to obtain pure water for employee use as Salemites complained about the contaminated Willamette River water.

Wool began to be scoured once more, and to insure an adequate supply, a buyer was dispatched to The Dalles, at that time the largest primary wool market in the United States. These purchases, with some sheep pelts, were stored in the old Wallace cannery across the street and in the old agricultural works building. When the tannery was discontinued, the pelts were burned.

The question of a wool tariff was being hotly debated in Congress. Because the commodity had been on the free list in the Cleveland administration, woolmen claimed that the recent hard times were in part caused by this aspect of the free trade policy. Later, with McKinely's election, wool began to move to Boston and other eastern points with a consequent rise in price, the result of increased demand and the turn of the political wheel to a protective tariff. Willamette Valley wool could be bought for eight to ten cents a pound; Eastern Oregon for twelve to fourteen cents. It was the custom of Boston merchants to advance eighty per cent of the price of the wool on consignment, then remit the freight charges and interest when sold, but this year there had been no market, with consequent paralysis of the Oregon wool industry.

This depressed situation was reflected in a decision of the board of directors meeting of August 6, 1896, when it was voted to suspend operation. The issue was forced by the First National Bank which requested that the company account be reduced on account of the uncertainty of the approaching presidential election and the fear that the free silver candidate, W.J. Bryan, might be elected. The mill's business was in such a condition that it could not run without more credit.

It was not until October when T.B. Kay returned from California with orders for cloth that the factory again resounded to the whir of pulley belts and line shafting. The probability that a Republican president would be elected gave assurance of expanding business, the full dinner-pail and happy workmen. Local evidence of returning business confidence was the rehiring of former employees, some of them on the night shift. Furthermore, an extra loom was brought in from the Waterloo plant and a wagonload of unfinished cloth from the same place was discharged at the Salem factory for finishing, a practice which continued until the former mill burned in 1898. The finishing department was enlarged, with some finishers coming from Waterloo, making twenty in all, or double the force which manned this department prior to the fire.

In November, the first worsted cloth manufactured west of the Mississippi River came off the looms and the forty-yard bolt was placed on display and sale in the Salem Woolen Mills Store. Owner C.P. Bishop immediately cut off three-and-one-half yards of the blue serge and took it upstairs to the tailor shop to be measured for a suit. The rest was advertised at $25 a suit. To develop this aspect of the business, Arthur Greaves of Moosup, Connecticut, was brought in. At approximately the same time James McDonald, a designer and manufacturer from Rhode Island, was added to the staff. In March of 1897, two carloads of machinery, mostly worsted looms arrived from North Andover, Massachusetts. Superintendents in the new mill were named Cameron and McGregor.

As the end of 1896 approached, the mill had eighty-eight people on the payroll. Machinery duplicating that lost in the fire was coming from the East and from Waterloo, especially finishing and dyeing equipment. The tax rolls showed the mill listed at $26,000 assessed valuation on which $890.80 taxes were paid.

Workers were getting a slightly higher wage; the average was $1.75 a day with experienced operatives paid not less than $1.00. Daily pay for boys averaged sixty-three cents with a minimum of fifty cents. Fifteen women averaged eighty-two cents per day with seventy-five cents the lowest pay in this group. Inexperienced girls were paid a flat wage of fifty cents each per day running one side of a spinning frame.

Experienced girls who could run both sides received higher wages. On some jobs women got one-and-one-half cents a yard. Weavers worked by the piece and made from $1.00 to $1.50 a day. There were at this time approximately 150 employees altogether in the Salem and Waterloo mills.

Full production in January, 1897, meant active market demand, especially from Pacific Coast buyers who dealt largely on a consignment basis. It was customary at this time for some of the Oregon woolen mills to sell their output on the above basis to jobbers, who in turn had the cloth made into suits; Chinese tailors did a flourishing business in Portland as a result of this practice. The San Francisco jobbers like Hoffman & Rothchild (later Hoffman & Alexander), and Louis Straus sent their cloth to eastern suit manufacturers after which it was returned to these middlemen and in turn distributed to the retail trade. It was this kind of arrangement which the Salem Woolen Mills Store had with the above-mentioned firms and which worked so satisfactorily for all parties.

In addition to suitings, the mill found a ready market for flannels, robes, twelve-pound China blankets, and mackinaws for miners bound for Alaska. Salem concentrated on mackinaws and flannels; Waterloo on bed and camp blankets. A four-pound blanket sold for $3.50 at the mill.

In the Pacific Northwest and the Rocky Mountain states, Fleischner, Mayer and Company of Portland were distributors for the Kay mill. To meet expanding miners' markets the above-named company leased a store formerly occupied by C.H. Dodd, part of which was a large second-story room converted to a clothing manufacturing department. Here, in September, 1897, forty electric sewing machines were installed for as many girl operatives, with plans to install forty more early the following year. Mackinaw suits, flannel underwear, and overalls were manufactured for the Klondike trade. Goods were forty ounces to the yard with old gold the favorite color, appropriately selected in view of the commodity which its wearers would seek.

At one time the above distributor had placed an order for 10,000 yards of forty-ounce mackinaw cloth and for unnumbered bales of blankets which sold readily in Utah, Montana, Idaho, Oregon and Washington. One Portland house made special reference to the Kay mill's cloth in its catalog.

Obviously, the Klondike goldrush and the less dramatic mining operations in the Pacific Northwest, including British Columbia, and as far east as Colorado, provided a market bonanza for Oregon woolen mills, hard-pressed for business along with other manufactories as the result of four years of a Democratic party administration. Evidence of this market awareness was shown by advertisements appearing in Portland papers. J.L. Bowman, manager of the recently opened Salem Woolen Mills Store, 102 Second Street, Portland, stated that his establishment dealt in Klondike supplies and was prepared to outfit 10,000 men with mackinaw suits, blankets, overshirts, and underwear direct from "our woolen mills" thus saving the customer the middleman's profits and commissions. Although this store by inference seemed to be directly associated with the Kay mill, there was no relationship except that it stocked the former's products.

In the spring of 1897, the management of the mill announced that T.B. Kay would be sent to New York to develop and expand that market, even though the mill was running full time on Pacific Coast orders. Nevertheless, there might come a day when national distribution would be desirable and the present seemed like a propitious time to expand. The assistant manager had been settled in his new position scarcely six months when he was ordered home; there was no need for continuing such expense in view of the stability of Pacific Coast business so he returned in January, 1898.

A rather specialized demand was for prison stripe cloth ordered by the Washington State and the California penitentiaries.

Increased market demand for the Kay products which now enjoyed a wide regional reputation, necessitated heavy wool purchases of 750,000 pounds for which from fourteen to fifteen cents a pound were paid for Valley wools. Of the above amount about 125,000 pounds were Eastern Oregon fibers which sold for slightly less than the western Oregon product. The company was also in the market for a certain amount of mohair which presumably was mixed with wool and which was bought for twenty to twenty-one cents a pound.

Wool prices reflected the position of sellers who were holding out for a continued rise, a position strengthened by increasing numbers of eastern and western buyers at The Dalles and other marketing points and by the possibility of a revived wool tariff. Political maneuvering in Congress added uncertainty to the market. American manufacturers were, therefore, buying abroad which partly accounted for the untenable position of sellers. The Salem company later paid twelve cents for Valley wool and eight cents for Eastern Oregon.

Under the pressure of an enlarged market, the factory was forced to expand its plant facilities in January, 1898, by building a two-story brick addition on the east end of the main structure. Here, fulling and finishing operations were housed as well as eight new looms. At the same time, two mules, a carding machine, a gig and other machinery were purchased costing altogether $10,000. This augmented productive capacity would make the plant the second largest woolen mill on the Pacific Coast, being exceeded in size by the one at Oregon City. This was in line with Kay's policy to eventually have 500 operatives in the establishment.

The full time operation required the services of 100 employees manufacturing among other fabrics the aforesaid miner's clothing, but an interesting sideline was sleeping bags. It is not known whether these were manufactured or were carried as a merchandise sideline. Weekly output was sufficient to clothe 1,100 men. It was Kay's opinion that the Klondike boom would probably be good for another two years before demand settled down to normal consumption. But this decline was not felt until the end of 1898 when jobbers' orders began to fall off; such dealers were well-stocked with goods purchased during the height of the gold rush. News came that Eastern mills were running half time or had completely shut down.

In the meantime, wages had been advanced ten per cent and worsted manufacture was temporarily curtailed in favor of the more profitable miners' goods.

The carefully managed mill, prospering in a sellers' market, was struck again by fire on Wednesday afternoon March 16, 1898. The sonorous blast of the factory whistle brought crowds of Salem citizens on the run down State Street where they viewed with understandable distress the huge billows of black smoke pouring from the picker room. Unlike the earlier fire, the mill force quickly had a stream of water playing, although they were handicapped again with only one pump operable, the other being repaired. The fire department was soon on the scene assisted by volunteers including Chief Justice F.A. Moore and Judge George H. Burnett, both of whom ably handled the nozzles directed toward the fire. That the entire layout was not again consumed was due not only to the effectiveness of the firefighters but to the wisdom of constructing the buildings with corridors between.

A $4,000 fire loss ensued composed of a small building, 10,000 pounds of wool and waste, as well as damage to two new picking machines and a lumper installed only the week before. Insurance coverage was only $2,500 in policies written by the Imperial Insurance Company, and the Continental Insurance Company. While Kay went to Portland to buy pulleys, belts and other needed equipment, the night shift was temporarily laid off pending repairs.

Embers of the picker-house fire had scarcely cooled when, at nine o'clock on the evening of March 28, 1898, the dryhouse was consumed. It started in woodwork adjoining the hot air pipes. Here again a space of twenty feet separated the frame structure from the main brick factory building. Two hot air fans, pipes and some stock were lost. This might have been averted had the mill pump been working properly and if the Salem fire department hoses had not burst due to age (it was reported that they were not less than nine years old). The loss in this instance was not mentioned but there was $3,000 insurance coverage. Kay immediately wired a $1,700 order to Sargent & Sons, Lowell, Massachusetts, for new machinery. James McDonald was superintendent at this time.

As might be presumed, accidents occurred from time to time, although the record appears to be remarkably clear in this respect. One such was when Jack Burrans, age seventeen, son of the head dryer, had three toes crushed in a spinning frame, and when S.R. Raistrick, sorting-room foreman (Kay's nephew) injured his leg in a fall from a ladder.

Nothing of particular interest marked the activities of the mill during 1899. It manufactured what the market demanded, for example, uniform cloth and overcoatings for the State Guards, the tailoring of which was in the hands of Charles Coopey of Portland, an ardent home industry enthusiast for Oregon woolen textiles. Most of the effort was directed toward supplying the market with blankets and flannels. There was so much business that the company was forced to reject the mounting orders. Considerable credit for this happy situation goes to T.B. Kay as sales manager with offices at 11 Sansome Street, San Francisco. Incidental features of the year were the sale of the Waterloo boiler to the Kay mill for $300 and declaration of a ten per cent cash dividend. J.P. Wilbur, soon to become superintendent of the Union, Oregon, woolen mill became loom boss at the Salem plant when the Waterloo factory was burned.

January of 1900 opened with the election of the same officers and directors, namely Kay, president; Farrar, vice-president; R.H. Coshow, secretary-treasurer; T.B. Kay, assistant manager and salesman. Directors were Thomas Kay, Squire Farrar, C.P. Bishop, T.B. Kay, J.K. Weatherford. Improvement of the fire protection system was ordered by the construction of a 15,000 gallon capacity redwood water tank and a $3,000 interior sprinkling system.

DEATH OF THOMAS KAY

The factory personnel and Salem citizens were saddened to learn of Kay's death in Portland on Friday, April 27, 1900, at age 63, as the result of a major operation. He had been ill for several months, had made a trip to California seeking medical aid, but finally returned to Oregon and the operation as a last resort. Salem's most eminent industrialist was widely eulogized in the Oregon press not only as a contributor to the commonwealth's economic growth, but as a citizen who participated willingly and generously in the broader aspects of its development. Although without formal schooling, he typified the intelligent, apprentice-trained Englishman who sought opportunity in America to display his inherent capabilities. The Oregon woolen textile industry presented that opprtunity and he made the most of it. Mr. Kay was one of the most important figures on Oregon's industrial frontier.

At the directors' meeting on May 14, J.K. Weatherford[10] introduced the following memorial:

Thomas Kay, President of this company, died on the 27th day of April, 1900, at the age of 63 years. He was an Englishman by birth coming to this country in early manhood, reaching Oregon in 1863 and located at Brownsville, Oregon, where he resided for many years.

From early youth he followed the occupation of a manufacturer and became more than ordinarily proficient.

For many years he was the general manager and superintendent of the Brownsville Woolen Mills of Brownsville, Orgon, and in its earlier days it required skill and energy to succeed. When others faltered he stood firm as a rock and wrested success out of apparent failure.

Upon a reorganization of the Brownsville Woolen Mills Company, Mr. Kay concluded to retire and organize a company and build and operate a woolen mill at this place. It was a large undertaking and a difficult task but nothing daunted he undertook it and soon his efforts were crowned with success.

Scarcely had this new and valuable enterprise commenced operation before it was swept away by fire.

Once more his push and energy secured the necessary means and a larger and better mill arose phoenix-like from the ashes of the former.

He became its manager and as such had full control of its affairs. To his genius and energy is due the success of the enterprise.

---

(10) Mr. Weatherford was a prominent Albany attorney, a close friend and legal adviser of Mr. Kay.

While like institutions were standing idle the Thomas
Kay Woolen Mills never stopped for a minute.

Mr. Kay was a man of iron nerve and indomitable
energy endowed with remarkable perseverance and deter-
mination; what he proposed he performed. He was honor-
able in all his affairs, honest, open and fair in all of his
dealings.

His conduct was such that he had the undoubted confidence of all his associates, the respect and esteem of this
community and the love and affection of his family and
neighbors.

No man did more for or is more deserving of the en-
comiums of this community than Thomas Kay.

He was blessed with but little education but possessed
those qualities of brain and heart that achieved success.

He was the architect of his own fortune and he carried
his name on the topmost rung of the ladder of usefulness.

He held high ideas of the capabilities of our State and he
stood the peer of any man in developing its resources.

Mr. Kay was sincere and frank in his convictions and
uncompromising where principle was involved.

To him duty well performed was the sublimest object of
his life.

It would have been as easy to swerve the sun from its
course as to move him from his faithful discharge of duty
committed to him. He was mindful of the rights and interests of others and with the many opportunities offered
no one can truthfully say that he ever did a mean act. He
left an unsullied name and a character free from even the
suspicion of a blemish.

In the death of President Thomas Kay this company has
suffered an irreparable loss, the community an honored
citizen and his family a true and faithful father.

Therefore, be it resolved that the foregoing memorium
be spread upon the minutes of this meeting as an expression of the respect and esteem in which Mr. Kay was held
by his associates and that this meeting do now adjourn.

R.H. Coshow, Sec.   Squire Farrar, Vice President

At the same time, T.B. Kay, son, was elected president and general manager at a salary of $2,000 per
year. O.P. Coshow was elected the new director and

ordered to draw up a set of by-laws. All promissory notes signed by Kay for the company were ratified.

Apparently the mill business ran smoothly under the new president. Employees totaled 115 happy people representing $45,000 annual payroll. Wool consumption was 500,000 pounds a year. Although water taken from the millrace was the source of power it was necessary to burn 1,500 cords of wood a year for the heating, dyeing and scouring processes. On one occasion slabwood was brought from Portland as an experiment in availability of supply and perhaps as to cost. By 1904, it was reported oil was being used as a cheaper fuel than wood, as the latter was becoming more difficult to buy in large quantities. Improvements were in the nature of a new sprinkler system, warehouse, and additional machinery. Small matters were noted in the minutes book but nothing of importance occurred. A ten per cent cash dividend was declared.

New stockholders' names appeared at the January, 1901, meeting: William Waldo, 25 shares; Fannie Kay Bishop (Mrs. C.P. Bishop), 25 shares; T.L. Davidson, 5 shares. Executors of the Kay estate were requested to fix a price on the Waterloo property, and the president's salary was determined at $2,400 annually. The months moved on, and another ten per cent cash dividend was declared.

Bishop continued to stock the products of the Kay mill, especially blankets which were always sold under the mill's label. Early in December, 1901, he advertised the opening of the store at a new location, 254-56 Commercial Street, Salem, emphasizing that blankets were sold directly from the factory with no middleman intervention, in gray, mottled, scarlet, white and vicuna, at prices ranging from $3.00 up to $8.55 a pair. They made beautiful Christmas gifts and were so advertised in the local newspapers, especially the virgin wool white ones at $4.00 to $12.25.

In addition to the Salem store he also owned the Salem Woolen Mills Store at 85 Third Street, Portland, where C.T. Roberts, Bishop's brother-in-law, was manager. Here, as in the capital city, the Kay fabrics and blankets were stocked and tailoring departments were maintained. In 1906 this store was sold to Ben Selling, a Portland clothier, who later had one of the largest stores of this kind in the city.

The appearance in January, 1902, of Asahel Bush's name as a new stockholder with 25 shares is significant. Bush was president of the Ladd & Bush bank. R.H. Coshow's salary was raised to $1,500 annually, and a stock dividend of twenty-five per cent was declared.

Perusal of the minute-book reveals the monotonous regularity with which cash dividends were paid; never less than five per cent, usually ten, and occasionally twenty-five, interspersed with a stock dividend now and then. These continued until the last declared ten per cent cash dividend on January 20, 1925.

New machinery continued to be added. It seemed as though new looms, cards and other necessary equipment were always on the move toward the Thomas Kay woolen mill. In this case, a new duster was installed as well as a scouring outfit, a hydro extractor, and two new looms which brought the factory up to thirty-two looms capacity or approximately three times the original figure when founded. A new brick boiler house was constructed twenty-eight feet square with a cement floor and an iron roof to house a new 100-horsepower boiler, thus making two to carry the heating and dyeing load. The company was grossing $200,000 a year, mostly as the result of the growth of the San Francisco market. The mill properties including machinery were valued at $85,000.

Along with T.B. Kay, Farrar, O.P. Coshow, Jr., and Weatherford, the name of Fannie Kay Bishop appears as a director on October 9, 1902. Kay's salary was increased to $3,000 in the January, 1903, meeting and shortly thereafter a question of water use of the millrace by state institutions occurred and was settled amicably. The same directors continued in office during 1903 and 1904 until the April meeting, 1905. Secretary Coshow resigned at this time and his offer to sell his shares at $150 was accepted. Mrs. Ann Kay likewise put her stock up for sale at the same price as did Mrs. Bishop with her small block of stock.

The most important business at the November, 1905, meeting was the sale of the Waterloo property to J.W. Cusick.

In February, 1906, it was reported that T.B. Kay and others had purchased the Eugene Woolen Mills Company, of Eugene, Oregon, a transaction confirmed in the minutes book by an authorization to buy $10,000 worth of the stock of this factory.

E.J. Swafford was hired as bookkeeper at $100 per month and later elected secretary of the company, a position which he held for many years. Six months later the record shows A.N. Bush a director. By the end of 1907 the company was reported in excellent condition with no outstanding bills, $30,000 accounts receivable, $6,000 cash in the bank, and with one $12,000 note payable for stock bought sometime during the year. There was a slackening off in business and the mill shut down for a week the day before Christmas (one of the very few times the factory had deliberately ceased operations), to reduce and revise the payroll.

In April, 1908, T.B. Kay made a proposition to sell the factory for $75,000 to the Bishops, who, at that time had not yet acquired ownership of the Pendleton woolen mill. Kay also offered the company's share in the Eugene woolen mill plus a division of the profits, and agreed to stay out of the business for two years. The transaction never materialized.

Other than this, the years 1908 and 1909 passed inconspicuously. In January, 1910, A.N. Bush was elected treasurer. The intervening years until World War I yielded nothing eventful in the history of the Kay mill.

The European conflict did spur the board to authorize contracts with the United States government for its products, presumably blankets and other woolen textiles. Squire Farrar died and the vacancy on the board was filled by Ercel W. Kay, son of the president. By 1918, the directors were: T.B. Kay, A.N. Bush, O.P. Coshow, Jr., J.K. Weatherford,

E.W. Kay, with T.B. Kay, president; Weatherford, vice-president; and E.J. Swafford, secretary. Ercel W. Kay was appointed assistant manager.

In the meantime, T.B. Kay had run for the office of State Treasurer, and ably held that position from January 4, 1911, until January 6, 1919. In 1925 he was in the same office again until his death in 1931.

In August, 1919, the board decided to discontinue the services of S.M. Merrill Company of Minneapolis as agent. Kay took over the management of sales at two-and-one-half per cent commission; his salary was cut to $350 per month as manager. E.W. Kay's salary was eliminated as assistant to his father. The secretary's salary was increased to $200 per month.

From this time through the following years there was little of interest to report. There was the usual regular declaration of dividends up to June 1925, but from then on these indicators of prosperity are not mentioned; in fact, there was talk of shutting the mill down in 1928. Secretary Swafford died and K.H. Pickens became secretary, a position he held until the mill was closed permanently in 1959. Asahel Bush became second largest stockholder.

Business picked up somewhat the next year, indicated by an authorization to purchase machinery from the defunct Matzen Woolen Mill Company of Kirkland, Washington, and to borrow money to carry on the affairs of the company. A $15,000 life insurance policy in the Oregon Life Insurance Company which the company held on T.B. Kay's life was transferred to him. In the meantime he had taken an extended trip to Europe returning in time to preside at the January, 1930, meeting of the board of directors. The annual report showed heavy financial losses through bad accounts amounting to $12,000, and business failures, but the greatest loss was on account of the decline in inventory taken at present market values: wool, dyes, and unfinished goods on hand. At the January, 1931, annual meeting it was decided to cut wages or shut the mill down. Upon the death of T.B. Kay in May, A.N. Bush was elected president and E.W. Kay, the son, appointed manager. A resolution of condolence was passed.

In 1931 Ercel W. Kay became president, a position he held until his death in 1965. In September 1959 the company announced it was closing the Salem factory; competitive conditions beyond their control forced the regrettable decision.

The old mill building was not destroyed but is part of the five-acre Thomas Kay Historical Park which also contains the restored Jason Lee house and parsonage, evidence of early Methodist missionary activity in Oregon.

THOMAS KAY DOCUMENTS

SUBSCRIPTION CONTRACT BETWEEN
THOMAS KAY AND THE CITIZENS OF SALEM
TO RAISE $20,000 BONUS.

We, the undersigned, in consideration of the advantages to accrue to us, and each of us, from the construction of a woolen mill in the city of Salem, Oregon, hereby subscribe the sums set opposite our respective names, as a subsidy for such purpose.

Whenever the amount of this subsidy shall reach the sum of $20,000.00, we agree to give our promissory notes for the amount of our subscription to such trustee as may be selected by the subscribers hereto, said note being drawn payable as follows: 12-1/2% on March 1, 1889; 25% on July 1, 1889, and the remainder on December 1, 1889 without interest until due.

This subscription is based upon the condition that there is to be a woolen mill established in Salem, Oregon, prior to January 1, 1890, capable of consuming 200,000 pounds of wool per annum; that the sum of $2,500 be paid on or before March 1, 1889 by the party constructing said mill into the hands of the trustees provided for herein, to be applied upon the purchase of the waterpower, and that the work of construction of said mill shall be begun prior to August 1, 1889; and that all payments on the part of subscribers shall become a lien upon all the interest in the mill site acquired or to be acquired by the recipient of the subscription for the construction of said mill to the satisfaction of the trustees, or the repayment of the amounts subscribed.

CONTRACT BETWEEN THE BOARD OF TRADE TRUSTEES AND THOMAS KAY

DRAWN BY HON. J.J. SHAW

The said party of the first part (Thomas Kay, and his associates O.P. Coshow, Jr., Squire Farrar and C.P. Bishop) hereby agrees with the said party of the second part (J.H. Albert, C.B. Moores, H.W. Cottle, W.M. Waite, and John G. Wright), trustees for and in behalf of the subscribers to the fund subscribed for the establishment of a woolen mill in Salem that the party of the first part his associates and assigns shall and will establish a woolen mill on the site known as the oil mill property, in the city of Salem, Marion County, Oregon, complete for the manufacture of woolen and worsted goods prior to January 1, 1890, capable of consuming 200,000 lbs. of wool per annum, and to pay toward the purchase of said site on or before the first day of Apr. 1889, sum of $2,500 in cash to W.T. Gray, George B. Gray and Charles A. Gray.

And in consideration of the above agreement on the part of the said party of the first part, the said party of the second part hereby agrees with the said party of the first part that said party of the second part shall and will pay to the said party of the first part the sum of $20,000.00 as follows to wit: The sum of $2,500 cash April 1, 1889; $5,000 on or before August 1, 1889; $5,000 on or before January 1, 1890; and in case the said woolen mill shall be completed and in good workmanlike manner on the said first day of January, 1890 by said first party, his heirs, associates, or assigns, then and in that case the said second party shall pay to said first party or his associates, heirs or assigns the further sum of $7,500.00.

But should said woolen mill not be so completed, the said balance ($7,500.00) shall not be paid until said woolen mill shall be completed.

It is understood by and between the parties hereto that said woolen mill shall not be used for any other purpose than that above specified for the term of five years from and after the time of its completion, but that any surplus power over and above that sufficient for the proper operation of said woolen mill may be used for any purpose desired by said first party, his heirs, associates or assigns, and said first party hereto binds himself, his heirs and assigns that the said power and woolen mill shall not for said period of five years be used or operated for any other purpose other than as aforesaid in the penalty of $20,000.00 to be paid said second party for the benefit of the subscribers to said fund in proportion to their subscriptions.

Witness our hands and seals the day, years first above written.

Chapter III

WATERLOO DEVELOPMENT COMPANY

"Cheap land and waterpower at the Falls
of the Santiam"

WATERLOO, Linn County, Oregon is a quiet, unobtrusive little community situated about 18 miles from Albany, the county seat. Neighboring towns of Lebanon and Sweet Home have recently felt the touch of modern progress as two great dams on the South Santiam River were constructed. But Waterloo has only casually responded to the economic vibrations which emanate from such projects. A new concrete bridge spans the river and adjacent is the inviting park, but the community still retains some of the quiet charm of the early days.

The Falls of the Santiam had invited pioneer power-minded Elmore Kees to build a gristmill and a sawmill there, but these had disappeared prior to the 1880s. Nevertheless, the power potentialities at this location were known to industrialists like Thomas Kay who had opened a new woolen mill at Salem in March 1890 after selling his interests in the Eagle woolen mill at Brownsville. Woolen mill men were always thinking in terms of cheap land and waterpower and there was an abundance of both at Waterloo.

With the demise of the Eagle mill Mr. Kay began to cast about for factory sites and may have given serious thought to Waterloo even before he selected Salem, for on August 25, 1888 a deed records the sale of one acre of land together with "1,000 inches of waterpower thereon" to Thomas Kay by John Leedy and his wife, and Jacob Sandner.[1]

More property was acquired on July 17, 1890 when Kay and J.K. Weatherford, a prominent Albany attorney and Kay's legal adviser and lifelong friend together purchased from Mark Hulburt and wife, one acre of property on the donation land claim of Elmore Kees and J. Albert Gibheard, in the town of Waterloo. The property was known as the Mack property and was purchased for $3,125. [2]

In April 1891, Kay and Weatherford began correspondence relative to the California Hosiery Company of Oakland which was anxious to sell its machinery.[3] This enterprise was established in 1881 and continued in successful operation until its purchase by the Waterloo Development Company in 1891.

The Oakland capitalists suggested the formation of a $45,000 company to donate the land, waterpower and to erect the buildings. The hosiery company would take stock in the new company in payment for the machinery which would be transferred to Waterloo. In other words, the Oregon promoters would provide the site and part of the working capital. At the time, the Oakland mill with its 200 employees was

---

(1) Deed Book 32, p. 536, Linn County Recorder
(2) Deed Book 38, p. 342, Linn County Recorder
(3) J.K. Weatherford Correspondence, Special Collections, University of Oregon Library

considered a high cost operation and was not making a profit.

Details surrounding this transaction were not always clarified in the correspondence, but in one letter from Kay to Weatherford he said "let the hosiery people put in their plant at $15,000, you and I $15,000", the estimated value of the land and waterpower, the remainder of $15,000 to be subscribed locally. This procedure would get the project under way. Kay felt he could not put more into it, but that cheap power on an excellent waterpower site, an abundance of fuel from nearby sawmills, and good quality wool made the proposition attractive.

The site selected for the new hosiery mill was on part of 200 acres owned by Mr. Kay on the south side of the South Santiam River where the old flour mill and sawmill had once been built, but discontinued in 1885.

Correspondence continued through the months into August between the hosiery company representatives and the Kay interests now formally organized as the Waterloo Development Company to facilitate the promotion. Incorporators were J. Wristman, an Albany insurance agent; W.C. Davis, and E.E. Montague. Mr. Kay's name does not appear in the articles of incorporation which were completed on August 11, 1891, and filed with the Oregon Secretary of State on April 14th. Capital stock was $70,000 divided into shares of $100 each. The principal place of business and office would be at Waterloo after January 1, 1892, but in the interim at Albany. Writsman became a director and was secretary-treasurer of the company.

At this point the name of J.H. Albert, an officer of the Capital National Bank, Salem, appears who suggested a trade of Salem town property for Waterloo land. His relationship to the project is not clear, but Kay thought he would be a good man to have in the company.

David Rutherford of the Oakland company said that if the town is once laid out the sale of town lots would pay for the mill. Whereupon Mr. Kay offered 100 acres of his land and included the water rights. All of which indicates that the project had other angles than just the establishment of a hosiery factory. But matters dragged on. The Oakland owners did not want to spend more time or money on the Waterloo proposition and announced that they had promising buyers in Mexico who had taken a 60-day option on the purchase of the machinery. Much to the relief of the Waterloo promoters the option was not exercised by September 28, 1891, the deadline, and negotiations were reopened with Kay and Weatherford.

Rutherford was becoming impatient to close the deal and urged Kay to make a formal proposition. It was thought $5,000 could be raised in Portland as the president of the Portland Chamber of Commerce was interested. In the meantime, the Oakland company's board of directors met and gave assurance that no one else would get an option and the Waterloo people could proceed without fear. "The Oregon people are slow in making up their minds but we like their proposition." A telegram to Kay on October 1, 1891 stated that a representative from Oakland would be in Oregon with full power to act, which prompted Kay to wire Weatherford at Albany "Good news from Oakland will be up (from Salem) tonight get men together."

The transaction for the purchase and sale of the hosiery mill machinery was completed and arrangements made to store the machinery and a warehouseman selected to watch over the property until it could be shipped to Waterloo. Insurance coverage expense was made on a 50-50 basis. A boiler was purchased for $841 in late November.

A letter to Weatherford dated December 11, 1891 stated that Kay enclosed a deed duly signed, but no reference was made as to whether this was for Waterloo property, although a strong presumption prevails that this was for the Waterloo land. In February 1892 Mr. Kay stated that he would deed the land but not the waterpower, but would permit use of the waterpower for five years.

Other promotional aspects developed in August 1892 when Kay and Weatherford discussed the possibility of a railroad from Lebanon to Waterloo via Sodaville, a distance of approximately eight miles. This would make a direct connection with the Southern Pacific's branch line to Albany.

Establishment of a textile factory in any western Oregon community always stimulated economic activity. In Waterloo's case a plot of the town was filed with the Linn County Recorder on February 23, 1892 and a charter received in March the following year. A hotel was built by Kay and Weatherford with A.P. Howe, manager.

Waterloo began to build up rapidly. Soon there were five stores, a butcher shop, two blacksmith shops, a shoe repair shop, a barber shop, a livery stable, dance hall, tavern and a saloon.[4] A year later in 1893 a four-room schoolhouse was built followed by an Evangelical church. The Census of 1880 gave Waterloo precinct 715 population which had decreased to 589 in 1900. Waterloo town had 59.

Perhaps the hosiery mill operation was not as profitable as the development company had anticipated, for on October 31, 1894 directors of the Thomas Kay Woolen Mill Company of Salem, were considering the purchase of the Waterloo hosiery mill and waterpower from the Waterloo Development Company.[5] After an investigation of the title, the mill building and all the machinery, fixtures, waterpower and river frontage were purchased. Payment would be made by an issue of $10,000 of the woolen mill stock.

An aspect of the transaction is revealed in the records of the Linn County Recorder wherein there was filed on January 30, 1895, the Waterloo Development Company's deed to E.P. McCornack, an Albany banker, for $3,600 covering the purchase of property in four blocks in the town of Waterloo with all water rights, water powers, flumes, ditches, and races; also the woolen mill property and its

(4) Interview with Mrs. Nettie R. Glass, Waterloo
(5) Minute Book, Thomas Kay Woolen Mill Company

Waterloo Woolen Mill at the Falls of the Santiam.

Eugene Woolen Mill, circa 1910.

machinery.[7] The document was signed by Thomas Kay, president of the Waterloo Development Company, and Writsman secretary.

On the same day McCornack filed a deed for the same property and the same amount to the Thomas Kay Woolen Mill Company.[8] Details of the McCornack transaction are obscure, but a reasonable assumption is, that he held a mortgage which was ultimately liquidated. The development company divested itself of Waterloo property during the year. Several lots were sold for $1,500. On March 21, 1895, the Albany *Disseminator* and other Willamette Valley newspapers carried a story that Thomas Kay would start a new $20,000 woolen mill at Waterloo.

Plans were drawn for a factory building 100 feet by 40 feet to house a 3-set mill to manufacture blankets, flannels, and other woolen fabrics. Waterloo was chosen because the plant could be run cheaper in a small community than in a city. Goods could be freighted by team to the Albany and Lebanon Railroad Company* station at Lebanon, a distance of about eight miles.

Published price for wool was ten cents for Valley and eight cents for eastern Oregon, and Kay needed 40,000 pounds to start. By June 12, the twelve looms were running full time on a blanket contract for a New York buyer which would keep the mill's sixty employees busy well into September. This mill would

---

(7) Deed Book 49, pages 172, 173, Linn County Recorder
(8) Deed Book 52, Linn County Recorder
(*) This was a short line which connected with the Oregon and California Railroad at Albany

add another to those already operating at Brownsville and Albany in Linn County making this area the center of Oregon woolen textile manufacturing.

Luckily for the Kay interests that the Waterloo mill was in full operation, for early in the morning of November 18, 1895, Salemites were awakened by the agonizing shrieks of the Kay mill whistle. A fire which had started in the dryhouse burned the structure to the ground. The loss was a severe blow to Mr. Kay, but within a month ground was broken for a new building.

Four Knowles fancy looms and a Park and Woolson shear were immediately ordered to be installed at the Waterloo mill to fill the orders of the Kay mill until it was in operation again, which was in May, 1896. The Waterloo mill not only took up the production slack of the Salem mill but it was a godsend to many of the temporarily displaced dyers and finishers who worked there while the new building was under construction.

With the two mills going, Mr. Kay shuttled back and forth between Salem and Waterloo as occasion demanded during 1896 and 1897. Waterloo was like a branch plant filling orders offered to it by the Kay mill and frequently obtaining its wool and other supplies from there. The smaller plant, on the other hand, sent some of its cloth to Salem to be finished after it was dyed. Costs were thereby reduced as one team of finishers handled the work of both mills.

Tight credit resulted in the presidential election year of 1896 when the ephemeral free silver doctrine was espoused by William J. Bryan against William McKinley's gold standard, protective tariff platform.

The First National Bank of Salem requested that the Kay woolen mill credit line be reduced for fear that the free silver candidate might win. As the business required more credit, the directors in August voted to suspend operations which temporarily threw more business to the Waterloo factory. When a Republican victory was assured the mill was reopened and four extra looms were removed from Waterloo to Salem. Unfinished cloth from there also dribbled in indicating close working arrangements between the two mills. The finishing and dyeing departments at the Salem factory were enlarged.

As orders began to pour into both mills, specialization was in evidence with Salem concentrating on mackinaws and flannels for the Alaska trade and Waterloo on bed and camp blankets. Fleishner, Mayer & Company of Portland, were the wholesale distributors for the Kay interests. Excellent markets prevailed for woolen goods as the Klondike goldrush gathered momentum. Retailers advertised Oregon-made mackinaw suits, overshirts, underwear and blankets. Good times came for all Pacific Northwest woolen mills. The spring of 1897 found the Kay mills working full time.

The prosperity which a seller's market brought to the fifty employees of the Waterloo woolen mill was dramatically cut short on Saturday April 9, 1898 by a fire which consumed the entire mill building and its contents. Thomas Kay, on his way home from Waterloo had just boarded the train at Lebanon when a man on horseback came galloping up to say the mill and hotel were burning. Upon arrival at Albany Mr.

Kay immediately telephoned his son-in-law, C.P. Bishop at Salem. The mill had shut down at 4:30 p.m. the regular Sunday closing time. About an hour later the fire was discovered in the dryroom. Although the mill building was completely destroyed, a bucket brigade was formed which saved the hotel owned by Kay and Weatherford. The loss was estimated as high as $60,000 with insurance coverage of $26,000.

J.P. Wilbur, later manager of the Union woolen mill at Union, Oregon, was working at Waterloo at the time of the fire. Mrs. Wilbur, who was home, heard the crowd yelling and saw a bucket brigade formed in a futile effort to stop the fire. A water pump in the basement which might have been effective was reported broken.

Fire was an ever present hazard at the woolen mills, and the Kay interests had their share. Although these misfortunes were frustrating, the employees at Waterloo were the real sufferers. The mill payroll had been a stabilizing influence in the community, and when Mr. Kay announced that the factory would not be rebuilt many families prepared to move. The record is not clear, but it may be presumed that some of the technicians may have been absorbed by the Salem operation.

Then hopefully, Waterloo citizens made the company a proposition to furnish brick for a new building providing construction could be gotten underway that summer. Former workers agreed to work at half pay if the plant would be rebuilt, but nothing materialized. The gloomy and disheartening situation which enveloped the town is best expressed by a news item in the Albany *States Right Democrat* which said that things have been quiet since the fire of a year ago. The reporter said he saw 17 men sitting on a fence watching a man gardening. Although Waterloo did not become a ghost town, people moved away including some of the city officers. All that were left were a schoolhouse, a churchhouse, and a store.

The only consolation Mr. Kay had was a painting of the mill building by Charles Devine which had been presented to him by the employees at an earlier date and which hung in his Salem office.

Mr. Kay died on April 27, 1900, age 63, approximately two years after the damaging fire. His son T.B. Kay undertook the active management of the businesses. In later years he divided his time between the woolen mill and as State Treasurer of Oregon.

Disposition of the Waterloo properties is evidenced in the Linn County Recorder's Deed Books wherein on November 15, 1905 deeds were filed to eight lots from the Thomas Kay Woolen Mill Company of Salem to Ann Kay two-sixths, J.K. Weatherford one-half, and Z.K. Rudd one-sixth; to J.W. Cusick 15 lots and property in Concordia. The documents were signed by T.B. Kay, president, and O.P. Coshow, secretary.[9] Transfers were then made of another block of lots to Cusick by the first three named above, all for the sum of $1.00.

Thus is concluded the history of the Waterloo woolen mill at the Falls of the Santiam, one of the

---

(9) Deed Book 80, pp. 223-31, Linn County Recorder

triad (including the Brownsville woolen mill) of such enterprises which made Linn County the center of woolen cloth manufacturing in Oregon during the 1890s and early 1900s.

Chapter IV

DALLAS WOOLEN
MANUFACTURING COMPANY

"Our people are determined
that the woolen mill will go"

DALLAS, county seat of Polk County, was no different than other Willamette Valley communities in its eager desire for a woolen factory. A lasting imprint had been left on the town by the earlier small pioneer Ellendale mill founded by Judge Reuben P. Boise in 1865.[1] The abandoned site on the Rickreall Creek with its aged flume, three miles west of the town, were constant reminders that the wasting waters of the stream should again be diverted to productive use. The need for payrolls to supplement the economy of a strictly rural community stimulated talk of a woolen mill in the late 1880s and early 1890s.

Said the Polk County *Itemizer* of November 6, 1891: "There was a good-sized meeting at the courthouse last night to talk the matter up." It was known that the Santa Rosa, California woolen mill had ceased operations and was for sale. The high cost of operation and scarcity of fuel were largely responsible for its closure. Whether by design or accident, two of the principal stockholders were in Dallas at the time, presumably with the intention of moving the plant to

---

(1) Alfred L. Lomax, *Pioneer Woolen Mills in Oregon*, Binfords & Mort, Portland, Oregon, 1941

Oregon providing a suitable site could be found with cheap power, fuel and a dependable supply of raw wool. Dallas had these prerequisites. The principal problem was finance as it always was with woolen mill promotion. Undoubtedly the two men attended the courthouse meeting where a bonus of $5,000 was tentatively set.

Within a week, $32,000 had been subscribed at $100 per share toward the $50,000 named in the articles of incorporation of the Dallas Woolen Manufacturing Company, drawn up on November 28, 1891. Incorporators were W.C. Brown, John J. Daly, M.M. Ellis, Adam K. Wilson and Peter Allison. Of the 61 stockholders in the enterprise, Allison, a former weaver in the Santa Rosa mill, held 120 shares; the remainder was taken by townspeople in small shares amounting to $20,200. The subscription list bore the names of such well-known citizens as John Ellis, J.W. Crider, Ed Siefarth, R.C. Craven, N.M. McDaniel and others.

Directors of the new company were not elected until January 18, 1892, when Peter Allison, W.C. Brown, R.C. Craven, A.K. Wilson, W.P. Wright, M.M. Ellis, and J.F. Groves were chosen. One week later R.C. Craven was elected president and Allison, foreman. Groves, Craven, and Allison were appointed a building committee which soon recommended the purchase of a strip of land on the Rickreall 156 feet by 325 feet from La Creole Academy for $900. The site was just east of the railroad bridge on the south side of the Rickreall, or as the little river was sometimes called the La Creole.

A combination stone and three-story frame building 60 feet by 110 feet was planned with a 75 feet by 40 feet engine and dye room adjoining. Construction was delayed until the inclement weather of January and February cleared.

The end of March, 1892 saw the completion of the solid masonry basement and the beginning of the frame superstructure. Allison left for Santa Rosa to ship the machinery north to its new location. One month later, the framework of the first story was in position. By the middle of May the roof was on and the building awaited the arrival of the machinery.

South of the main building a picker room was built, and nearby a platform for drying the wool. Compared to most of the buildings in Dallas, the structure presented a massive appearance.

Six carloads of machinery sufficient for a 3-set mill arrived the latter part of May with the building ready to receive it. "Ere long the plant will be put in operation and it will be a grand old day for Dallas," bubbled the *Observer's* editor; and "Our citizens ought to go and see the great piles of machinery waiting to be put in their proper places," enthusiastically urged the *Itemizer's* editor, on a topic which for once both were in agreement.

Upon Allison's return he brought with him three skilled workmen from Santa Rosa to help install the machinery. In anticipation of the whir of the spindles and clatter of looms, raw wool in great woolbags began to make its appearance on the factory premises.

In June 1892 financial problems began to appear with the directors voting a stock assessment to clear current debts. It was gossiped about that matters were not quite right on the Rickreall; stock subscriptions were not being paid up as fast as was desirable. The immediate shortage of cash for operating expenses was a deterrent to the operation of the mill.

The big engine had been tested, its hissing exhausts and humming flywheel pleasant preludes to the regular rhythm of flying shuttles and spinning bobbins. Ten thousand pounds of raw wool were on hand by September, the machinery was in place and in spite of monetary difficulties the woolen mill appeared to be ready for operation.

Public apprehension that all was not well at the mill was voiced by editorial comment in the local paper in October which urged stockholders to stand by their investment. "Everything is in readiness to start as soon as the balance of the stock is paid up. The mill should be running to its fullest capacity and paying its owners a handsome investment instead of standing idle at a loss and as a travesty on the good name of our people. The cry of hardtimes is past . . . and all our flourishing town requires is a monthly payroll from manufacturing enterprises and the woolen mill will be the opening wedge."

The situation reached a climax the latter part of October when the mill property was attached by the sheriff to be held for claims. Notice was sent to all delinquent stockholders to pay up. President R.C. Craven called a stockholders' meeting for February 4, 1893 and again on the 15th when it was decided to circulate a stock subscription list to secure more capital. "Let those now give who never gave before;

and those who gave, now give the more," desperately urged the *Observer's* editor in a rhyming mood.

Some stock was sold but not enough to forestall legal action, for in March the mill was bought at sheriff's sale by John Walker, a California capitalist who bid in for the amount of the claim at $5,784.36. Judgments against the company amounted to $4,000 more. It was hoped the stockholders would redeem their factory before the May term of the Circuit Court when the sale would be confirmed. A hopeful note in the midst of despair was from the home-industry-minded Portland *Oregonian* which said: "Dallas has a woolen mill which will in the near future be a source of revenue to Polk County farmers and citizens of Dallas. Dallas will have 10,000 inhabitants within five years."

A few days after the Walker transaction, twelve citizens purchased the sheriff's certificate to forestall final closure. News came in May that the court had confirmed the sale back to the stockholders, and with the clearance of legal entanglements the woolen mill would now surely begin operations "that will make Dallas the happy home of hundreds of mill employes." But the community was understandingly remorseful and bitter toward its investment losses.

From September 1893 to June 1896 the factory building stood full of idle machinery, a monument to civic ambitions and a constant reminder of a non-paying investment. Disappointment and disgust characterized the feelings of the people. Appeals to start up the woolen mill appeared week after week in editorial brevities reminding negligent stockholders to fulfill their obligations. An attention-getting rhythmical outburst entitled "The Woolen Mill Will Run" broke the dull monotony of the personals and other local news just before the Christmas holidays, December 1894:

> The woolen mill will run
> You hear it on the breezes whichever way they blow,
> Our people are determined the woolen mill will go.
>
> And e'een the pattering raindrops encourage every heart
> They say in silent language: The woolen mill will start.
>
> Our people are rejoicing, and every mother's son
> Has felt the glad assurance the woolen mill run.

Then on January 4, 1895 another burst in lieu of solid news about the mill:

> Our poet he is anxious, he wants the folks to know
> Why people are determined the woolen mill won't go.
>
> He told in storied verses a month ago or two
> To make the spindles rattle we certain things should do
>
> These things are not accomplished, the mill still idly
> stands;
> And if the owner don't soon act we soon will wash our
> hands
>
> Of woolens, linens and all else that soon would raise the
> town
> To one that old John Gilpin called "A City of Renown."

In contrast to the tangled affairs of the Dallas enterprise were the highly successful woolen mills of the Thomas Kay interests at Salem, Marion County, and Waterloo, Linn County. Also in Linn County was the then successful Albany woolen mill.

In March 1895, Judge Hewitt sustained a demurrer to a complaint to allow certain plaintiff creditors of the woolen mill until May 1 to file an amended complaint and to have the balance of the outstanding stock collected and applied against the accounts of the company.

With the dull winter days gone the editor moved to one final versifying spasm:

It Won't Do It

Dallas woolen mill, don't bereave us
Neither wilt thou answer to the call;
Bless the enterprise that's always with us
While we balance eight and circle all.
(The looms won't run)

A spirit of frustration possessed the town which in turn manifested itself in ridicule as someone suggested that the woolen mill be moved to the courthouse grounds and used as a temple of justice as the front end of that building was about to cave in and should be condemned. Year's end found the factory building standing idle, an unwanted memorial to a promising manufacturing project gone sour.

A little brighter prospect turned up in 1896 when Charles Sheperd, owner of a Woodland, California woolen mill came to Dallas and began negotiations. The optimistic pronouncements accompanying his visit did not materialize and the town took another blow to its industrial ambitions.

The situation literally glowed in June when James Shaw of Oregon City with his two sons completed arrangements for buying the Dallas woolen mill. As usual, the most optimistic statements began to appear in the local newspapers as to population increases, the movement of real estate, and the demand for empty houses. The situation looked so good it reminded everyone of 1892 when the mill started up.

The Shaws did a good job of renovation. The machinery was dirty from having stood idle for so long. The accumulations of gummy oil and caked grease to say nothing of dust, kept them busy cleaning during most of July. But at month's end, Shaw was getting out samples of flannels and blankets for distribution to the market. Delinquent stockholders were requested to pay their subscriptions to the Dallas City Bank.

Five looms were added in October and the labor force increased. November saw William McKinley's election as president of the United States, a prophecy of good times to come under a Republican administration as contrasted with the hard times of the past four years associated with the Democratic party. "The woolen mill whistle sounds better since McKinley's election" chortled Republican-minded editor Hayter.

The mill, now running full time, had built a new storeroom and workshop. Orders were on hand from eastern buyers of woolen cloth and blankets. Miners' goods, 12-pound blankets, heavy flannels and other cloth were also in demand. A market had blossomed at the opportune time. It looked like Shaw was the right man. The mill operated successfully through 1897.

Shaw's announcement two weeks before Christmas 1897 that he was hiring 60 more workers for day and night shifts was welcome news to a payroll-hungry community. Several carloads of raw wool were piled high on the unloading platform of the factory, bulky fodder for the steam scouring tubs and voracious carding machines which awaited it on the inside. A large shed was added for the picking department. Night work was facilitated by the plant's own electric power plant. A tailoring establishment was added under the supervision of W.C. Brown and his son Alonzo, Shaw's brother-in-law, who also ran a dry-goods store.

Intermittent operations characterized the mill until May 1898. In July, there was a rumor that a group of Portland and eastern capitalists were interested in purchasing the factory and would operate it full time. In September, sheriff Van Orsdal was still trying to settle the business of the stockholders.

In October, word got around that some Tacoma men had shown an interest in the Dallas properties. The Tacoma woolen mill in which these men had a substantial interest, was completely gutted by fire on October 1, 1898, and were now looking around for another mill. These were Fred Carter, Charles H. Carter, brothers, and William Walker. The Carters came from a family of textile workers in Dewsbury, Yorkshire, England. After a short sojourn on the Atlantic Coast, they came to Tacoma where they had leased the woolen mill of that city. The father and mother were also skilled textile workers; the father was a weaver and the mother an expert loom operator.

After refusing a Tacoma bank's offer to sell them the remnants of the destroyed mill for the amount of the mortgage or less, the banker told the brothers about a woolen mill in Dallas, Oregon which he thought was for sale. Fred went immediately to the Polk County town and began negotiations with James Shaw which ended in the lease of the Dallas Woolen Manufacturing Company for one year with the privilege of purchasing.

The sum of $10,000 was paid and the Dallas factory came under the control of the Carters and Walker with Fred as manager. These three then incorporated the Pioneer Woolen Mills Company for $10,000 on October 29, 1898 with the principal office in Portland. As soon as this news was reported the *Observer* blazoned the fact in a 24-point headline. Then editorially skeptical it said: "This is an old song of the Observer, but recent events seem to indicate that we are telling the truth this time." November 1, 1898 was set for the opening day of the mill under new management.

Five carloads of machinery arrived together with some household goods; the Tacoma machinery was too badly damaged to justify its transfer to Dallas. Additions were a machine shop for repairs, a new picker room for shoddy, and an electric lighting system. Opening date was extended to the middle of the month.

Dallas now had about 1,500 population. Typical small-town manufacturing plants were a sash and door factory, flour mill, foundry, tannery, sawmill, wagon factory, electric light plant, brick and tile factory and fruit evaporating plants.

Better transportation facilities were in the offing with the construction of the Luckiamute Valley and Western Railroad from Falls City via Dallas to Salem

Spinning frames (mules) in Eugene Woolen Mill.

[Lane County Pioneer Museum]

Bandon Woolen Mills, Bandon, Oregon, facing the Coquille River.

[*Victor C. West collection*]

with a proposed westward extension to the small coast river port of Yaquina. The town stood to gain as a supply point for logging camps and sawmills which were moving into the vast stand of Douglas fir and hemlock which blanketed the Coast Range.

For several years Dallas had been served by a narrow gauge rail line from Portland, later acquired by the Southern Pacific Railroad and converted to standard gauge. The woolen mill was without a rail siding, consequently, both incoming grease wool and outgoing finished cloth were carted to and from nearby Independence on the Willamette River from which point sternwheeler steamboats ran to Portland. Sometimes outgoing freight was transshipped at Salem, 15 miles distant, where rail connection was made with the Southern Pacific.

Just before Christmas two new boilers were installed to furnish power for the mill and the electric light plant. Eight new looms were added. There were now 60 people on the payroll with wages 10 cents an hour for men, 75 cents a day for women. Orders were on hand for eight months ahead.

Dallas was a happy and prosperous little community as 1898 came to a close. Its industries were operating full time, but best of all the woolen mill kept steam up day and night. No one minded the early morning shriek of the factory whistle as it called the people to work. Never before had Dallas seen such busy days, nor the farmers who were paid the highest price for their wool.

This contentment was manifested in the lack of news about the woolen mill. The full dinner pail was a reality under a Republican administration. The Spanish-American War, Admiral Dewey, Cuba, Hawaii, and how best welcome home the heroes of Manila and the Malabon made more interesting copy than a drab woolen mill and workers in overalls.

News brevities announced the transfer of some acreage to the Pioneer Woolen Mill Company; the refurbishing of a room formerly occupied by Judge Hardy Holman as a clubroom for the young men of the woolen mill; and the issuance of naturalization papers to Fred and Charles Carter.

The new year 1900 opened auspiciously as orders for heavy suitings, overcoatings and other cloth poured in which forced the mill onto a day and night shift basis. There were now 100 employees which turned out 125,000 yards of cloth in six months.

Several months of idleness followed this surge of prosperity and key personnel quit when it was rumored that the factory would close down and move to Portland. When it was disclosed that Fred Carter, William Walker and Raleigh Stott had incorporated the Portland Woolen Mills for $90,000 on July 3, 1900 a further disquieting note was added to the situation. But the company was never activated.

The Carters evidently saw the futility of trying to revitalize the Dallas mill and looked elsewhere to use their talents. In December, 1900 Fred Carter and Walker became the incorporators with others of the Marysville, California Woolen Mills, Carter with a $5,300 subscription and Walker with $2,700. On March 4, 1901 Fred Carter's name was affixed to the incorporation papers of the Portland Woolen Mills with those of Portland capitalists.

At this time Portland business men were agitating for a woolen mill. Some expressed an interest in moving the Dallas plant, others opposed the idea for fear of creating small town enmity toward the big city whose businesses were benefitted by their trade. In spite of these assurances, with the formation of the aforesaid Portland Woolen Mills, the machinery was removed from the building, disassembled and shipped to Sellwood, a Portland suburb where it was installed in a new factory building. But these moves broke the spirit of Dallas business men who never again promoted a woolen mill.

Fred's association with the new company was brief, as was that of his father, mother, and son John, Jr. all of whom moved to Marysville where Fred became superintendent. Charles stayed in Oregon as vice-president of the Sellwood mill and later became the company president.

The woolen mill building in Dallas was eventually purchased by the LaCreole Academy (Dallas College) and used as a gymnasium until it was consumed by fire on Christmas Day 1910.

Chapter V

PORTLAND WOOLEN MILLS COMPANY

*"Local capitalists should take advantage of
woolen mill investments"*

PORTLAND, a city of 65,000 population in the late
1880's had burgeoned into a small but important
manufacturing and marketing center with flour mills,
sawmills, breweries, foundries, and small clothing
establishments which served an expanding regional
and local market. Wheat and wool from the agricultural hinterland flowed down the Columbia and
Willamette rivers on sternwheelers to be picked up by
the newly built railroads to California and the East,
and the small coastal steamers which discharged at
San Francisco.

Raw wool from the ranches, washed wool from the
scouring mills at Pendleton and The Dalles, and
finished cloth from the woolen mills at Oregon City,
Salem, and Brownsville were distributed through
Portland middlemen. Oregon ranked seventh in the
nation in number of sheep by June, 1900, with a total
of 2,139,504 fleeces shorn. The wool clip had
expanded to over 18,000,000 pounds, valued at
approximately $2,400,000.[1] With so much raw
material available it seems odd that Portland did not

---

(1) *Twelfth Census of the United States*, 1900, Vol. V, *Agriculture*, Part I,
pp. 320, 673. Vol. VIII, Manufactures, Part II, p. 734, gives 1899 figures

have a woolen mill. Perhaps the Oregon City mill was sufficiently near for Portlanders to claim it as their own. Perhaps this community indifference to the then popular woolen mill movement can be explained in terms of "mossbackism," a local, faintly opprobrious expression directed at the self-satisfied elements in a community who seemed opposed to progress and remained happy in their isolation.

At any rate, the rhythmical clacking of shuttles and looms was yet to be heard in competition with the staccato whine of saws in the riverfront sawmills. The promotional vigor which raised the pioneer woolen factories was lacking in Oregon's metropolis.

The first organized effort to promote Portland's industrial potentialities was the organization of the Manufactures' Association on April 16, 1895.[2]

Panics had left their scars; payrolls were urgently needed to stimulate and stabilize business. "Develop home manufactures for home patronage" was the slogan, with special reference to woolen mills.

There was no dearth of capital. First families had established fortunes firmly rooted in transportation, banking, drygoods, and the professions. Ladd & Tilton, First National and Ainsworth National were already locally powerful banks, their letterheads displaying the names of leading citizens as officers and members of the boards of directors.

R.D. Inman, head of the big Inman, Poulsen Lumber Company, was president of the newly formed association; A.H. Devers of Closset & Devers,

---

(2) *Morning Oregonian*, Portland, April 17, 1895

wholesale grocery firm, was vice-president; R.J. Holmes, manager of the Northwest Cold Storage & Ice Company was treasurer; and A.C. Master was elected secretary.[3] Monthly meetings were held in Room 524 Chamber of Commerce Building, a gray sandstone structure which filled half a block on Stark Street between Third and Fourth (the building was razed several years ago to make space for a parking lot).

Two years elapsed before the subject of woolen mills was revived. At its March 9, 1897 meeting a favorable report was made on the qualifications of a locally organized company called the Pacific Woolen and Clothing Company and incorporated for $100,000.[4] Incorporators were Lewis Russell of Russell & Blyth, a real estate, insurance and loan firm; John Eben Young of Garratt & Young, woolen goods manufacturers' agents; and Charles Coopey, prominent tailor and woolen mill enthusiast, who submitted a prospectus of the project.

The plan was to dismantle a ten-set eastern woolen mill and ship it to Portland for reassembly. From 200 to 300 people would be employed on a monthly payroll of $5,000 to $7,000.

Considerable enthusiasm was evinced for the proposition with one member promising to take $5,000 in stock if the company would select his property as the site for the mill. Much of the discussion centered around financing and the indifference of Portland capitalists toward woolen mill promotion.

(3) *Morning Oregonian*, April 30, 1895
(4) Filed in the office of the Secretary of State, Oregon, March 10, 1897

Woolen mills were under way in Salem and at Union in eastern Oregon. Surely, Portland with its superior financial resources could do as well or better than the smaller towns which had displayed enviable community enterprise.

Prosperity was returning; the Klondike gold fields offered a market for heavy clothing and a tariff law protected home industry. Oregon woolen goods, especially blankets, were achieving both a local and a national high quality reputation.

Coopey argued that the mill could produce cloth for uniforms for policemen, firemen, trainmen, and the National Guard. That he was a tailor and specialized in this kind of outfitting perhaps lent emphasis to his remarks. The mill could also make Irish frieze, a coarse cloth with a shaggy nap on one side used for skirts and other outer garments. Knitting machines for underwear were also included in the project.

A common argument in these discussions was that Oregonians were dependent upon eastern manufacturers to supply local clothing needs. Oregon wool was shipped east, both in the grease and scoured, manufactured into cloth and suits and shipped back, thereby necessitating the payment of freight costs two ways. West Coast stores sold the suits for $12 to $17 each, an exorbitant price to pay for a factory-made suit, so it was said.

Entrenched retail and jobbing interests countered by stating that eastern manufacturers could place quality clothing in the Portland market cheaper than could the local textile mills. Nevertheless, suitings continued to be made by Oregon woolen mills, notably the Kay mill at Salem, which for a time had its own store there and in Portland.

Emphasis was placed on the natural resources of the state. The high quality of Oregon's woolen textiles, especially blankets, was accountable not alone to the craftsmanship of skilled workers, but in part to the mineral-free, soft waters of the streams which coursed out of the Cascade Mountains. Fleeces washed and scoured in this crystal-pure water carded and spun better and held their dyes in greater brilliance than where less favorable conditions prevailed.

Another resource was the moist, temperate climate which provided the necessary humidity in the factory and tended to free the fibers from the ever-present static electricity in the carding and spinning operations.

As steam and electricity gained prestige, the use of water-power on millwheels declined. Wood as a fuel for boilers was plentiful everywhere in Oregon; waste from sawmills could be obtained at a ridiculously low price and sometimes free. Electricity, generated at Willamette Falls near Oregon City by the Portland Electric Company, provided dependable power for any factory which chose Portland as a site for a woolen mill or other kind of factory.

The pool of 2,000 skilled textile workers and technicians which had its beginning in the pioneer mills first built at Salem, Brownsville, Oregon City and elsewhere included the descendants of these self-trained workers, augmented by immigrants from eastern and mid-western woolen mills.

Meetings were held and discussions continued by the Manufacturers' Association, but the mill promotion plans failed to materialize. In January 1898, woolen mills were again discussed when David Dalgleish, retired Brownsville woolen mill executive then living in Portland, stated that an eastern mill owner was ready to move to the city providing a free building and site and free power would be donated, but that no cash bonus would be required. The proposition was roundly discussed with the suggestion that every property owner on the east side should contribute not less than $25 toward the purchase of a site for the mill; that east siders had better wake up as St. Johns, six miles down the river, already had a standing offer and a large bonus available as an inducement for woolen mills and other factories to locate there. This prompted an inspection of several east side sites between East Burnside and East Clay Streets.

That area was lightly industrialized and included a box factory, a sawmill, leather, tinsmith and other shops and an occasional warehouse. Business sites were somewhat impaired by sloughs or arms of the Willamette River and in times of high water were flooded. Until these indentations were filled with dredgings from the river channel, the streets and buildings were built on pilings. Any business established in the area would have the advantage of both railroad switching service and waterfront facilities, it was argued.

Again, the discussion failed to bear fruit, and nothing more was heard of the Pacific Woolen and Clothing Manufacturing Company or any other proposals which came before the association during 1898 and 1899. When the subject was revived in January 1900 with another report recommending the organization of a company with $100,000 capital stock, there was some enthusiasm, but the Portland Woolen and Clothing Company, like its predecessors, was stillborn on paper.

Nor did the possibility of working out a deal with Dan Wagnon, the Siuslaw Railroad and Eugene woolen mill promoter, materialize. "We raise the wool, we have the labor, and our rapidly growing trade, local and export, is reaching out for the product, and local capitalists should take advantage of this opportunity," editorialized the *Oregonian*,[5] and the *Pendleton East Oregonian* crackled that Oregon's chief city had been lamentably lacking in public spirit and enterprise.

In spite of the well-meaning efforts of the association which read prospectuses, inspected factory sites, and heard committee reports without end, at the turn of the century the metropolis on the Willamette was still without a woolen mill.

An interesting divergent development was Felix Flemery's proposal to establish a weaving and dyeing school under his direction and instruction. He was From Aachen, Germany, (a centuries-old woolen manufacturing center) and believed that the education and training of skilled workers was a sound basis upon which to build the industry.

(5) *Morning Oregonian*, January 5, 1900, editorial

When J.W. Cook magnanimously donated a seven-acre tract in Albina for the school, it was pronounced unsuitable for such a purpose. Flemery's choice was Crystal Springs Farm owned by the W.S. Ladd estate, "where a dozen or so springs of the purest water conceivable and surpassingly adapted for woolscouring and cloth-washing"[6] made the site perfect in his eyes. Neither the school nor the anticipated reservoir of technicians materialized.

Nevertheless, the publicity which the association's meeting received did not fall on sterile ground, for presently Fred Carter, president of the Pioneer Woolen Mills of Dallas, Polk County, Oregon, with William Walker, part owner, and Raleigh Stott, became interested in Portland's plea for a mill. On July 3, 1900, articles of incorporation of the Portland Woolen Mills Company were drawn up which provided for $90,000 capital stock divided into 9,000 shares of $10 each.[7] This project created an immediate appeal, but like the others, lacked vitality to survive and nothing more is heard of it.

The months slipped by without incident, but by April, 1901, the long-looked-for factory appeared to be a reality. Money had been raised and a site selected for the recently incorporated (March 4, 1901) Portland Woolen Mills with capital stock of $50,000 divided into 500 shares under the presidency of William P. Olds, Portland department store owner. Vice-president was Fred Carter, second vice-president,

(6) *Sunday Oregonian*, January 14, 1900
(7) Filed in the office of the Secretary of State, Oregon, July 11, 1900

Charles Coopey, and secretary-treasurer, E.L. Thompson, real estate and insurance, principal promoter of the enterprise. Charles Carter, Fred's brother, was superintendent. These, with Ralph Wilbur, a lawyer, were the incorporators. Other stockholders were Walter F. Burrell, capitalist; W.M. Ladd, banker; Gordon Voorhies, retired army officer; Frederick Nitchy, manager for Crane & Company; M.C. Banfield, head of a large fuel company.

Fred and Charles Carter were the only trained woolen mill men in the group. Similarity of the Willamette Valley environment to the north of England sheep and mill country, had attracted these skilled technicians to the Pacific Coast. The family, with the exception of Charles, spent very little time in Portland but moved to Marysville, California, where Fred had obtained an interest in a woolen mill.[8] Charles H. Carter spent a lifetime with the Portland Woolen Mills, first as operative, then superintendent, later as president, and prior to his death, as chairman of the board.

The decision to close down the Dallas plant was coincidental with the Manufacturers' Association's efforts to attract a woolen mill. To eliminate as many of the promotional features as possible, it was publicly announced that only a limited amount of stock would be sold to the public, thus keeping control in the hands of a small interested group. Charles Carter divided his time between Portland and Dallas to su-

---

(8)   Refer to Chapter 6, Dallas Woolen Mill, for Carter biography

perintend the filling of the last of the orders at that plant and to dispose of the remaining stock of goods, mostly blankets. Presumably also, he superintended the dismantling of the machinery which was shipped to Sellwood.

Accompanied by Carter, Thompson selected a site on Umatilla Avenue near Johnson Creek in Sellwood, a suburb on the southern edge of the city, where the Oregon Worsted Company now stands. The choice was influenced by a $5,000 bonus offered by the Sellwood Board of Trade. The company planned to start in a small way and if successful to expand as the need arose.[9]

By the end of June, 1901, work had commenced on the flume to bring water from Johnson Creek to the turbine waterwheel, and the Southern Pacific Railroad Company was constructing a siding along the east side of the factory site. Close at hand were the tracks of the electrified Oregon Water Power & Railway Company which ran southeast for about 25 miles to Estacada, Clackamas County. Construction progressed so satisfactorily that announcement was made that the mill would be ready to operate by February, 1902.

In the meantime, Olds had made an extensive tour through most of the important textile centers in New England and the Mohawk Valley to observe the latest machinery in operation, plant layout and construction.

---

(9) Interview with Charles H. Carter, Sr.

The one-story frame structure built to house a six-set mill to produce 1,000-1,500 yards of cloth a day, was 120 by 170 feet, and just east of it connected by a wide extension was the two-story warehouse. In between were the boiler and enginehouse, thirty-five by forty-five feet. A pullery, dryroom and scouring tubs were in separate buildings constructed of wood, brick, and iron. All shafting, gears, and belting were placed beneath the floor. Although the main power source was a late model McCormick turbine water-wheel, a 150-horsepower steam standby plant was considered necessary in case of water shortage or damage to the flume, foresightedness which proved valuable later on. A large water tank connected to an automatic sprinkler system, supplemented by the installation of a watchman's clock, gave complete fire protection.

Entrance to the office and packing room was on the north side of the building. The seven rows of north-ward facing sawtooth windows on the roof broke the Sellwood skyline to give it a most modern industrial appearance. An innovation was the installation of a women's lunchroom and a restroom, and an employee time clock system patterned after the large eastern mills.

Huber and Maxwell, a firm of civil engineers, were in charge of the power installations including the construction of the 1,500-foot flume. A twenty-four-foot fall at the entrance to the tailrace gave sufficient head to turn the turbine waterwheel controlled by an automatic governor, and to generate 150 horsepower. The power site was obtained through the cooperative efforts of the Sellwood Board of Trade. The factory was designed by Richard Martin, Jr., architect.

Although the mill had been in operation since March with fifty people on the payroll, formal opening was delayed until May 2, 1902, when a big celebration and banquet were held on the second floor of the Firemen's Hall sponsored by the Sellwood Board of Trade and the Women's Auxiliary. On the committee for the arrangements for this momentous affair for 225 guests were Professor Edward D. Curtis, W.E. Pettenger, Dr. F.C. Sellwood, W.J. White, and Russell Campbell. Weber's orchestra furnished the music and Judge Hennessy rendered a vocal selection.

On the platform were officers of the company and such well-known, distinguished citizens as Frank B. Gibson, Judge W.M. Cake, Harvey W. Scott (strong willed editor of the *Oregonian* and persistent advocate of home industry), T.C. Devlin, and M.C. Banfield. Messrs. Olds, Scott, J.M. Long, and Major T.C. Bell were the speakers.

Olds' speech was appropriately enthusiastic:

> . . . the suit of clothing I wear tonight is made of Oregon wool which was scoured, carded, spun, woven, dyed, and finished into cloth at the Portland Woolen Mills, and tailored in our own city . . . the day is not far distant when it will be the boast of our best men that their clothing is home-made and better made than any similar kind that comes from afar, and I also hope that the busy swish of the scourer, and the soft hum of the cards, the whirr of the spindles and the rattle of the looms of the Portland Woolen Mills are but the advance guard of the industrial music that in the future will greet the visitor to Sellwood's manufacturing district.[10]

(10) Scrapbook 35, p. 65, Oregon Historical Society

References were made to the forthcoming Lewis and Clark Centennial Exposition planned for 1905, and the stimulating influence it would have upon the growth and development of Portland's industrial economy. Sellwood property owners would do well to erect dwellings to meet the demand for housing which would come inevitably as new residents sought work and places in which to live. Forty new homes had already been built in the Sellwood community in the past months at a cost of $500 to $2,500 each.

Vice-president Coopey recited the difficulties in raising money to launch the new enterprise and related how his friends would dodge out of sight when they saw him coming. For him, this day was one of the highlights of his life. Born in England, Coopey could never forget the similarity which the Willamette Valley bore to the woolen textile country of his native land, and was forever talking and writing about the advantages which such an industry would bring to Oregon. He later became the promoter of the ephemeral Gordon Falls project in the Columbia River Gorge where he envisioned a great textile plant employing hundreds of happy workers turning out fabulous yards of fine cloth from the superior fleeces of Oregon sheep.

During July, the first full month the plant had run, 20,000 yards of cloth were produced, much of it high grade suitings. Employees numbered 100. By September, the president was able to report a fat sheaf of unfilled orders and prophesied the employment of 200 workers, and the expansion of the mill properties. Much credit was given to the Carter

brothers who typified the young blood deemed so
necessary to put Portland on the industrial map.

In the meantime a question arose as to the legal
rights of the Johnson Creek waterpower, but it was
amicably settled between John Adolphson and Nels A.
Pearson, joint claimants, who received $1,150 from
J.W. Nickum, a stockholder, in settlement of their
claim.

Some time in January, 1903 the two-story, 75 by
100-foot main building annex was finished and most
of the eleven carloads of machinery installed, making
it necessary to hire seventy-five more people. Factory
personnel now numbered 175 men and girls. Charles
Carter, who now was superintendent, announced
that when all forty-five looms were in place the mill
would make 1,500 yards of cloth every twenty-four
hours, and that approximately half of this output
would be shipped east and the remainder sold on the
Pacific Coast. So enthusiastic was Charles Coopey
over the success of the mill that he began to organize
a clothing company which would take most of the
output of suitings. A considerable portion of the
output was sold through W.I. Pettis of San Francisco.

Fred Carter had resigned in the meantime to go to
Marysville, California. Gordon Voorhies was elected
first vice-president, and E. L. Thompson became
secretary-manager.

In March, labor trouble began to disturb the mill.
An employee organization had been effected called
the Textile Workers Union, over the pronouncement
of the company that labor unions would not be
tolerated. Request for an American Federation of

Labor charter brought J. H. Howard of Oregon City, organizer for the American Federation of Labor, assisted by Harry Rogers of Portland. E. L. Thompson pointed out that he could see no particular cause for dissension among the employees, that they were drawing ten percent more wages than any other textile workers on the Pacific Coast. The plant, slightly more than one year old, was a model of working conditions and sanitary improvements. The workers would continue to receive good pay and the company would continue its policy of taking small profits.

Howard's contention was that the textile workers should be protected against the employment of cheap Chinese labor which was characteristic of the California mills and with which Oregon mills were in competition. Oriental labor had never been much of a problem in this state except at the Oregon City mill more than thirty years previously, so that the organizer's statement sounded specious.

As a matter of fact, Pacific Northwest woolen fabrics competed with the California product most favorably, so much so that a movement to combine all the California and Pacific Northwest mills into a gigantic $3,500,000 organization patterned after the American Woolen Company of New Jersey, had made some headway. J. M. Martin, president of the Marysville woolen mill and said to be a promoter of gas and electric combinations in California, was the originator of the idea. Thomas B. Kay (son of the founder of the Thomas Kay Woolen Mill, Salem) principal stockholder in the Salem mill, was chairman of a committee representing all the mills of both states which investigated the proposition. There were three representatives from California and two from Oregon.

In 1903, woolen mills were in full operation on the Pacific Coast: nine in Oregon, seven in California, and one in Washington, as follows.[11]

	Set of cards	Value of plants
Oregon City	14	$400,000
Portland	6	175,000
Salem	5	150,000
Pendleton	2	75,000
Eugene	3	75,000
Union	2	50,000
Albany	2	40,000
Bandon	2	25,000
Brownsville	2	10,000

California mills were located at Marysville, San Jose, San Francisco, Napa, Santa Rosa, Eureka. Ellensburg was the only Washington town mentioned.

The plan was to incorporate with the stock held in approximately equal proportions by the California and Oregon mills. All of the latter were inclined to join with the exception of the Portland Woolen Mill which had satisfactory local and eastern market connections and so could see no advantage in participating. About the only gain would be that of increased specialization of production. As far as the directors of the Portland company were concerned, the mill was working on a ten-hour shift and had more orders than it could fill. Nothing more is heard of the plan.

---

(11) *Portland Oregonian*, June 5, 1903

About this time it was decided to install a steam power plant on account of water deficiency in Johnson Creek in spite of the fact that a dam had been built to assure a head of power. Two hundred horsepower was needed which the pond could not furnish; all the water would be drained out by noon each day. Close by was a sawmill which could furnish all the slabwood and free sawdust which the factory could use.

Labor trouble continued to smolder for the next two months with a threat from management that if organization of the workers was perfected the plant would be shut down. The situation was aggravated by demands for higher wages at the Oregon City mill. The situation was somewhat ameliorated after Mr. Thompson addressed them as a group whereupon a committee of seven was appointed, one from each department, to discuss grievances with the management. A short time later the committee reported back it did not want to disrupt the present cordial relationships which existed within the factory in spite of the strenuous efforts of labor organizers to effect unionization. No further repercussions of the problem occurred.

On February 18, 1904, less than two years after it had begun operations, the prosperous, well-managed mill burned to the ground during the noon lunch hour; only the wool-house was left standing. A $6,000 monthly payroll was lost, 150 people were thrown out of work, and property worth $150,000 (covered by $100,000 of insurance) was consumed. A frictional spark which had ignited dust in the mixer was reported as the cause of the fire.

Valiant efforts were made to save property and records including fabrics worth $80,000. Spectators, which included most of the employees, viewed with dismay the inadequacy of the Sellwood fire department, the tiny streams of water from the mains, and the ineffectiveness of the automatic fire extinguishers. Although Johnson Creek was running full and the February rains contributed bountifully, the property could not be saved. A reporter with an eye for color and details wrote that "the blazing frame of the mill looming brilliantly against the background of fir-timbered hills . . . and the procession of operatives wearing bright waists made a picturesque sight. Several of the men had put on gay blankets in the Mexican serape fashion and nearly all carried bundles of woolen materials."

On April 26, 1904, the Portland Woolen Mills increased its authorized capitization from $175,000 to $350,000 divided equally between common and preferred stock.

The principal stockholders at this time were W. P. Olds, president; Gordon Voorhies, vice president; E. L. Thompson, secretary-manager; Charles Carter, superintendent; W. F. Burrell, W. M. Ladd, Charles Coopey, R. D. Larrabee, J. H. Mills (Deer Lodge, Montana, banker), Nellie G. Mills, R. W. Wilbur, H. W. Hogue, F. A. Nitchy, M. C. Banfield, Dr. A. N. Fisher, Dr. W. S. Wood and W. G. Thompson.

The directors lost no time in deciding to rebuild, but not at Sellwood. Six miles downstream from

Portland on the east bank of the Willamette River, was the bustling, industry-minded community of St. Johns, recently incorporated with a population of 1,500. Subsidies amounting to $20,000 together with seven acres of land deeded to Mr. Thompson by a public-spirited donor were heavy factors in the decision.

Others were the availability of fuel and fire protection. Waste wood could be conveyed from the Douglass and Cone Brothers mills directly to the boiler house. Waterfront facilities were also attractive.

There was spirited competition between the two towns, the older one trying to retain its industrial prestige, the other seeking to gain it. St. Johns had an edge in land values, and although the company owned twenty acres of land with waterpower rights in Sellwood, the latter was not a factor any more in plant site selection with the installation of modern steam and electrical equipment. The Sellwood property was eventually sold. The site selected fronted on what is now Baltimore Street immediately north of the modern suspension bridge which spans the Willamette River.

Thompson and Carter immediately left for the East to purchase machinery at Louisville, Kentucky, and to visit mills for ideas on modern methods of manufacture. It was anticipated that the new woolen mill would be the largest and most modern on the Pacific Coast, and would tend to strengthen the position of the industry in the Pacific Northwest as compared to the competitive California mills. The annual output was estimated to be $300,000.

On the evening of July 13, 1904 the people of St. Johns met in the grove at the end of the recently completed City & Surburban Railway Company's electric line to celebrate the inauguration of work on the new woolen mill and the Jobes flour mill. Decorations of flags and colored lights added a festival atmosphere to the occasion which included the usual speeches by prominent citizens, as well as selections by the St. Johns band and the Haywood quartet.

Plans for the $250,000 factory showed a two-story concrete and brick structure 100 by 200 feet with a dyehouse attached; a boiler and engine room forty-five by fifty feet; a two-storied wool pullery and warehouse forty by one-hundred feet, all to cover about five acres of land. Operations did not begin until November 1, 1904. No difficulty was encountered in obtaining workers who delighted in the modern appointments of the factory which included lunch and restrooms.

By February 1905, a night force was added to increase output in order to meet incoming orders. Catastrophe nearly struck again when the entire manufacturing district of St. Johns was threatened by fire the latter part of August; fortunately, only two sawmills burned.

The woolen mill with its 200 employees and $75,000 annual payroll was now firmly established in an expanding industrial community in spite of its financial and personnel problems. During one such period Carter resigned to become superintendent of the Oregon City mill and Robert Paris of Prairie du Chien, Wisonsin was brought in. Shortly thereafter Carter returned and a necessary refinancing of the company was accomplished by William Olds.

The company continued to prosper under the management of Olds and Carter. Earlier stockholders had dropped out so that these two men guided the company through good times and bad. In 1915 it was a $600,000 company employing 300 workers creating an annual payroll of $130,000. The consumption of 1,500,000 pounds of raw wool each year made possible the production of approximately $1,000,000 worth of auto robes, blankets, suitings and mackinaw cloth.

The company has been recapitalized a number of times since its original incorporation culminating in the dissolution of the old Portland Woolen Mills founded in 1901, and the organization of the present Portland Woolen Mills, Inc., whose articles were filed February 23, 1928. Incorporators were W. P. Olds, Charles H. Carter, Willis K. Clark, D. E. Stewart, J. N. Edlefsen, Edwin J. Neustadter, Arthur A. Goldsmith, R. T. Montag, Max S. Hirsch.

The mill has continued to operate at its Baltimore Street site, augmented by additional buildings as the business grew. The company established a record for continuous operation up to 1928 and was turning out annually 1,250,000 yards of cloth from approximately 4,000,000 pounds of wool. John W. Powell was vice president and sales manager.

In 1946 Charles H. Carter, Jr. succeeded his father as president and general manager, the latter retiring to the position of chairman of the board.

Announcement was made in October, 1960 that the mill would close permanently on December 1, 1960. [12]

(12) *Portland Oregonian*, October 16, 1960

Chapter VI

EUGENE WOOLEN MILLS COMPANY

"Looms and spindles on the Mill Race"

EUGENE, county seat of Lane county, was founded
by Eugene F. Skinner who built a log cabin at the
foot of Skinner's Butte in 1846, and in 1851 plotted
the town of Eugene City. The town grew naturally as
a trading center for a tributary farming and lumber-
ing area at the southern end of the Willamette Valley,
approximately 112 miles south of the then embryonic
metropolis of Portland. Between the two geographic
extremities other towns like Albany and Salem were
emerging from the pioneer push. Flour mills, black-
smithing, and other crossroads industries were established to meet the everyday demands of the surrounding agricultural economy, an important segment of
which was sheepraising.

With the introduction into Polk County in 1848 of
Joseph Watt's plainsdriven flock of 330 head of
Merinos, pioneer sheep husbandry in the Willamette
Valley received its first substantial impetus.[1] These
animals, augmented by those which came with the
wagon trains, established the small farm flock pattern
of sheep husbandry in the Valley. Natural increases
followed. By 1870, Lane County claimed 52,745

---

(1) Alfred L. Lomax, *History of Pioneer Sheep Husbandry in Oregon*, Oregon
Historical Quarterly, Vol. 29, No. 2, 1928

sheep and 167,893 pounds of wool, second only to Douglas County with 94,963 sheep and 321,643 pounds of wool.[2] Furthermore, the county statistics reflected a growing manufacturing economy.[3]

With the rapid production of wool a surplus appeared which forced the settlers into a marketing situation. Woolen mills made their appearance, the first at Salem in 1857, followed by one each at Brownsville, Oregon City, Ellendale (near Dallas), Ashland, and The Dalles, in that order. It is not surprising that Eugene, like other Willamette Valley communities, persistently encouraged the promotion of such an enterprise as an important phase of industrial advancement.

This habit of industrial imitation was stimulated by an available wool surplus from heavy-fleeced sheep; abundant waterpower for turbine water-wheels; clean, mineral-free water for washing and dyeing; and a favorable, moist climate similar to that of the great north England woolen textile manufacturing area. Eugene, Lane County's growing commercial center had all of these.

Waterpower was a most important natural element in attracting manufacturing to a community, and where the town was situated on a river as was Eugene on the Willamette, it was apparent that sooner or later such power potential would be used. This occurred in June 1869, when the Eugene Water Ditch

---

(2) Ninth Census of the United States, 1870 volume 1475, Table IV, pages 230-31

(3) Ibid, General Statistics of Manufacturing, by counties, Oregon, Table IX (A), page 560

Company was organized based on a rumor that certain parties were looking for a woolen mill site. Three years later Messrs. Underwood and Osburn built a canal to the town from a point on the river about two-and-one-half miles to the east.

Flour and lumber mills were the first industries in the state to use this source of energy, followed by woolen mills. Such establishments installed turbine waterwheels of which there were eighteen in Lane County in 1870.[4] One who took advantage of this power was Charles Goodchild, age 35, an English carder and spinner who operated a small, woolen manufacturing enterprise on a $1,500 investment. A one-set carding machine processed the wool for 8,000 rolls valued at $4,000 during its five months operation. One male over 26 years of age and two children were the employees, probably members of the Goodchild family.[5]

The latter's sojourn was of short duration in Eugene, for in 1872 the family moved to Ashland where he and G. N. Marshall bought the Rogue River Woolen Manufacturing Company for $32,000. This mill, which had been in operation from 1868 to 1872, had lost money, although fully equipped as a one-set operation.

With Goodchild's departure for Ashland, textile manufacturing ceased in Eugene, and it is not until February 1874 that revival of interest was manifested

---

(4) Ibid Table IX(A)

(5) Original Schedules of the 9th Census of Population, 1870, microfilm, University of Oregon library; Schedules of Industry, Lane County, Oregon, Oregon State Archives, Salem

with a query in the Eugene *Oregon State Journal,*
"Shall we have a woolen factory? Albany is making
liberal offers to persons in this vicinity to induce them
to start a woolen manufactory in their town. Eugene
needs manufacturing and local people should get
behind a project."

A partial answer came with the announcement by
William Irving that he had purchased the machinery
of C. Goodchild, and ran the following advertisement
until September 19:[6]

CARDING AND SPINNING

Having purchased the machinery owned by C. Goodchild,
I am now prepared to make all kinds of yarn, batts,
Hosiery, etc. for customers at the lowest living costs.

William Irving

He also advertised for 10,000 pounds of wool for his
Eugene City yarn mill. The advertisements then
ceased to appear, and it may be presumed that the
little mill closed down. Almost a year elapsed when
announcement was made that parties with money
and machinery were negotiating for waterpower and
a woolen mill site.[7] This may have been William
Skelton, an Englishman, who had come to Eugene in
1874 and who became the proprietor of the Eugene
City Woolen Mills.[8] Apparently he had bought out
William Irving (although this would be difficult to
substantiate) and ran the plant until 1878 when he
left Eugene for Jefferson, near Albany, to operate a
yarn mill.

(6) Oregon State Journal, June 27, 1874
(7) Oregon State Journal, May 8, 1875
(8) Walling, *History of Lane County,* page 501

The Portland *Oregonian*, ever alert to promote home industry, commented that Brownsville had recently raised money for a woolen mill and that Eugene is left out in the cold, but voiced the hope that the town would eventually get a mill. Woolen mill news does not appear again until 1881 when the *Oregon State Directory* carried an advertisement of Charles Goodchild, who apparently had returned with his family from Ashland when that mill changed ownership in 1878. He probably bought Skelton's mill with the money from the sale of his interest in the Ashland factory. The 1880 Census of Lane County lists Goodchild as a woolen manufacturer. His advertisement in the Eugene papers read as follows:

CHARLES GOODCHILD'S HOSIERY AND
YARN FACTORY
EUGENE, OREGON

The trade throughout the northwest and California supplied with the hosiery, yarn, etc. of superior manufacture at prices which are bound to give satisfaction. None but the best of wool used, and the best of machinery known are used in the manufacture of these goods.

This was followed by an explanation that the mill had been established "some seven or eight years ago by W. M. Skelton but it did not prosper. It is three years since the present owner purchased the works and added machinery."[9] Carding and knitting machines and a spinning frame of 150 spindles were included. Goodchild probably put his family to work, a 14-year old daughter and 12-year old son.

---

(9) Oregon State Directory, 1881, page 547

The operations were conducted in a small building leased from the Eugene Flouring Mill Company. About two o'clock Sunday morning, May 29, 1881, the old firebell pealed out an alarm as the structure and its contents became a total loss estimated at $6,000-$7,000. The volunteer hook-and-ladder company stood helplessly by unable to reach water. Goodchild was covered for $2,000 on the machinery, and $800 on the inventory by policies written by the Commercial Insurance Company, and Hamburg-Bremen Insurance Company.

In 1882, William Skelton returned to Eugene and with his son Joseph C. Skelton, commenced to manufacture yarns and hosiery in a building formerly occupied by the Eugene Mill Company. Machinery had been ordered and it was expected to arrive about June 1st, but it did not come until the last of that month, then more came in September. Power was derived from a turbine waterwheel mounted in the millrace. Production was 100,000 pounds of wool annually which was manufactured into socks, yarns, batts, and wool beds.

Eugene now boasted of various industries such as flour milling, sash and door factory, furniture, brewery, fruit drying and canning, tanning and an iron foundry. By 1885 it was the thriving big town of the upper Willamette Valley with about 2,000 population in the heart of the highly productive wheat, fruit, and sheep country. It was on the main line of the Oregon and California Railroad (later the Southern Pacific) from Portland and building toward Ashland. The Oregonian Railway, popularly called the "Narrow Gauge" (later absorbed by the Southern Pacific), had been completed to Coburg seven miles north of Eugene, with prospects of advancing to nearby Springfield.

The Portland *Oregonian's* New Years Edition of 1885 reported that 80 new houses had been built in Eugene the past year, and 40 more were planned immediately. Four hotels, two banks, and three newspapers placed Eugene beyond the category of a little village. A cultural element had been added with the opening of the University of Oregon in 1876. The paper commented upon the industrial opportunities, especially the waterpower. George Melvin Miller, brother of Joaquin, the poet, emerged as the most vociferous and prominent real estate booster for the town.[10]

Eugene could now be considered one of several communities which either supported a woolen mill or was eagerly promoting one. Mention woolen mills anywhere in western Oregon and immediately there was a flurry of interest and affirmation that they were the answer to sustained payroll prosperity. There was something about the industry which stirred the towns as no other factory project did. "Woolen mill fever" is an apt descriptive term applicable to the situation.

Indications of this interest were observed during 1888. The Eugene Mill Company enlarged the tail-race below the woolen mill which for some unexplained reason had closed its doors late in 1887 after having run for approximately five years. The mill

---

(10) Lomax, Rail Plan Gave Birth to Fairmount Area, *Eugene Register-Guard*, February 28, 1971

could be restored to operating condition for $3,000 pleaded a news story. Interested parties should address Patterson, Edris & Company, owners of the flour mill and millrace.

Business men held meetings during the spring of 1889 to discuss industrial promotion projects including a potato starch factory, a shingle mill, and a woolen mill, the latter prompted by a Kankakee, Illinois mill owner with a sizable payroll who was interested in locating in Eugene.

Another was the Ashland woolen mill which rumor said was interested in relocating its factory operations in Eugene providing a $15,000 bonus could be raised, which prompted the editor of the *Eugene City Guard* to quip "and we'll bet a nickel that Eugene will raise the bonus in three days." The superintendent of the Ashland mill came north to discuss the matter. As this looked like a promising project a special meeting was called for April 26, 1889 with T.G. Hendricks, chairman; D.W. Coolidge, secretary; and J.F. Robinson, assistant secretary. The meeting was as bare of accomplishment as the Ashland proposition was indefinite; but correspondence was authorized in the hope that a favorable deal could be consummated. Aspirations in this direction were blasted when the Ashland owners said they preferred to remain in southern Oregon.

Nevertheless, sufficient interest had been created among the business men to empower a committee to investigate the cost of new woolen mill machinery as a basis for underwriting any future projects. Authority was also given to test the local citizenry's interest in and willingness to contribute to a stock-selling campaign should any woolen mill proposition develop in the near future.

This was a sensible move in view of the fact that the pioneer-founded Brownsville woolen mill had ceased operation, and one of its owners, the reputable Thomas Kay, was looking for a location in which to build his own mill. Competition was keen for Kay's favors among Pacific Northwest communities which included Albany, Salem, Eugene, Pendleton, and Spokane Falls. Bonuses were usually stipulated as an inducement for plant location.

Kay selected Salem with its $25,000 bonus for the new Thomas Kay Woolen Mill. This moved the editor of the *Eugene City Guard* to say that unless the town encouraged manufacturing it would be out of the running, and proposed that "every holder of real estate should contribute five per cent of its value to start manufacturing establishments." With a population of 4,000, a millrace, pure water, abundant raw material and a main line railroad north and south, the town was in an excellent position to demand industrial recognition.

No specific woolen mill news appeared in the local papers during the next decade. The millrace changed ownership in 1898 as George Midgley and Frank L. Chambers became the new proprietors. They immediately began to widen and deepen it, dug out the stumps, and raised the bridges for the benefit of university student canoeists.

Mr. Chambers had come to Eugene in 1887 from Dallas, Polk County, Oregon, and with his father opened a hardware store on Willamette Street, later moving into their own building. Over the years he became one of the town's leading business men with interests in real estate, banking and manufacturing.

Six years later another young man, Robert McMurphey, came to Eugene to marry Alberta Shelton, daughter of Dr. Thomas W. Shelton of Salem. The doctor had moved here to organize the Eugene Water Company in March, 1886. The son-in-law became manager of the business.

Although the usual small-town industries of a tannery, a couple of foundries and machine shops, a cooperage shop, a furniture factory and two lumber mills contributed to the economy, there was no woolen mill at the turn of the century.

This textile deficiency was broken in September 1901 when H.D. Wagnon of Portland, a promoter, came to Eugene representing a nameless company composed of himself, his brother W.S. Wagnon, and George W. Hirst, owners of a woolen mill in Iowa. Wagnon met with a group of business men at the Hotel Eugene and stated that he wanted to move his $45,000 factory to the Willamette Valley, but preferably to Eugene. This was a 3-set mill which employed from 50-75 people and had a monthly payroll of $3,500. Fifty cords of wood per month would be required for fuel. A $15,000 bonus must be guaranteed. A public meeting was called for September 27 to discuss the proposition in detail.

T.G. Hendricks, J.M. Shelley, and J.H. McClung were appointed a soliciting committee for the bonus. These were augmented by F.M. Wilkins, J.M. Williams, M.L. Campbell, Councilman Mel Green, C.S. Frank, and S.F. Kerns. First efforts were disheartening but improved as the committee persisted. People were reminded how gallantly they had responded for contributions to the University of Oregon building fund in earlier years, and the bonus of $1,000 raised for the excelsior mill. Both Boise, Idaho, and Portland were ready to meet Wagnon's demands, especially Portland whose Board of Trade had spent months discussing sites and bonuses and finally won the Portland Woolen Mill for the Sellwood location.

In the meantime, the bonus requirement had been reduced to $8,000, but November came before the pledges totalled this amount. Among the subscribers were the First National Bank $600; Robert McMurphey $500, F.L. Chambers $250, Frank Dunn $250, George Midgley $250, S.H. Friendly $100, Eugene Mill and Elevator Company $100, followed by a long list of names of people who contributed from $5 to $100.

As the project seemed assured a rumor was circulated that W.H. Hirsch, former superintendent of the defunct Eagle Woolen Mill at Brownsville and now at Sigourney, Iowa, would move his 3-set mill to Eugene, but the story was without foundation.

The first meeting of subscribers was held in the parlors of the First National Bank on November 21, 1901 to confer with Wagnon and to draw up a contract. The contract committee was J.H. McClung, Frank E. Dunn, Robert McMurphey, S.B. Eakin, F.M. Wilkins, and J.M. Shelley. It was agreed that the new building would be frame construction 60 by

110 feet dimensions, and two stories high. The site was on the millrace next to Day and Henderson's old furniture factory which would be converted to a dye house and picking department. Wagnon agreed to operate a 3-set mill to be ready by July 1, 1902.

The committee stipulated that the mill must run a minimum of ten hours a day with an approximate payroll of $3,500 per month, and that the factory would not be removed or dismantled for a period of twenty years. If the mill ceased permanent operation within one year from the completion date, Wagnon was to refund eighty per cent of the $8,000 bonus. The same penalty prevailed if the mill failed to operate within two years any year thereafter for five years. Fifteen per cent of the $8,000 was to be refunded if it ceased operation permanently within the second five years, the exception being destruction by fire. Wagnon was to be paid $8,000 on or before the completion date of July 1st.

Articles of incorporation for the Willamette Valley Woolen Manufacturing Company were drawn on November 29, 1901 with capital stock of $60,000. Incorporators were Frank E. Dunn, Robert McMurphey, Hamilton D. Wagnon.

Construction bids were opened in McMurphey's office with the successful contractor N.B. Alley whose bid of $2,449 was lower than those submitted by L.N. Roney $2,549 and J.M. Eddy $2,595. Hirst was appointed superintendent.

The first formal corporation meeting was held in McMurphey's office in the Eugene Loan and Savings Bank building on December 3, 1901 with all directors present ready to elect officers. These were: Robert McMurphey, president; H.D. Wagnon, vice-president; George W. Hirst, secretary; and F.E. Dunn, treasurer. Wagnon left immediately for the East to purchase machinery. Alley started work on the foundation of the building.

News broke about the middle of January 1902 that eight carloads of machinery would arrive in two weeks, purchased at Fremont, Nebraska; Pittsfield, Massachusetts; and Philadelphia. Two carloads arrived on the 25th from Fremont and included one set of cards, two spinning jacks of 240 spindles each, one ten-foot gig, one mixing picker, one spooler, a dresser, a grinder, and six looms. Four more carloads came in February, freight on which was $600. A.B. Rintoul of the Oregon City woolen mills displaced Hirst as superintendent.

More machinery arrived in March and was installed. A boss carder, James Denton had been hired to set up the carding machines. He had twelve years experience in Scotland woolen mills, nine years at the Kay mill in Salem, and four with the Jacobs Brothers Oregon City mill.

A boiler was installed in the old furniture factory just east of the new factory building. A new, two-story building for scouring, picking and dyeing was erected. McMurphey moved his office to the factory. The millrace owners spent $6,000 improving that waterway.

A two-year contract was made with the Eugene Lumber Company to supply sawdust for fuel; it was cheaper than cordwood and slabwood.

McMurphey suggested that a custom scouring plant be built. Most of the woolen mills had their own scouring tubs, but the proposed operation could scour wool for all of the Willamette Valley mills. It would be a seasonal business to run only four months of the year and employ sixteen men. As there were at this time only two other scouring mills in the state, namely, at The Dalles and Pendleton in eastern Oregon, the idea had considerable merit. Both of these plants scoured Oregon, Idaho, and Washington fleeces for Pacific Northwest consumption, but shipped most of the output to Boston and the East. Unscoured wool paid freight on burrs, ordure and other extraneous matter collected in the fleeces, whereas scoured wool was delivered in a clean condition at a somewhat higher price ready for processing.

About the last of May, a final carload of machinery arrived from Philadelphia. By the end of June 1902 the mill was operating with two sets of cards and a third almost ready. The lack of local experienced help was a handicap to the full operation of the factory, a not uncommon situation when a new woolen mill came to town. But there was now a pool of skilled textile workers in Oregon which could be drawn upon, augmented by local unskilled laborers who could be trained. Although itineracy was not a serious factor among woolen mill workers, names of those who had worked at other mills were often duplicated on the payrolls of Oregon woolen mills.

Late in October repairs at the Judkins Point intake of the millrace disrupted manufacturing operations.

Not a wheel turned so that the stillness reminded people of preceding hard times.

In the meantime, fire extinguishers had been installed in the main building and a contract let for a 15,000 gallon water tank on a 60-foot tower. Delinquencies appeared on the woolen mill bonus list which set the committee to work again collecting.

During the early part of December the Willamette River went on its annual rampage and caused damage to the industries along the millrace. When the waters had subsided it was discovered that the foundation of the woolen mill needed repairing. A shutdown followed until the first of the year. A contemporary advertisement stated two dozen pairs of slightly damaged blankets, some torn and off color, were for sale cheap, an aftermath of the flood.

On September 3, 1903 the capital stock of the woolen mill was increased to $100,000 with 1,000 shares valued at $100 each. Incorporators were Hamilton D. Wagnon, Robert McMurphey, Frank E. Dunn. Officers of the company were Robert Mc Murphey, president, F.E. Dunn, secretary-treasurer.

Not much is heard of H.D. Wagnon except that he continued his promotion activities by endeavoring to start a woolen mill at Boise, Idaho.

Changes occurred in both personnel and machinery in December. J.F. McGuire, an experienced woolen mill man from Jamestown, New York succeeded J.D. Ladly as superintendent and immediately installed a new engine and other equipment. Business was so good that the mill worked overtime on blankets and flannels and had orders ahead for three months.

But these outward appearances of prosperity did not reveal the inner problems of management, for on March 19, 1904 L.N. Roney, Eugene contractor and builder, through his attorneys Woodcock and Harris, filed an action in the Circuit Court of Oregon against the Willamette Valley Woolen Manufacturing Company, to satisfy a claim of $1,800.45. This was the balance due for construction and material costs for a building which he had erected. Attachment papers were served by Sheriff Fred Fisk on March 29 on the real property and other assets including an inventory of blankets, mackinaw cloth, flannels and miscellaneous supplies. F.E. Dunn, secretary, accepted the summons.[11]

On May 21 the National Woolen Company of Cleveland, Ohio, through its Eugene attorney George B. Dorris, served attachment papers against the woolen mill company for $983.03 for unpaid merchandise.[12]

On June 10, Jerry Bronaugh, a Portland attorney, filed an involuntary bankruptcy against the company for three petitioning creditors: the National Woolen Company, J.C. Albee Company of Portland, and the Oakes Manufacturing Company. Five days later five other creditors joined the above three in filing an amended petition alleging that the woolen mill corporation was in debt to them. It was alleged that the stock of the corporation was entirely owned by F.E. Dunn and Lena Dunn, his wife, and Robert McMur-

(11) L.N. Roney, plaintiff vs. Willamette Valley Woolen Manufacturing Company, Circuit Court Case No. 5192, Lane County, Oregon
(12) National Woolen Company vs. Willamette Valley Woolen Manufacturing Company, Circuit Court Case No. 5215, Lane County, Oregon

phey and Alberta McMurphey, his wife, all of Eugene, Oregon. The petition further referred to the fact that McMurphey as president and general manager of the company had filed suit in the Circuit Court of Oregon for Lane County, alleging insolvency of the said corporation and asking that a receiver be appointed for conservation of its assets. Robert McMurphey filed an answer through Charles A. Hardy, his attorney, denying that the company was insolvent and had not committed an act of bankruptcy.

Roney in the meantime had stated that he had not taken judgment but had stipulated that the matter should remain open until the next term of court, stating that the corporation had sufficient assets with which to pay its debts. He further said that he was willing to let the corporation sell the property and to apply the proceeds in satisfaction of the corporate debts.[13]

In October, A.C. Woodcock advertised that he would sell the machinery, buildings, ground lease, and the stock on hand to the highest bidder on October 15 at one o'clock in the afternoon on the woolen mill premises, but there were no takers.

Weeks passed until January 9, 1905 when J.P. Wilbur, superintendent of the Union Woolen Mill Company, Union, Grant County, Oregon, and Will Wright, cashier of the First National Bank of Union, registered at the Smeed Hotel and stayed just long

(13) Acknowledgement is made to Estes Snedecor, Referee in Bankruptcy, United States District Court, District of Oregon, for data on the above-mentioned proceedings

enough to negotiate with Woodcock for the purchase of the defunct factory, taking a ten-day option on the plant.

Prior to coming to Eugene they had stopped at Hood River where the enterprising citizens had ready a $20,000 bonus guarantee for a woolen mill. The two men had discussed the possibility of moving the Eugene establishment to the Columbia River town, but decided against the idea after they had appraised the situation.

Over a week elapsed before the final papers were signed giving ownership to the two promoters who promised that woolen textiles would be coming off the looms by May 1st. Their plan was to operate the Eugene mill in close cooperation with the one at Union. The local factory was to specialize in flowered dress goods, blankets, and robes. A large scouring mill was proposed for Union whose product would be shipped to Eugene. One hundred hands would be employed in the Eugene plant thus creating a monthly payroll of $4,000 and producing with the Union mill goods valued at $20,000 a month. With an experienced management backed by adequate capital, it was apparent that smoke would soon be billowing out of the tall chimney on the millrace. The rejuvenated plant would offer a ready market for Lane County wool and this demand would in turn stimulate sheep-raising. The monthly payroll would tend to stabilize the town's economy as the employees distributed their earnings among the local merchants.

In the meantime, on February 8, 1905, the petitioning creditors had filed a motion for an order dismissing the involuntary petition in bankruptcy. A dismissal order was entered on the above date.

Notwithstanding promises that the plant would be in full operation by September or October, nothing materialized; the Wilbur and Wright deal proved to be purely speculative.

Toward the latter part of January 1906, a group of Salem people headed by Thomas B. Kay, son of the founder of the Thos. Kay woolen mill at Salem, together with some selected employees, began negotiations for the purchase of the Eugene properties. With Kay was Emil Koppe, a German-trained woolen textile man whose family had worked in the woolen mills, of Saxony.

When Mr. Koppe came to Oregon in 1887 he went to work for the Brownsville woolen mill in which Thomas Kay had a substantial interest. His wage there was $1.50 for a ten-hour work day. Upon the dissolution of that company in 1888, Kay built a mill at Salem which began operation in March 1890, whereupon the Koppe family moved to the capital city where Mr. Koppe became acting superintendent in the new factory. When this plant was destroyed by fire in November 1895, Koppe worked in the Kay-owned Waterloo woolen mill located on the South Santiam River in Linn County. With the completion of the rebuilt Salem plant in May 1896, Mr. Koppe resumed employment there.

In 1902 he and two other employees of the Kay mill purchased the Brownsville woolen mill but sold out to their two partners two years later and returned to Salem where he opened a men's clothing store. In addition to the retail department, a hand knitting machine for socks and a hand loom for shawls were in operation. The two sons and two daughters continued to work at the Kay mill.[14]

Eugene business men were eager to get the woolen mill in operation again. To that end S.H. Friendly, merchant, T.G. Hendricks of the First National Bank, Frank L. Chambers and Darwin Bristow of the Chambers-Bristow Bank assisted in closing the deal. Kay signed a ground lease early in February 1906 as well as a contract for millrace waterpower in which utility Chambers was part owner.

In the meantime, formal dissolution of the five-year-old Willamette Valley Woolen Mill Company was recorded in the Secretary of State's office, Salem, January 20, 1906.

On February 15, 1906, the Eugene Woolen Mill Company was incorporated with the aid of Carson, Adams and Cannon, a Salem law firm, with Thomas B. Kay, Emil Koppe, C.J. Howe, and Arthur W. Lord signers of the articles of incorporation. Capital stock of $40,000 was divided into 400 shares of $100 each. The papers were filed with the Secretary of State on February 19, 1906.

The company records reveal the following names of the stockholders:[15]

(14) Acknowledgement is made to Mr. Carl Koppe for the biographical data pertaining to the family

(15) From the original corporation book and stock record in the Special Collections division, University of Oregon library

Certificate no. 1—		
Thos Kay Woolen Mill Company—100 shares—$10,000		
Certificate no. 2—		
Emil Koppe	50 shares—	5,000
Certificate no. 3—		
Lizzie J. Owens	30 shares—	3,000
Certificate no. 4—		
H.J. Ottenheimer	20 shares—	2,000
Certificate no. 5—		
F.L. Chambers	10 shares—	1,000
Certificate no. 6—		
C.J. Howe	20 shares—	2,000
Certificate no. 7—		
Mrs. Sadie Howe	20 shares—	2,000
Certificate no. 8—		
Mrs. Bessie Baillis	20 shares—	2,000
Certificate no. 9—		
A.W. Lord	10 shares—	1,000
Certificate no. 10—		
Theo. Bernheim	20 shares—	2,000
Certificate no. 11—		
Asahel Bush	20 shares—	2,000
	320	$32,000

The first meeting of the corporation was held in the Thos. Kay Woolen Mill Company offices at 4:30 p.m. March 2, 1906 with Kay, Howe, Lord and Chambers present to elect directors, who with Emil Koppe became the policy-making body. Ten minutes later a board meeting was called when the following officers were elected: T.B. Kay, president and manager; C.J. Howe, vice president; Emil Koppe, secretary and superintendent; F.L. Chambers, treasurer. Stock certificates were authorized to be issued at par when the stock was fully paid up. The manager's salary was fixed at $75.00 per month beginning April 1st, and the superintendent's at $100 beginning May 1st.

The president was authorized to purchase the Willamette Valley Woolen Mill Company property for

$12,000 of which $10,000 was the Thomas Kay Woolen Mill Company equity.[16]

A contract was made with the Chambers Power Company for a lease of not less than thirty years from February 1, 1906 at a yearly rental of $900 for 60 horsepower, and to include ground for an additional rental of 40 horsepower at the same rate. This contract continued until the power company was purchased some years later. Corporation by-laws were adopted at the same meeting. Offices were located at E. Sixth and Mill Streets.

Organization matters engaged the attention of the superintendent and the manager. Some of the old machinery was discarded and technicians from the Salem mill were brought in to repair the remaining equipment. When Koppe learned that a Provo, Utah woolen mill had closed down he bought from them yarn, dyed wool ends, and prepared stocks, and at the same time ordered wool from the Salem mill until the spring clip was available. Preparations moved right along so that the superintendent could promise that yarn would be on the spindles before the end of the month.

The Provo woolen mill was one of several manufacturing industries established by the Latter Day Saints in the 1850s and 1860s.[17] It had been successfully operated until about 1902 when it lay idle until 1910.

---

(16) From the Annual Statement of the Thos. Kay Woolen Mill Company, 1906
(17) The Utah State Historical Society and the Provo Chamber of Commerce supplied the above data

Contractor W.O. Heckert had cement blocks and other building materials on hand for a new one-story fireproof picker house, 30 feet by 34 feet, to be located between the main building and Midgely's planing mill. The blocks, the first of their kind to be used in Eugene, were made in the local A.J. Daly plant.

Monday, April 23, 1906 was an auspicious one for the industrially ambitious town. To the whine of saws and planers at the Midgely mill was added the welcome clatter of looms in the revitalized woolen mill as the flying shuttles carried the bright new yarns for blankets and other yard goods. The hoped-for payroll with the names of forty employees had at last been achieved.

Matters looked so propitious that Mr. Koppe moved his family from Salem to Eugene where they lived in the C.S. Frank house on East Seventh and Pearl Streets. Later the Ingham house on East Third and Pearl was purchased.

During May, a running advertisement in the local papers asked for wool deliveries to keep the 14 looms going and to feed the new machinery which had just arrived. It was now a 4-set mill and ranked as one of the larger woolen mills in the state.

Most of the wool originated in Lane and Douglas counties augmented by eastern Oregon fleeces purchased through wool dealers in Portland. The local mill, like all woolen mills was dependent upon dyes imported from Germany and Switzerland prior to World War I.

The factory performed reasonably satisfactorily but not up to the expectations of the new owners, for in August Mr. Kay wrote O.P. Coshow of the Salem mill, as follows:[18]

> Everything is running nicely here (Salem), but the Eugene people are not doing very well. They are not getting out as many goods as they expected to and as they find some of the machinery very poor they are having more troubles than I had figured on. It will take some time, but I think they will get on a good running basis in time.

At the close of the year 1906 Eugene could boast of an industrial nucleus composed of a woolen mill, two iron foundries, two sawmills, three planing mills and sash and door factories, a flour mill and grain elevator, one excelsior factory, a soap factory, a fruit cannery and dryer, a vinegar and cider plant, an ice plant, one water plant, an electric light plant, and a gas plant.

In this setting the Eugene woolen mill prospered as evidenced by the annual statement of the Thos. Kay Woolen Mill Company for 1906 and 1907 which listed its equity in the Eugene company as an asset worth $10,000. A footnote at the bottom of the 1907 statement reads: "The annual report from the Eugene mill shows a good profit and though undivided, we figure our stock in that company worth at least $12,000."[19] This figure was carried in the annual statement through 1909, but increased to $14,000 in 1910 and then not listed thereafter. The stock was purchased by Emil Koppe and his sons Paul, Louis, and Otto.

---

(18) From the files of the Thos. Kay Woolen Mill Company, Salem, Oregon
(19) From the files of the Thos. Kay Woolen Mill Company, Salem, Oregon

During the above period the same stockholders and directors were in charge except that F.L. Graham became treasurer in place of Frank Chambers. In 1910, the latter resumed office. Various items were discussed at the directors' meetings such as installation of a sprinkler system and an increase of electric power from the Chambers Power Company. Koppe's salary was increased to $125 a month and Howe was appointed assistant superintendent at $100.

With the withdrawal of the Kay interest, Koppe became president, and superintendent; Howe vice president and assistant superintendent; and Lord treasurer. The stockholders felt that Mr. Kay was selling the production of both mills and possibly apportioning the least desirable order for fabrics to the Eugene mill. By controlling their own sales the Eugene management felt they could develop a better line of fabrics.

Piece goods were sold direct to garment manufacturers on the Pacific Coast and through a Minneapolis broker for the eastern trade. Blankets were distributed through wholesalers on the Pacific Coast. Over the years a large variety of fabrics was produced such as shirtings, men's suitings and coatings, ladies' coatings, mackinaws, and sport coatings. One line of blankets was successfully sold under the registered trademark "Three Sisters."*

The company had now established itself as a successful family controlled enterprise, making money for its stockholders and maintaining a stable payroll

(*) Three snow-capped peaks visible from Eugene and associated with the area

for its employees. Labor problems, if any were minor. Eight per cent dividends were declared regularly, some as high as forty percent on the capital stock. In 1918, the capital stock was increased to $150,000 with 1,500 shares at par value of $100 per share. Stockholders in 1918 were Emil Koppe, C.J. Howe, Mrs. Baillie, Theo Bernheim, F.L. Chambers. In 1919, there were minor stockholder changes and Bernheim was elected secretary. In 1923 Carl Koppe was elected to the board of directors and appointed assistant manager. Paul Koppe became vice president.

Purchase of the Chambers-owned Eugene Power Company's millrace was a transaction which involved a one-half interest in the water right for $5,000, the other half by the Eugene Excelsior Company for the same amount together with land purchases from the Southern Pacific Railroad. In 1928 all water wheels were discontinued and the two mills operated exclusively on their own electric utility.

Details of operations, labor, finance, marketing and other managerial relationships are embodied in the company's records in the custody of the Special Collections Division of the University of Oregon library. These records will reveal how a family-controlled company built a defunct, poorly managed woolen mill into a highly profitable enterprise until it ceased operation in 1950.

Chapter VII

THE STAYTON WOOLEN MILL

"The welcome sound of the woolen mill whistle"

STAYTON, Marion County, Oregon, on the North Santiam River, is 17 miles southeast of Salem, the state capital. Mill Creek, a tributary which flows through the town, was an open invitation to pioneer industrialists like Drury S. Stayton who invested $2,000 in a carding operation composed of one carder and one extender, which were brought from Springfield, Oregon in 1866 or 1867. This was an 8-horsepower machine operated by two men who turned out 10,000 pounds of wool valued at $5,000.[1]

The original building is still standing adjacent to the Western Batt and Bedding Company premises. The machine-carded wool was a boon to the pioneer housewives who were relieved of the arduous, time-consuming hand carding. By 1870 a sawmill and flouring mill had been built, and by 1872 Stayton had laid out the townsite which bears his name.

Drury Stayton died in 1875; his son Drury E. Stayton thereafter ran the mill, but the following year the business went to D.F. Campbell for $5,000.

In 1880, John and David Grier had a carding machine operating on $1,700 capital which employed three people including one child. They worked ten

---

(1) U.S. Census 1870, 1880 Schedules of Industry

hours a day at an average daily wage of $1.50. The annual payroll was about $350; value of material $425; value of product $1,362. A 20-horsepower waterwheel furnished the power. The little factory made yarn and knitted wool socks which sold for 50c-75c a pair. Five years later John Grier's carding mill was still operating.

The next decade is silent concerning Stayton woolen mill activity, but in late April 1905 a meeting was held in the City Hall with Fred A. Carter, formerly with the Portland Woolen Mill Company, and S. Philippi, farmer and sheepraiser, to discuss plans for promoting a woolen mill. On April 29, 1905 the Stayton Woolen Mills Company was incorporated by S. Philippi, Fred Carter, and W.L. Freres, for $100,000. Enthusiastic local response to the stock-selling campaign brought in $65,000 by the middle of May, with $10,000 yet to be subscribed.

The citizenry visualized a monthly payroll of $4,000, a population increase, and the elevation of real estate prices. Such publicity brought in enough stock subscriptions to warrant actual planning of the factory building. Stock books were kept open at Gardner's grist mill and Brown's sawmill.

The site selected was on the Whitney property northeast of the Gardner mill not far from the site of the present woolen mill. Contract for quarrying the foundation stone was let in June, 1905.

As planned, the main building would be 120 feet by 69 feet and two and one-half stories high. The lower floor would house the weaving and finishing departments; the second floor carding and spinning;

and the upper floor would be reserved for clothing manufacture. A separate one-story building would be built for scouring, drying, dyeing, and picking. Automatic sprinklers would reduce the cost of fire insurance by two per cent, which on a $75,000 investment meant an annual saving of $1,500. Fire regulations required the building to be whitewashed.

The structure was not finished until the latter part of October 1905. By December, the penstock was completed and the 100 horsepower 30-inch Sampson waterwheel was installed. The penstock had been built large enough to accommodate three waterwheels if additional power should be needed. The buildings were soon finished and ready for the installation of machinery. Carter and Philippi had, in the meantime, left for San Francisco and Los Angeles to purchase machinery.

The boiler was installed in March 1905 and the smokestack raised. Four carloads of machinery arrived from California late in July, but not until the last of September did the final shipment come to complete the installation, nearly eighteen months after the project started.

No record is available by what means the machinery at Stayton was delivered as the town had no railroad service. Presumably it was hauled from Salem by dray or truck as neither Stayton or West Stayton had railroad service from that town. A conjecture is that it could have come by the Southern Pacific from Portland via Silverton to West Stayton. This was the old narrow-gauge built in 1880 which ran to Coburg and Springfield and was later standardized when the Southern Pacific assumed ownership.

On February 8, 1907 president Philippi called a meeting of the stockholders to elect directors, to amend the by-laws and retire or purchase the outstanding stock. Philippi and secretary Davis resigned and a new board of directors was elected as follows: A.D. Gardner, G.L. Brown, W.L. Freres, Charles Streff, George Spaniol. Directors then elected the following officers: A.D. Gardner, president; W.L. Freres, vice president; Charles Streff, secretary-treasurer.

Philippi, one of the original founders of the company retired because he felt a more competent person should fill the office as he had no knowledge of the woolen textile business. There was some indication of petty jealousies which were not revealed in the publicity.

Not until the last of May or the first week of June did the looms start turning out blankets. Advertisements for wool began to appear in the local paper, the *Stayton Mail*. G.D. Trotter purchased the first ten blankets and had an appealing display in his store windows.

On July 20, 1907 reincorporation occurred. Personnel changes were made in all departments and George Sault became superintendent. Knitting machines to make stockings were installed.

The following months saw a 65-foot high tower and a 15,000 gallon water tank constructed for fire protection, and wiring for an electric system installed. The factory was enjoying full employment on orders for blankets and hosiery, especially bright colored blankets sold to the Portland and San Francisco Chinese trade, some of which presumably could be credited to J.H. Davidson's selling prowess. At the December stockholders' meeting the same directors and officers were elected.

On February 4, 1908 the *Stayton Mail* published a special edition describing the town and its industries in which a photograph of the mill was shown. It had been in operation a full year as a 3-set mill which made 125 pairs of blankets and 35 dozen pairs of stockings a day. Sixty people were employed. Officers were A.D. Gardner, president; Charles Streff, secretary. Directors were W.L. Freres, G.L. Brown, George Spaniol. Sault was still superintendent.

Stayton's textile economy was given a slight nudge late in October 1909 when G.R. Emmons from Waterloo entered into partnership with A.J. Caldwell of Stayton to make socks. The organization was known as the Santiam Carding and Knitting Mill. This was an agreeable addition to the 1,000 population town which now boasted two flouring mills, an excelsior mill, and a rawhide chair factory whose product was in much demand throughout the Pacific Northwest.

The woolen mill ran intermittently through 1909 and 1910 evidenced by some employees leaving for steadier employment at other Oregon woolen mills. In July 1910 the welcome sound of the woolen mill whistle gave renewed hope that regular operations would begin, but the three-day run was solely to process 3,000 pounds of wool to prevent spoilage by moths.

Principal stockholders met in January 1911 to reorganize the company but without much success. This disheartening condition of affairs was optimistically dispelled about a year later when J.P. Wilbur, former manager of the Union Woolen Mill Company, met with a large crowd of citizens at the City Hall and made them a proposition to operate the mill.

He proposed that the town bid in the mill and an $8,000 mortgage about to be foreclosed and deed the property over to him. In return, Wilbur would invest $35,000 in new machinery and equipment and would operate the mill continuously for five years. He pointed out that the property was not a very attractive investment unless the factory could be rehabilitated and the water rights confirmed. Letters were read from T.B. Kay, president of the Kay mill at Salem, and from bankers at Union. A committee was appointed to solicit subscriptions and if successful, a bid would be entered. The local newspaper ran a front page story itemizing the benefits of a going woolen mill and republished the photograph of the factory building.

At another public meeting $2,500 was reported to have been raised, following which the names of subscribers and the amounts pledged which ranged from $5 to $200, were published. This promotion was augmented by a meeting at the Opera House on February 13, 1912 when T.B. Kay made a strong appeal for support of the project. All stores, pool halls, and the theater closed for the occasion.

The situation looked a little brighter in March when the Court affirmed the proprietorship of the mill company to the water rights. Plans were divulged for a railroad from Stayton to Salem, a distance of 17 miles. If and when completed it would facilitate the marketing of the woolen mill's products.

Matters lay dormant until May 1912 when announcement was made that the mill's creditors had accepted Wilbur's private offer of $5,625 at a Salem meeting, thus foreclosing an earlier threatened public sale to the highest bidder. About the same time J.F. Mounce, promoter of the Salem, Stayton and Eastern Railroad received a 30-year franchise to build into the city, but it never materialized. Years later the Southern Pacific built a connecting line from West Stayton to Salem.

Not until the latter part of September 1912 did the situation crystallize when Wilbur announced the incorporation of the Santiam Woolen Mills with himself, his wife and J.H. Evans as incorporators. Capitalization was for $50,000 with stock fully paid up. Wilbur was president and manager, O.F. Phillips, a stockholder, secretary-treasurer.

Evans of Salem, an experienced woolen mill man, had been with Wilbur at Union for several years and undertook the job of overhauling the Stayton plant. A few new pieces of machinery were purchased to replace the old equipment. An addition to the woolhouse was made and the machinery harnessed to the waterwheel. Silk labels which were sewed on each blanket, robe, mackinaw and other products read:

"Made in Oregon by the Santiam Woolen Mills, Stayton, Oregon."

The first week of October saw the mill ready for work with 6,000 pounds of fine grade merino wool ready to be run through the cards, the spinning frames and the two looms. At year's end the factory was preparing for a big 1913.

National and regional market response was good as was the local patronage which was consistently solicited through newspaper advertising worded as follows:

> Blankets, flannels, dress goods and wool batts retailed at wholesale prices. We will save you 30% on your woolen purchases if you deal with us. Patronize home industry.

Published prices for mill-end sales were: wool blankets $8.00-$10.00; others as low as $3.00; dress goods 10% off. Slightly damaged blankets were sold at less than cost.

On October 10, 1913, the name was changed to the Wilbur Woolen Mills Company.

The new year brought expansion plans with a new warehouse and a wool mattress factory planned to employ 100 girls at sewing machines. No record exists that this program materialized. Nevertheless, two salesmen were kept on the road whose orders kept the mill satisfactorily productive.

Wilbur advertised consistently that highest prices would be paid for wool and that wool would be carded for mattresses and comforters. A feature of these advertisements was that new wool sacks would be furnished gratis "if we buy your wool." Valley wool was selling for 17-18 cents a pound; Eastern

Oregon 15-20 cents. Later, fleece twine and wool sacks were advertised for sale.

Increased business was evident in 1915 as four salesmen on the road covered the Rocky Mountain states, Texas, and the Pacific Northwest. Alaska, Hawaii and the East Coast also bought the fine quality goods produced at the factory. Indicative of this interest was a substantial repeat order from Wellesley College, Massachusetts, for blankets.

Local retail business was encouraged by the issuance of a trade card for $40 which, when completely punched entitled the holder to a $5 bonus of free merchandise. Prizes and blue ribbons were won at the Linn County Fair held at nearby Scio. Before year's end a contract was made to supply all state institutions with Wilbur woolen mill blankets.

Wilbur's personal fortune progressed with that of the mill enabling him to build a modern California type bungalow for $3,000 on a slight rise overlooking the Cascade foothills and distant Mt. Jefferson.

World War I caused prices of woolen goods to soar and Wilbur used this economic lever in October 1917 to advertise a closeout sale at the previous year's prices of 250 suits of men's and women's underwear and 300 mackinaw coats, and soliciting mail orders. White, gray, brown and plaid blankets regularly priced at $5-$15 sold for $4-$12. Immediately afterward he advertised a new stock of coats for children, youths and adults, also loggers and mackinaw shirts.

Up to the present, the Stayton mill had been free of fire, but in late February 1918 a spark from the picker ignited the cotton and, fanned by the draft from the machine, created a $1,500-$2,000 uninsured loss.

In June there was a repetition in which Wilbur was severely burned. As he threw a pail of water on the blazing machine he slipped and fell on the greasy floor and severely burned his left arm and face. A steam jet system was immediately installed to prevent any more such accidents.

Wilbur, always an active man, announced his filing in March as a candidate for Republican representative from Marion County in the state legislature.

With 1919 came the announcement that the woolen mill would close, but that the batt and comforter departments would be kept open and a new batt machine would be installed. In June Wilbur bought 50,000 pounds of wool at a government wool sale held in Portland.

A closeout sale of the entire stock of manufactured goods was held in the J.R. Gardner store building.

In the latter part of October 1919 Wilbur sold the woolen mill to a company called the Santiam Woolen Mills of Portland, the personnel of which was J.W. Creath, J.V. Burke, William Agnew, and Theron E. Fell. C.J. (Boss) Webb, a Philadelphia wool dealer was the principal financial backer. Wilbur stayed on for about a month and Mr. Fell, formerly manager of the old Pendleton scouring mill, acted as manager. During the winter of 1919-20 he constructed a new building for the finishing operations, added a women's restroom, and hired a Mrs. Davis to teach weaving techniques to local women who wanted to work in the mill.

Webb's reputation as a promoter was borne out at this time when he acquired the Portland Wool Warehouse Company of which Creath was president; the Portland Hide and Wool Company; and most of the outstanding stock of the Santiam Woolen Mills Company.

Another of his operations was the proposed amalgamation of the Portland Woolen Mills, the Pendleton Woolen Mills, and the Kay mill at Salem, into an organization to be called the Northwestern Woolen Mills, but nothing came of it.

About this time the Stayton mill had a contract with Montgomery Ward and Company for blankets, but when that account was closed the mill operated intermittently until 1926 when it was sold to a group of Portland people which incorporated the Western Woolen Mills on September 22, 1926. These were Leonard Andrus (a civil engineer); Glenn Fox, a former Portland Woolen Mill Company salesman; and R.S. Clark, who became superintendent. The venture was not profitable and closed down.

Shortly thereafter, Robert D. Paris came to Oregon from a Prairie du Chien, Wisconsin woolen mill and became superintendent at the Portland Woolen Mills. He was there for a short time and then in 1923 leased the Brownsville Woolen Mill and was running it in 1928. In that year Mr. Bowman, owner of the Brownsville mill died, and when Paris' offer to buy the property from the Bowman estate was refused, he bought the Stayton factory in 1933. Since then it has been called the Paris woolen mill.

The machinery was in such poor condition that he

junked most of it and replaced it with practically new equipment from the Knight Woolen Mills of Provo, Utah, which operated but a short time before liquidating in 1932. Three sets of cards, looms and mules were items in this transaction.

There is a dearth of woolen mill news at this time, but in October 1935 a rare casualty occurred to the physical plant when a carbonizer* blew up with a roar and partially demolished the small building in which it operated. The carbonizer was German-made and was one of the very few of this kind in the United States. At the time of the explosion a lot of vests which contained a large percentage of rayon linings was being processed for the Brownsville woolen mill, and it was this material which caused the explosion. With the acceptance by the industry of the inclusion of synthetic fibers in wool fabrics, Mr. Paris developed a process for removing latex (rubber) from sweater and wool swimming trunks clips.* These were mostly from Jantzen Knitting Mills in Portland and after carbonizing were reworked into robes and blankets.

Welfare of employees was an inherent policy factor during the Paris administration which was expressed in employee profitsharing and an annual bonus distribution at the end of the year, a practice which continued with the Powells, the succeeding owners.

In March 1944 John W. Powell, formerly vice

(*) Carbonizing—the use of either hydrochloric or sulphuric acid to remove extraneous vegetable fibers other than wool, leaving the wool content intact. Vegetable synthetic fibers do not respond to the treatment, but cotton does. The hydrochloric method is preferable as it is simpler and less costly

(*) Waste accumulated in the manufacture of wool garments

president and sales manager of the Portland Woolen Mill Company, and his son John E. Powell, bought the Stayton factory and proceeded to reorganize operations on a three-shift basis. To modernize production in robes, pram robes, and blankets, automatic looms were installed. Among the superintendents at this time were Wilbur Berry, a part owner until he resigned and sold his interest to John W. Etzel. The Powells operated the woolen mill until 1947 when Mr. Etzel, a Stayton farmer, bought the Powell's interest and incorporated the Paris Woolen Mills on August 11, 1947 with members of his family.

Mr. Etzel, who had worked as a wool buyer and sorter in the Stayton factory but had no training or experience in the manufacture of fabrics, depended upon his superintendents for technical aspects of the business. Superintendents followed in quick succession, among them Eddie Stephen, who died shortly after Mr. Etzel became the owner, followed by a Mr. Calvert from the Portland Woolen Mills, and he in turn by Alex Etzel (brother of John), a former weaver with the Portland woolen mill, who was superintendent at Stayton until April 1, 1956. Carl Koppe, former owner of the Eugene Woolen Mill followed.[2] That year new machinery was installed including comparatively new Whitin cards and two Whitin spinning frames from the old Botany Woolen Mills, Passaic, New Jersey. New automatic looms were purchased for $20,000 after being delivered by truck

---

(2) Acknowledgement is made to Carl Koppe, Eugene; Lee Brown of Stayton; and Mrs. Claude Phillips formerly of Stayton, for their assistance in writing this chapter

from Massachusetts. Twenty-four looms were now in operation with the mill running on a one-shift basis and 65 on the payroll turning out auto robes, pram robes, blankets, worsted and cooler cloth for race horses. The purchase of blankets by the state of Oregon for its institutions pushed the business along and a Jantzen Knitting Mills order for 100,000 yards of cloth gave added impetus to the operations. In 1960 the obsolete spinning mules were discarded and four Davis and Furber spinning frames were installed.

Mr. Koppe resigned in 1963 and a new superintendent from an eastern woolen mill was hired, but resigned in December. Mr. Etzel's son Elmer replaced him and in turn was succeeded by Paul Koppe, Carl's nephew.

Property improvements have been made from time to time including strengthening the factory building against flood waters of the mill ditch by the addition of a bed of gravel under the floor topped by concrete.

At the present writing, the mill is operating full time. The buildings stand today unique in the history of Oregon woolen mills never having suffered a serious fire loss as did so many of the other mills. The Stayton woolen mill stands as a kind of monument to its durability through the vicissitudes of fluctuating policies of no less than seven ownerships over sixty years of its existence.

PART II

The Oregon Coast Woolen Mills

Chapter VIII

THE BANDON WOOLEN MILL

"The Chico *steamed up to the wharf"*

BANDON, Coos County, at the mouth of the Coquille River, is a rural seashore town 368 miles north
of San Francisco. Population in the 1890s was approximately 700. This southwestern county is brushed by
the Pacific Ocean on the west and flanked by the
Coast Range on the east. Before the advent of modern
highways the community was isolated from the more
populous Willamette, Umpqua, and Rogue River,
Valleys. The most accessible contact with the outside
world was by sea.

Evidence of sheepraising is found in an item in the
Coos Bay News of October 18, 1876 that the first consignment of wool grown in the county was shipped by
the *Mose* to San Francisco. In 1898 there were 13,500
sheep and probably included F.M. Langlois' flock of
purebred Cotswolds. The availability of locally grown
wool even in limited supply, was sufficient incentive
among some enterprising business men to promote a
woolen mill. The proximity of fine quality Umpqua
wools in adjacent Douglas County may also have
been considered.

On September 16, 1893 Theodore W. Clark, H.Z.
Burkhart, Fred E. Palmer, and W.B. Kurtz incorporated the Bandon Woolen Mills Company for
$75,000. Scarcity of research material leaves an ac-

tivity gap of several years from the date of beginning until the mill closed down in 1903. However, in December 1894 the *Port Orford Tribune* stated that the Bandon woolen mills is turning out a fine assortment of buggy robes, blankets and flannels and that the weaving was done mostly by women. In 1898 the factory produced 1,778 pairs of blankets, 236,125 yards of flannels, 2,260 yards of mackinaw cloth of a total value of $84,000.

The woolen mill had a stimulating effect in counteracting dull times and was instrumental in attracting small industries: a salmon cannery, a broomhandle factory, and shipbuilding. "Prosperity and goodwill reign in Bandon" chortled the editor of the Bandon *Recorder* and announced that the woolen mill was paying the highest price for wool.

Clark was still president of the company at the turn of the century and, as was his custom, made periodic trips to San Francisco to buy wool and supplies and to solicit orders from wholesalers. These trips were made on the *Mandalay*, one of several small coasting steamers which ran on schedule to San Francisco. Occasionally the less direct land route was used, sometimes by horse and buggy to Myrtle Point, thence by stage to Roseburg; or a combination of riverboat from Bandon to Coquille City; or by the 26-mile railroad* which ran from Marshfield to Myrtle Point. Upon arriving at Roseburg the Southern Pacific was taken to San Francisco, or north to Willamette Valley points and Portland.

(*) This was the Coos Bay, Roseburg & Eastern Railway and Navigation Company, built in 1891-93. It was never completed

Such a transportation situation underscores the isolation of southwestern Oregon communities. Millions of pounds of wool were available at Pendleton, The Dalles and Portland, but the inadequacy of transportation by either land or water from interior shipping points, literally forced coast towns to trade with San Francisco. When Clark took off on one of his missions, the woolen mill usually closed down for two or three weeks for lack of wool. He also made order-taking trips to Detroit; fulfillment of these orders assured the mill full-time operation for months ahead.

Hundreds of cords of wood were needed for fuel. Although the Coos Bay coalbeds were just a few miles north, it was much easier and probably cheaper to haul the four-foot lengths of fir and hemlock from the surrounding forest than to undertake the transshipment of coal from the mines to the factory. Another factor may have been the poor steam-raising quality of the lignite coal.

In October 1901 Clark visited Willamette Valley woolen mills to find weavers.

With the mill running full time the town enjoyed a real estate boom; $10.00 lots were selling for $100.00. Small payrolls resulted from the salmon cannery, broomhandle factory, match factory, foundry, brewery, and woodpipe factory. Sawmills, shingle mills, and shipyards augmented the payroll income.

In June, 1903 Clark returned from an eastern trip and announced he was closing the Bandon factory and moving it to North Bend, a new community 25 miles north on Coos Bay. While in the East he had purchased machinery for installation in the new plant. Not until January 28, 1904 was the Bandon mill machinery moved, stowed aboard the chartered steamer *Chico* and carried to North Bend along with 200 sacks of wool.

A disconsolate note pervaded the town as employees began to move to their new jobs. "What will Bandon people do now to repair the loss?" wailed the *Recorder's* editor. In answer to the plea, Robert E. Lee Bedillion, a well-known citizen, left for San Francisco early in February 1904 on the new steamer *Elizabeth* purportedly to find capital for a new Bandon woolen mill. March came and the project was still indefinite.

Bedillion had a varied background of miscellaneous jobs including the management of a Bandon hotel. He had no knowledge of textile manufacturing, but under his direction the Bandon Woolen Mills was incorporated on May 7, 1904. The other two incorporators were C.Y. Lowe and W.D. Marshall. Capital stock was $40,000 divided into 400 shares of $100 par value each.

Unlike the feverish promotion which characterized so many of the Oregon mills, there is no evidence of a soliciting committee pressuring people to buy stock, although $1,200 more were needed to complete the financing. On June 21st the stockholders held a meeting to elect a board of directors who in turn elected officers of the company. Directors were Elbert Dyer, R.E.L. Bedillion, and W.D. Marshall. The latter was elected president.

Immediately a man was dispatched east to buy machinery. Soon word came that ten carloads had been purchased for $48,000 from a defunct Rochester, Minnesota woolen mill. The old woolen mill building was too small so plans were drawn for a new building to be constructed near the site of the former mill just east of Timmon's cannery on the waterfront.

While the Rochester machinery was being disassembled, construction went ahead on the new building. This waterfront site was decidedly advantageous because all wool and supplies came from San Francisco by water. Direct handling from ship to mill thus saved additional wharfage charges, and vice versa on outgoing finished products. Piling was driven to connect with Rosa's wharf and the foundation dug. Progress was slow on account of the weather and the non-arrival of windows and sheeting. Not until December was the structure with dimensions of 104 feet by 66 feet with a 60-foot by 60-foot L. covered. The roofing was pushed as fast as possible in order to cover the machinery when it arrived from Rochester. Word came that it was routed by way of Seattle to San Francisco, thence by the steamer *Chico* to Bandon. To help matters along the steamer's owners generously agreed to ship the machinery free of charge and to take $1,000 in stock in the enterprise. Meanwhile, the concrete foundation for the boiler and engine was laid.

On December 15, the shrill whistle of the *Chico* as she steamed up to the wharf brought crowds of happy townspeople to the mill to watch the unloading of 600 tons of machinery, balance of 200 tons to come later.

A stonemason was brought in to do the bricklaying for the boiler foundation which was completed the following month. The bricks came from Henry Schroeder's brickyard at nearby Arago.

On January 5, 1905 the *Elizabeth* brought the remaining 200 tons of machinery instead of the *Chico* which was laid up for repairs.

While the building was being painted and the brickwork completed shafting was installed to run the looms and spindles.

The year 1905 was a stimulating one what with the woolen mill giving assurance of a renewed payroll and the probability of a sulphite paper mill being built. Word came that a congressional appropriation had been made to build the much-needed north jetty to improve channel depth. Equally stimulating were the Southern Pacific's survey crews on the line from Roseburg via Drain to Marshfield, and the Santa Fe's project to run a line along the coast.

February, March and April and most of May were used to finish installation of the machinery and to make test runs with superintendent Levar, "King Bob" Bedillion, and J.A. Maplethorpe of Albany, spinning department head, on hand. Official opening was promised for May but was extended to September and still no operation. Lack of working capital was given as the reason, but a dynamo was purchased in San Francisco for the electric lighting system.

In the meantime, the North Bend woolen mill was having troubles. The unused stock of wool, yarn, dyes and chemicals was for sale and was brought to Bandon. On March 19, 1906 the whir of pulley belts and clatter of looms shattered the months of silence in the big building. "The whistle of the mill and the rattle of machinery will make the kind of music that Bandonians like to hear" chirped the patient editor of the *Recorder*. Two weeks later, the first shipment of goods went out on the *Elizabeth* for San Francisco.

Considerable enthusiasm was created at this time over the prospects of improved transportation to the outside. Portland merchants began to take notice of southwestern Oregon and put on the steamer *Alliance* with a ten-day service to Coos Bay. The Portland & Coos Bay Steamship Company was organized as a Southern Pacific subsidiary. About the same time a proposed electric line from Roseburg was reported and, like others, never came into being. Rail connection to the outside seemed assured when twenty cars of bridge steel were unloaded at Drain, a station on the Southern Pacific.

The sale by the Spreckels family of the Coos Bay, Roseburg & Eastern, for $1,000,000 to the Harriman interests gave assurance of completion beyond Myrtle Point. Contracts were let in August for the first twenty miles beyond Myrtle Point.

The woolen mill was running full blast on orders for several months ahead. The town never looked better as the products of the area were shipped out: 23,000,000 feet of lumber, 706 tons of broomhandles, 3,307 tons of matchwood, 355 tons of coal, 639 tons of shingles, augmented by livestock, dairy products, vegetables and fruits. News that a 10-ton paper mill was planning to move in gave further proof of the town's industrial attractiveness.

A temporary shutdown occurred in April 1907 when the coal supply ran out and not until May was the shortage remedied when a company scow went up the Coquille River and brought back a load of coal. This was purely a matter of transportation and not a lack of resource as there was plenty being mined in the nearby coalfields. Another shutdown occurred while waiting for wool shipments from San Francisco. The Woolen Mill Addition to the city was put on the market.

Except for shutdowns matters were going smoothly. The annual election of officers was held in December 1907 as follows: Elbert Dyer, president; W.D. Marshall, vice president; George P. Topping, secretary; C.Y. Lowe, treasurer. Directors were Dyer, Marshall, R.H. Rosa, A. McNair; Bedillion, general manager. These were all local business men. The mill had a monthly payroll of 35 employees and $2,000. Cassimeres, flannels, and men's suitings were made, but its principal product was carriage linings.

In March 1908 the mill closed down temporarily for the installation of a new 150-horsepower boiler needed for additional machinery which Bedillion had purchased from the defunct North Bend woolen mill. In the latter part of June or early July the plant again closed to install the machinery and make repairs in preparation for an $80,000 contract, $65,000 of which was an order for carriage cloth from a Detroit carriage and buggy builder. Presumably, this was the same company which had placed orders with the North Bend mill before its demise. This order was the largest ever filled and kept the factory running from 7 a.m. to 9 p.m. four days a week for several months.

Bedillion sandwiched in his duties at the woolen

mill with that of representative in the state legislature and as a delegate to the Rivers and Harbors Convention, Washington, D.C. as well as trips to San Francisco. Cases of woolen goods went out regularly on the *Elizabeth.* In August 1909 a temporary shutdown was necessary while two spinning jacks and a steam finishing machine were installed. Some of the production on carriage cloth could then be diverted to the manufacture of blankets. A touch of pride in home industry was manifested when George Cornwall, editor of *The Timberman,* and John F. Carroll, editor of the Portland *Evening Telegram* ordered suitings while attending a convention at Bandon. Just before Christmas a dynamo burned out and was taken to San Francisco for repairs. This prevented night work so the hours were changed to 8 a.m. to 5 p.m.

In June 1910 another big order came from the Detroit carriage maker which put the mill in running order for a full year.

The *Elizabeth* continued to take either cases or bales of woolen goods to San Francisco and an occasional lot of locally-grown wool during November and December 1910 and the next seven months of 1911.

Another big order for carriage cloth came, but before undertaking production Bedillion closed the mill for repairs. In addition to the carriage cloth the mill made suitings, gray, white and scarlet blankets. The factory ran steadily all through 1911 and well into 1912 without repairs. In July, another big order came but from a Dubuque, Iowa firm which had heard about the fine quality of carriage cloth which a far western Oregon woolen mill had been selling in Detroit. By year's end the Bandon mill had shipped 9,960 pounds of woolen goods by coasting steamer to San Francisco. It was estimated that the annual value of goods produced in 1913 was $75,000 with a monthly payroll of $2,000.

Disturbing rumors were reported in 1914. One was the announcement the woolen mill was going to move to Cooston, a new townsite across from North Bend promoted by three Roseburg people. A new building would be erected by August and Bedillion would be manager under a five-year contract. Late in May, Bedillion went to Klamath Falls proposing that a site be donated for a woolen mill with a guarantee of fuel and water. He outlined his proposition to the chamber of commerce directors and a group of business men impressed with the availability of raw wool from the great flocks of sheep which pastured in Lake and Klamath Counties. The Klamath Development Company offered a free site of 3-1/2 acres along the railroad right-of-way. A discussion of the financial aspects followed, after which Bedillion left for the coast. Since nothing more was heard of this deal or that of Cooston, they presumably never materialized.

The town had a couple of fires, one in June which destroyed part of the business, but neither the old, first woolen mill building built in 1893 nor the new one constructed in 1905 were lost. However, in October, fire took the older building which had stood as a landmark but in later years had been used as a plumbing shop and secondhand store.

Just when the Bandon factory ceased operations is not clear, but apparently Bedillion had severed his managerial relations and in January 1915 went to Eureka, California. He returned home with a six-months lease for the idle Humboldt Bay Woolen Mill. At that time Bedillion announced that he would not reopen the Bandon woolen mill.

This disturbed the Commercial Club which met with John C. Kendall of Marshfield representing E.H. Tryon, said to be the principal owner at that time of the Bandon factory. Here again the record is not clear just when Tryon became owner, whether he assumed the debts of the enterprise, or how the stockholders felt.

But in June the Knights of Pythias tendered a reception to Bedillion their respected fellow citizen who had spent twenty-five years among them, and wished him success in his newest venture in promoting sheep and wool and a possible woolen mill in China. His oriental sojourn ended, Bedillion returned to Bandon and was postmaster there in 1917 encouraging the establishment of a shipyard.

Early in February 1917 the New Era Club began the promotion of a local company to operate the woolen mill, idle after Bedillion's resignation. A spontaneous response for pledges brought forth $5,000 in $100 subscriptions. The committee immediately got in touch with J.D. Ladely, a woolen mill man of San Francisco who was hired as superintendent and manager.

Following Bedillion's management, the property was placed in the hands of W.J. Sweet as Receiver, but whatever litigation was involved was settled in Judge J.S. Coke's Circuit Court when it appeared that a company would be organized and the factory operated under competent management. The news even got as far as Portland where a distributor offered to advance $5,000 against an order for blue flannel cloth, and at the same time a San Francisco house placed a $1,500 order for blankets.

These moves were very encouraging and fitted into the over-all business conditions of the town which reported nearly $900,000 in exported products, mostly ties, piling, matchwood and shingles. But cheese and butter, canned salmon and small amounts of wool and mohair also went out over the bar.

Enthusiasm for the woolen mill did not lag. The committee proposed a moneyraising dance for March 31 proceeds of which were to go for wharf repair and property overhaul. "The woolen mill rag will be a popular dance at Dreamland—be sure to get a yard of it" bubbled the editor of the *Western World*. The occasion was a rousing affair and netted the magnanimous(?) sum of $132.85, not quite enough to meet the $600 necessary to complete the fund.

Ladely arrived about April 1 and after a survey of the property reported that the mill would probably be in operation in ten days, Actually, May arrived before the machinery was in working order and the boiler and engine overhauled. Telegraphic orders went out for warp yarn and other supplies simultaneously with advertisements for bids for 75-100 cords of wood for fuel.

A new corporation was formed the latter part of

April taking the name of Sunset Woolen Mills which leased the plant. At a stockholders meeting the following named directors were elected: F.S. Perry, George P. Laird, W.S. Wells, Guy Dippel, E.H. Boyle. Election of officers followed with Laird president, Wells vice president, Dippel secretary, Boyle treasurer, and I.N. Miller attorney. The most important item of business was finishing the collection of $6,000 in subscriptions.

The third week of June came before the warp yarn and supplies arrived by the *Elizabeth* and shafting turned. Presumably operations continued throughout the year, but in December superintendent Ladely quit and Matthew Farley, an experienced employee, became superintendent. Shortly thereafter, at a stockholders meeting, Ladely offered to buy stockholders' interests on the installment plan and purchase all raw materials on hand. But certificate holders were cold to the proposition and accused him of not running the plant efficiently, tantamount to a no-confidence vote. Future prospects of the company were discussed and must have been appealing, for W.L. Crowe of the Pacific Waste Company, Portland, bought a block of stock. Encouraged by this bolstering of the company's financial status, the directors voted to continue operations and elected two new members, W.J. Sweet and Crowe. Farley, who it was agreed was running the mill satisfactorily, was retained as superintendent.

Optimism continued at the annual meeting of stockholders on January 15, 1918 when it was shown that the mill was on a paying basis. Although there had been a deficit during the preceding months, January started out with orders on hand for the next six months. Lack of working capital restricted the acceptance of future orders which were reluctantly turned down. John Nielson was elected to the Board in place of Sweet who resigned. In March Dippel resigned to become manager of the Burroughs Adding Machine Company's office in Eugene.

Financial affairs brightened in August when E.N. Smith, capitalist of El Centro, California with Coos and Curry County holdings, purchased E.H. Tryon's interest in the company. With financial stability assured in the $80,000 plant, it was agreed that Bandon would now have a first-class woolen mill. Affairs of the old Sunset Woolen Mill Company were closed with this transaction handled by the Bank of Bandon, and a new start made with promises of full operation in thirty days.

Whether the promise was kept is not revealed in the columns of the local newspaper the *Western World*, always eager to print news of the progress of home industry. The Coos and Curry Woolgrowers Association was organized to market the 30,000 pounds of fleeces on hand as the result of a slow market. The last mention of the Sunset Woolen Mill Company was in February 1920 when L.L. Langdon of Albany was in town to buy the surplus stock for his tanning company which handled wool, cascara bark and hides. About 1923 when John L. Bowman bought the Brownsville woolen mill he also purchased the Bandon woolen mill machinery and moved it to the old pioneer factory.

Except for the later years, the Bandon woolen mill

made an excellent industrial record considering its early isolation. While the Clark ownership established in 1893 ran for ten years, and Bedillion's ten did not quite equal the tenure of some of the Willamette Valley mills, nevertheless it was a good record.

Chapter IX

THE NORTH BEND WOOLEN MILLS COMPANY

"There is no more working capital"

NORTH Bend came into existence as an incorporated town when a charter was granted by the County Court of Coos County in June 1903 to Louis J. Simpson, son of Captain A.J. Simpson, San Francisco millionaire. The Coos Bay forest-lined mudflat was not the most inviting place for a townsite, but sawmill settlements provided a nucleus. The elder Simpson had earlier established logging camps and sawmills in the area and was operating coasting vessels to carry the lumber to San Francisco. Marshfield, two miles south of the townsite was considered the commercial center of the area.

When Theodore W. Clark, president of the successful Bandon Woolen Mills Company, learned that the settlements on Coos Bay were to be amalgamated into an incorporated community he abruptly announced in June 1903 that the Bandon mill would be closed. He had just returned to Bandon from a trip east to purchase machinery for the proposed North Bend factory. Presumably he and Simpson had talked about the latter's backing a woolen mill in the new town.

On April 16, 1903 the North Bend Woolen Mills Company was incorporated with $100,000 capital stock by Theodore W. Clark, R.P. Clark (son), and Louis J. Simpson. A site was selected in one of the city blocks bounded by California, Sheridan, and Virginia Streets and the waterfront, on the southwest corner of which was the City Dock. A three-story frame 60 feet by 200 feet building was immediately constructed but not until January 1904 was some of the Bandon mill machinery moved into the new building with 200 bags of wool carried by the steamer *Chico*.

The progressive, promotional spirit of the town soon attracted a milk condensery, a furniture factory which used the abundant myrtle and maple of the adjacent forest, and the possibility of a paper mill.

In the latter part of November steam was up for trial runs in the new factory with some of the transferred Bandon employees operating the equipment. Orders were on hand for a year in advance and it was anticipated that the plant would be in full operation by the end of the year. The carding machines were working preparing the fibers for the spinning jacks.

Suspicion that something was wrong was aroused in December 1904 when M.J. Smith, weaving superintendent, returned to Bandon. Two months later a receiver was appointed for the defunct North Bend Woolen Mills Company with a $60,000 indebtedness.

The townspeople and especially the 135 employees of the mill were naturally bitter and accused Clark of having no consideration for community welfare and being a promoter. Some justification for the accusation was based on his moving to Portland to promote a $200,000 scouring mill on the site of the former Portland woolen mill at Sellwood.

The Simpson Lumber Company wanted to operate the mill under the Receiver, but a petition addressed

to the Court was denied. Before Clark left he stated
that the company had reached its limit in borrowing,
but that if he could have gotten $2,000 a month he
could have operated. Just what the differences were
between Simpson and Clark are not revealed, but it
would appear that Simpson refused to contribute any
more working capital even though the family fortune
was adequate to meet the emergency. On May 5,
1905 an order of sale was entered in the Coos County
Circuit Court directing C.H. Merchant, Receiver, to
sell the property, and June 19th set for auction at Coquille, the county seat.

There were no takers. In July, Simpson gave an
option on the mill property to eastern parties who required test runs before purchasing. At this time, R.W.
Berr, operator of a Eureka, California woolen mill
claimed to be representing the buyers and it was to
him that a $50,000 option was given in which Cashier
Winsor of the Bank of Oregon was involved. Berr
promised to go east for the money. Simpson had concluded in the meantime that he would not sell the
property unless the owner would guarantee to operate
the mill for five years.

Apparently nothing came of this and the next news
is that early on Sunday morning, July 19, 1908 the
woolen mill structure and its contents were destroyed
by fire at an estimated loss of $80,000-$100,000 borne
by the Simpson Lumber Company, without insurance. The factory had not been operating the past
two years and the building was used as a warehouse
for Simpson's logging supplies and machinery, wire

rope and cable. Other losses were shingles and lumber piled on the adjoining City Wharf.

It was unfortunate that the woolen mill enterprise did not endure to benefit from the economic development of the area. A list of manufactories in North Bend showed:

	Employees
The Simpson Lumber Company	160
Shingle mill	50
Sash and door	50
Machine shops and foundry	12
Shipyards	60
Woolen mill	125
Furniture and veneer	150
Milk condensery	20
	602

Transcontinental railroads' survey crews were driving stakes on proposed rights-of-way leading to the Coos Bay country. The one that finally materialized was the Eugene-Marshfield branch of the Southern Pacific which reached that town in 1915; all others dried up including the hoped-for Roseburg-Drain-Coos Bay project of the Southern Pacific.

Small coasting steamers were still relied upon to carry passengers and freight, mostly to San Francisco, although Portland interests ran a service to southwestern Oregon ports.

The good roads movement offered relief in the second decade as automobiles chugged their way across the Coast Range dirt roads.

In later years Marshfield took the name of Coos Bay with the municipal boundaries and those of North Bend indistinguishable, twin cities of the area. Coastal vessels have all but disappeared, ocean

freighters now call to carry lumber cargoes to
Oriental and domestic ports.

PART III

Eastern Oregon Woolen Mills
and
Scouring Plants

Chapter X

THE UNION WOOLEN MILL

"Wages were paid in gold coin"

ON the night of January 5, 1897, in Union, Oregon, business men, farmers, and other interested citizens gathered in the City Hall to discuss the promotion of a woolen mill. Ten years had elapsed since the Inland Empire Woolen Manufacturing Company's plans had stirred the town with visions of a payroll. L.J. Davis, editor of the Union *Republican* was chairman, C.S. Marsh, secretary. An incorporating committee was appointed composed of Abel Eaton (wealthiest man in the county), James Hutchinson, J.H. Odale, E. Draper, and S.A. Pursel. At the same time L.B. Rinehart, N. Schoonover, W.H. Ostrander, S.A. Pursel, and Sol Seamans worked on the stock subscription committee. Both bodies were to report the following Monday at a public meeting to be held in the City Hall.

On February 23, 1897, articles of incorporation were filed with the Secretary of State for the Union Woolen Mill Company with $20,000 capital stock divided into 800 shares of $25.00 each. Incorporators of this newest of Oregon woolen mills were J.H. Hutchinson, Abel E. Eaton, W.R. Hutchinson, N. Tarter, H.C. Susiwend, J.M. Carroll, and Samuel Truesdale. By-laws were adopted and a board of directors elected composed of Abel E. Eaton, president;

F.E. Foster, vice-president; C.H. Marsh, secretary; Will Wright, cashier of the First National Bank, treasurer; and William Hutchinson, F.W. Davis, Joseph Wright, S.A. Pursel, and G.F. Hall.

Union, county seat of Union County, boasting a population of 1,500, had the basic resources and other requirements on which to promote such a factory. The community was situated in the heart of the productive Grande Ronde Valley agriculture and live-stock section of Eastern Oregon. Thousands of Merino sheep grazed on the hillside pastures of the encircling Blue Mountains. Catherine Creek could furnish both power and pure water for washing the fleeces prepa-ratory to carding and spinning. There was money in the valley, too, attested by the fine homes both in town and on the nearby ranches owned by the live-stock men and wheat farmers who were financially able to support such a factory. Fulfillment of Union's industrial aspirations seemed imminent.

Soon after the Catherine Creek factory site was selected near the corporate western limits of the town, Mr. Eaton left for the East to order the necessary machinery, although all the stock had not been fully subscribed or paid in. The first week of March, 1897, brought the joyful telegraphic news that the purchases had been completed, tangible evidence that it would not be long now until another payroll would be added to those of the flour and lumber mills. Reports of this newest of woolen mills spread throughout all of Oregon to spur other communities into the growing list of towns with such factories.

Ground for the new mill was broken on March 17 with W.H. Ostrander foreman of the construction, while a short distance upstream L.R. Rinehart was in charge of flume and other work on the waterpower. To bring the water to the mill and to obtain a better head, Street Commissioner Wilkinson superintended the construction of a new channel where Catherine Creek curved north through the Lewis property just west of the bridge. Here also was the raceway intake, and a short distance upstream was the reservoir which had been nearly demolished by the spring freshet, an annual occurrence in the otherwise friendly little stream.

Actual construction on the building did not begin until May, when excavation was completed and rock from the quarry east of town was delivered for the foundation. By the first week of June this work was finished and teams were hauling the big floor timbers into place. By August, the building had assumed a more complete form as the 50 feet by 100 feet three-story structure's flat top was covered by artificial roofing. The rustic pine siding, painted dark red, and the white-trimmed windows showed colorfully against the summer greenery. Front entrance was gained on the southeast corner, while another on the northeast side was used for manufacturing materials and supplies.

In the meantime, J. Frank Lever, an experienced textile man from Fremont, Nebraska, had been engaged as superintendent and joined Eaton in the purchase of the secondhand machinery at Waterloo, Iowa, which town, during Civil War days had supported an unsuccessful woolen mill when Iowa was a sheep state and was taken by the woolen mill craze. Three carloads of machinery presently arrived and were installed by Lever and his brother Walter S. Lever, who became boss carder and spinner. This shipment was followed by another one containing the waterwheel and the looms purchased in Illinois. In the meantime overhead shafting and pulleys were hung, a large threshing-machine boiler was installed, and with the arrival of the power plant, tests were run on the machinery. When recently hired woolen mill operatives appeared in October and E. Draper of High Valley delivered 16,000 pounds of wool purchased for ten cents a pound, the mill appeared to be ready for full operation, but Christmas and New Year were celebrated without benefit of a woolen mill payroll.

Although production of the first blankets came in February 1898, it was July before all five looms were fully at work producing seventy pairs of blankets daily. Editorial exuberance over the benefits of home industry could not be restrained: "It will not be long until Union County can wear Union-made coats, pants and vests," said Lewis J. Davis, *Republican* editor.

The annual meeting of the stockholders was held in the City Hall on February 24 when Mr. Eaton reviewed the year's work and a board of directors was elected as follows: A.E. Eaton, Joseph Wright, William Hutchinson, G.F. Hall, J.F. Lever, J.W. Kennedy, J.H. Cowan.

It was soon discovered that the present boiler capacity was unequal to the demands for hot water needed for heating, dyeing and scouring. President Eaton left for Portland to purchase a 100-horsepower boiler to be installed in a 40-foot by 60-foot annex on the northeast corner of the main building.

The usual machines and processes were employed, among them steam-driven centrifugal extractors turning at 3,000 revolutions per minute which partially dried the scoured wool before picking and mixing on the top floor. Two sets of cards on the second floor prepared the fibers for the spinning mule after which the bobbins were taken to the first floor for later use in the looms.

As the blankets came from the looms in lengths of six pairs each, they were placed in fulling machines to be washed, shrunk, and dried. To give the blankets a soft, downy surface texture, they were passed through a teasle napper[1] after which women at sewing machines attached the edging.

Except for a temporary shutdown in October to install an electric lighting system, the mill ran more or less regularly for the rest of the year. Another closure came in April 1899, awaiting the arrival of five looms which would practically double the weaving capacity. With this installation, the mill would have two four-shuttle looms, three one-shuttle Knowles,

---

(1) Napping was done by teasle burrs clamped in frames and inserted in a machine. The teasle is a plant which bears a large burr head covered with stiff, prickly hooked bracts or awns, which when dried were used for gigging, the process for raising a nap on woolen cloth. They were occasionally grown as a crop in the Willamette Valley. At the turn of the century a Molalla farmer had 150 acres under cultivation but lost his market when metal nappers were introduced.

one second-hand Jacquard,[2] one second-hand shuttle Crompton, and two six-harness Knowles. Other machines installed were a planetary wire napper, the second in Oregon, which could handle cloth 100 inches wide; a Miller rotary cloth presser; a measuring and winding machine for the finished cloth; a spooler, and washing machine, and a special kind of sewing machine for wet blankets.

The years 1898 and 1899 brought Yukon gold-hungry migrants to Pacific Northwest ports, especially Portland and Seattle, where complete outfits of clothing, blankets and tools could be obtained. Miners' supply houses in these and other cities stocked their shelves with Oregon-made blankets and mackinaws. Such orders came to the new Union mill and other Oregon factories and were important in keeping them in production.

Now that the woolen mill was engaged in full-time operation with twenty-five employees working on "wool that is produced on the thousand hills of Eastern Oregon," the *Republican* editor was moved to survey and comment upon the future of Union County with its vast natural resources. Here was the county seat situated near the main line of the Oregon Railroad and Navigation Company, 318 miles from Portland, in the center of an area three times as large as Rhode Island with only 15,000 people. "These alone will make it an inland metropolis," he noted with enthusiasm. Catherine Creek was Nature's richest gift to the city with power sites extending for eight or ten

---

(2) A loom controlled by a chain of perforated cards for weaving intricate designs. One of the three designs was a horseshoe with crossed riding-whips

Union Woolen Mill, Union, Oregon, circa 1904.   [*Oregon Historical Society*]

J. P. Wilbur, superintendent of the Union Woolen Mill, 1900-1907, and owner of the Stayton Woolen Mill, 1912-1919.

[*Author's collection*]

miles along its banks. "The day will come when this great energy now going to waste will be utilized by factories and mills employing thousands of operatives. No town in the West is more favorably situated for a great manufacturing center," he bombastically wrote, not realizing that the day of direct water power for factory use was already outdated and steam was the dominant power source with electricity making a bid in some industries. A little more factually, it was pointed out that two new railroads would serve the community: the Union, Cove and Valley Railroad whose spur connected with the O.R. & N. about two and one-half miles from town; and the Union, Cornucopia and Eastern, projected to tap the rich copper ledges in the Snake River area, but never built. It was the kind of evangelistic journalism which most of the newspapers of the day employed on the subject of home industries, not even excepting the conservative Portland *Oregonian*.

As the end of the year drew near, open dissatisfaction with the management of the woolen mill was voiced throughout the town. Why was the mill idle so often when other plants like those at Salem and Albany were overrun with orders? Several of the stockholders had disposed of their stock, among them the Lever brothers who were talking about establishing a knitting factory either at Union or La Grande. It was soon discovered that Mr. Eaton had been buying up the certificates of the disinterested stockholders and was now sole owner of the Union Woolen Mill Company.

Although manufacturing had ceased, orders continued to be filled from the accumulated stock of remaining blankets. March 1, 1900, was the announced date for reopening, with J.P. Wilbur, superintendent, but it was a week later before the rhythm of shuttles and looms could be heard along the creek.

Mr. Wilbur, a thorough-going New England trained textile man born at Potter Hill, Rhode Island, in 1856, brought to the Union mill his family background of wool manufacturing and many years of experience in the industry. When fifteen years of age he started learning the business and was soon proficient enough to become a weaver. After graduating from business college, John Wilbur became a bookkeeper for two years, but a desk job was not to his liking so he headed for California about 1875 where he worked temporarily in the mines and as a river front laborer at Stockton.

In a short biographical sketch Mr. Wilbur said:[3]

> My first job was in the old Sacramento woolen mills owned and operated by Sylvester Tryon. There were at that time (1876) about ten woolen mills in California located in Sacramento, Marysville, Stockton, San Jose, Petaluma, Santa Rosa and the Pioneer and Mission mills in San Francisco. I served time in them all as it was no trouble to get a good job in any of them, as good competent hands that could work in different departments were in demand. In 1881 I got the roving spirit again and went on a steamer to the Oregon country.

Wilbur had also worked in the Brownsville woolen mills and while there married Emma Kirk, daughter of H.H. Kirk, Halsey, Oregon, in 1883. The Wilburs

---

(3) "Making the Grade," Eavenson & Levering, Camden, N.J., August 1934, Volume 5, Number 9 (pamphlet)

returned to New Jersey where a daughter, Pearl, was born. The family then returned to Oregon a short time later, went to the Middle West and California before entering Oregon again in 1893 when Wilbur went to the Bandon woolen mill. His next move was to the Thomas Kay Waterloo mill on the south Santiam River and when that mill burned in 1898, he went as loom boss to Kay's Salem factory. Some time in between he worked in the Oregon City woolen mill. A visit to Union in October, 1898, no doubt influenced him to accept the management of that establishment when the opportunity came in 1899.

Thus, his early New England apprenticeship, the several years in California mills, and his wide acquaintanceship with all the important Oregon factories placed Wilbur as one of the ablest Oregon woolen mill executives of his time. His knowledge of the Pacific Coast industry enabled him to establish production and marketing policies which were reflected in the prosperity of the Union mill during the seven years he was its superintendent and sales manager. His talent for designing blankets and Indian robes coupled with his sales ability were the vital elements which made the Union mill so successful. He did all the designing, buying and selling, as well as attending to repairing looms. One day a representative of a large store came into the mill and asked a man under a loom for Mr. Wilbur, the superintendent. "Well, you're looking at him," replied Mr. Wilbur.

Wilbur made some changes, among which were the installation of steam-heating facilities, a boon to the workers accustomed to the ineffective warmth of twelve Rochester stoves.[4] Others were the installation of a soap-making machine capable of producing one ton of soap or a week's supply; a thread-winding machine; a flannel press; a dye tube and an extractor; a wool sorting room; elevator to the top floor; and a storage warehouse just south of the main building.

Labor was a problem. Union was a ranching and livestock town situated in the heart of a fertile wheat and extensive grazing lands; it was not a manufacturing center. Under these circumstances, Wilbur had to start from scratch in building his working force with agriculturally-minded, unskilled, townspeople. He was so distressed over this situation that Japanese were imported, but this move so angered the Unionites that they ran the Orientals out of town. The problem was eventually solved when skilled operatives from some of the Willamette Valley woolen mills augmented those hired locally.

Mrs. Wilbur was head of the finishing room and worked steadily in the mill from the time her husband assumed its management until it closed in 1907. Helena Pearl, the daughter, worked part time as a spooler. The family set an example of industry and leadership in the mill which must have been highly gratifying to Mr. Eaton, whose personal fortune had been made in part at least, by strict adherence to the principles of hard work and thriftiness. Wheat harvest took its seasonal toll when employees temporarily

---

(4)   A type of hanging kerosene lamp originally intended to be suspended from the ceiling, but in this case the hanging attachment was discarded and the lamps mounted on a table placed in the northeast corner of the factory.

abandoned their factory jobs and hired out to the ranchers.

Punctuality was a principle of work with the superintendent, who, at a quarter to seven every morning could be seen by the neighbors as he cut across the vacant lot, pipe smoke trailing behind and his little dog "Mickey" trotting faithfully at his heels. In an hour or so Mrs. Wilbur would be observed heading for the factory and her job as head finisher.

Factory hours were from 7 a.m. to 12 p.m.; and from 1 p.m. to 6 p.m. Saturday closing time was at 4:40 p.m. The whistle would blow at five minutes before seven to get the girls to their looms. There would be forty-five minutes for lunch, with resumption of work at 12:55 until the whistle announced quitting time at six o'clock, making a long working day of over ten hours.

Wages were approximately the same as paid by other Oregon mills. The starting wage for a woman blanket finisher and sewer was eighty-five cents per day which was raised to $1.00 as soon as she gained experience. Carders and weavers received $2.00. The prevailing daily wage was about $1.50. Piece work never paid more than $25.00 a month. Because of Mr. Eaton's lack of faith in banks, wages were paid in gold and silver coin. The payroll for approximately thirty employees was from $1,000 to $1,300 a month.

Wilbur set high standards of quality and design. His frequent absences on business trips were a welcome relief to the employees from his rigid factory discipline. A fine of five dollars per defective blanket was invoked upon the careless weaver if he could be caught, a severe penalty indeed, in view of the prevailing wage scale. His unpopular reputation as a taskmaster was accountable in part to the aggravations created by unskilled help, occasionally poor workmanship, and payroll separations, to say nothing of the production, maintenance, and marketing problems which he faced daily in the dual position of superintendent and sales manager.

In contrast to his factory personality, was his pleasure in being with people, his reputation as a good story teller, and the respect in which he was held by his business associates.

Working conditions were not the best judged by present day factory standards. Sanitary washrooms and patent toilet facilities were non-existent at the factory. Two outside privies built near the creek, sufficed, one of which, the men's, was a three-sided structure without a roof; a strip of burlap on the fourth side provided a modicum of privacy. Nor was there much comfort as a lunchroom. Women employees ate their midday meal grouped on the factory stairs, and on cold winter days would try to find a warm place in which to pass the all-to-short lunch period. Former employees still recall with some bitterness the poor conditions under which they had to work, especially during the winter. The uninsulated frame building was an inefficient barrier to the below-freezing temperatures of an eastern Oregon winter day; the twelve Rochester lamps while helpful, were not the most efficient heat producers.

There were pipes around the walls, but the old boiler had difficulty in supplying enough hot water to wash the grease from the wool, let alone heat the building. In spite of these unsatisfactory conditions, the little factory was always clean.

Wilbur personally supervised all operations from the purchase of the raw wool and supplies to the sale of the finished product. Upon taking over the management of the mill, he immediately converted its output entirely to blankets and robes. Contrasted with the first two years of intermittent operation, the business was now in a thoroughly prosperous condition.

Orders continued to roll in for the beautiful pure white, virgin wool blankets bound with silk ribbon. Wilbur insisted on quality, positively no shoddy, and it is a tribute to his craftsmanship, in spite of the difficulties he faced in obtaining skilled woolen textile operatives, that orders came from metropolitan eastern, middle western, and Pacific Coast stores for this high-grade merchandise. Among the largest buyers were John Wanamaker and Son, Philadelphia; Marshall Field and Company, Chicago; Jordan, Marsh and Company, Boston; Simpson-Crawford Company, New York and leading San Francisco and Portland stores. Such orders kept the mill in high production through 1901 and 1902. Union merchants sold the blankets for $12.50 a pair; the pure white ones from $16.50-$18.50. Some were extra heavy, weighed fifteen pounds and had very thick napping.

Another profitable source of income was from the sale of blankets to Indian agents on the various reservations. These blankets were so designed and colored as to meet the approval of the most fastidious brave or squaw. The beauty and fastness of the colors were attributed not alone to expert dyeing skills, but largely to the purity of Catherine Creek's water.

Although the national market and even Hawaii continued to buy, Mr. Wilbur did not neglect the regional market. He and Mr. Eaton were gone weeks at a time servicing accounts in Oregon, Washington, and California. At other times they took extended trips to the East and Middle West where they successfully solicited large orders, typical of which were the 2,000 pairs of blankets ordered by a Chicago house and 500 pairs by Wellesley College. Of special interest was the order from a steamship company plying the Pacific for blankets for one of its liners.

So pleased was Mr. Eaton with the prosperity of the enterprise that he hired Mr. Wilbur for a two-year term beginning in January, 1903.

During the above market promotion period the usual factory routines were evident. In the late summer of 1901 the mill was temporarily closed for repairs and the installation of $4,000 of new machinery among which were a new electric lighting system and a dynamo to be operated off the surplus steam power. Several months later a carload of looms, pickers, and scouring machinery arrived, which meant that the plant would resume operations with a crew of forty-five and a night shift. Among other improvements was an H.J. Reedy elevator; also a wool pullery based upon a survey Wilbur made of the availability of sheep pelts in the area adjacent to Union. Altogether $8,000 worth of improvements were made in 1903. Later, a new fifty horsepower engine was purchased in Portland as standby equipment in case of a water shortage. During 1903 the mill ran full time; 500 cords of wood and seven cars of coal were used as fuel.

Improvements were made to the plant with the addition of a ceiling to insulate the factory building in cold weather and the construction of a 30- by 50-foot one-story warehouse immediately south of the main building. The reservoir embankment was raised to guarantee a steady flow of water in case of a low stage or a seige of slush ice threatened.

The early spring months were spent by Wilbur and Eaton in buying wool. The season's supply was purchased in part from ranchers in the vicinity, namely, Miles Lee of Eagle Valley who represented a pool of sheepmen, Mrs. Florence Dobbins of Union, and others as far away as Huntington, Oregon, the Palouse country, Washington, and Lewiston, Idaho. One deal was closed with the Cunninghams in Umatilla County for 180,000 pounds at twelve and one-half cents a pound. Both large and small lots were bought from as low as 12,000 pounds to as high as 100,000 pounds. It was estimated that the annual wool consumption of the little mill was 350,000 pounds.

The factory had been operating nearly six years with few interruptions, adequately financed by Mr. Eaton's fortune and capably managed by Mr. Wilbur. Mr. Eaton had made his money as so many other pioneers had, in the community where he had chosen to reside, and had contributed generously toward improvements in Union and the surrounding area. At age seventy he began to talk of retirement, although three years were to elapse before the mill would be closed down permanently.

The second week of January 1905, saw Wilbur and Will Wright, cashier of the First National Bank of Union, in Eugene looking over the five-set bankrupt woolen mill of that place, idle now for almost a year. The two men took an option on this, the property of the Willamette Valley Woolen Manufacturing Company, with privilege to buy for $50,000 and eventually to consolidate the two mills under one management. A scouring plant was planned for Union which would then ship the cleaned Eastern Oregon wool to the Eugene plant to be mixed with the coarser Willamette Valley fleeces. The Eugene factory never operated under this scheme.

Wilbur's interest in Eugene and Mr. Eaton's contemplated retirement no doubt were disconcerting to the community, especially to the operatives in the woolen mill in their well-settled jobs. Reports began to be circulated during the spring that outside parties were looking at the factory and were prepared to buy up the stock. By the end of 1906 no deal had been made; the cheerful sound of the woolen mill whistle continued to reverberate across the rich farmlands of the Grande Ronde Valley, giving assurance that Union still had a payroll.

In the meantime, lucrative orders continued to be filled for well-established accounts, one in April for $12,000. Wellesley College continued to purchase the fine, white blankets now nationally known partially evidenced by a gold medal won at the Lewis and

Clark Exposition the year before. A $6,000 order came from a San Francisco merchant for a carload shortly after that earthquake and fire-sticken city was recovering from the holocaust. The little town of Union had contributed $3,700 toward the relief fund, a part of which no doubt were warm, comfort-giving blankets from the woolen mill.

In August 1907, true to his word, Mr. Eaton reluctantly closed the factory with a big celebration including a dinner, dancing and speech making by the pricipals. The mill had, in the earlier part of the year, been leased to Wilbur for a six-months period during which time he went on the road to dispose of the remaining stock of blankets. Eaton had encouraged his superintendent to buy the mill by generously offering to back him financially, but the latter felt this was too much responsibility to assume, so, coupled with the persistent pleadings of his wife who had been urging him to get out of business, he decided to refuse the offer, much to his later regret.

In June 1908, a Portland syndicate headed by a Dr. J.F. Bailey bought the idle factory for $25,000, said to have included 840 acres of land in Morrow County, the Commercial Hotel and a furniture store in Newberg, and thirty lots in Newport. It was Bailey's idea to bring his brother-in-law, a technically-trained woolen mill man, to Union to operate the mill.

The plant had now been idle for about a year, and the prospect of it being operated by a medical man and his friends made little impression on the Catherine Creek community. It was not surprising that, as the fall of the year broke, Bailey was dickering with parties to lease the plant but nothing materialized.

In the meantime, inquiries continued to be made by outsiders concerning the woolen mill but no concrete results followed. Bailey continued to make numerous trips to Union, his appearance there creating a revival of hope that the plant would resume operations, followed by disappointment that nothing ever came of these visits. Finally, it was publicly admitted that Dr. Bailey was unable to finance the project and asked the people of Union to assist him. This led to some conferences with leading citizens of the town, but they, being conservative merchants, farmers and livestock men, kept their dollars to themselves and Bailey went back to Portland to incorporate the Union Woolen Mills, with Arthur C. Burgess and B.A. Churchill. A deed from J.F. Bailey to the new company was filed with the recorder of Union County.

By June 1910, enough stock had been sold to insure the reopening of the mill on Catherine Creek; at least that was the assurance given to E.T. Kaster of the Union National Bank, and the company was ready to buy $100,000 worth of Union and Wallowa County wool. Bailey, president of the new company, Burgess, secretary, and Churchill, superintendent, were in Union that month to make repairs. It was claimed enough orders were on hand to keep the mill going for a year.

Bailey's promotion came to naught and the news broke the first of October, 1910, that Bailey would move the woolen mill machinery to Washougal,

Washington, at which place a $2,000 bonus had been offered if the mill would locate there. The people of Union were again given an opportunity to redeem the mill but there were none who would venture their capital.

Neither Eaton nor Wilbur took an active interest in the woolen mill at any time after its sale to Dr. Bailey. With Eaton's retirement, the business effectiveness of the two-man team which brought such prosperity to Union was broken. It can safely be said that the original Union Woolen Mill Company not only had a fine production and merchandising record, but it is one of the few such mills which survived the ever-present hazard of fire that consumed so many of the Oregon woolen factories. During most of its existence, Eaton and Wilbur made an excellent team, the one always ready with adequate cash to keep the mill financially strong, the other contributing his expert technical knowledge and sales ability, so that the mill made money. If it had not, it is doubtful if Eaton would have been so eager to continue his support.

After the factory was closed both Eaton and Wilbur continued to make Union their base of operations. The former settled a $50,000 endowment on Willamette University at Salem and was honored by having a new building named after him and the degree of Doctor of Laws conferred upon him. He continued to administer his various properties up to the time of his death on January 14, 1917. Appropriate services were conducted at both Union and at the Willamette University where Walter Pierce, later Governor of Oregon, gave the formal funeral address.

Wilbur continued to circulate in the Union and Umatilla county sections and was frequently seen in the Pendleton and Echo wool markets. The success of the Union mill attracted the attention of the Pendleton Commercial Club which body had asked him to assume the management of that factory which he declined; and again at Vale and Burns his advice was asked in the possible promotion of a $150,000 woolen mill to be located in one of these towns.

His woolen mill activities in Oregon were concluded with the purchase of the factory at Stayton, Oregon, in August 1912, where he remained approximately five years, then selling and moving to Portland, where he engaged in the real estate business for a time and then operated a chain of bakeries. In 1926 the Wilburs moved to Oakland, California, where he owned and operated a small wool batt factory, and at the same time acted as distributor for the Kay mill at Salem, Oregon, until his tragic death in an automobile accident in California in 1940.[5]

The former millsite is now a horse-lot which encloses the board-patched warehouse building. Nearby is an unsightly chunk of rock and cement, once a foundation corner of the building, together with a few of the weatherworn timbers which supported the superstructure. These are all that remain of one of the most successful woolen mills in the history of such enterprises in Oregon.

---

(5) Correspondence with Mrs. E.H. Thomas (Pearl Wilbur, daughter) Walnut Creek, California

Chapter XI

THE DALLES WOOL-SCOURING
MILL COMPANY

*"It was a sight to see the freight teams
pulling out for The Dalles"*

AS early as 1888 The Dalles claimed it was the largest
primary wool market in the United States, and in
June 1890, 5,000,000 pounds were reportedly handled
at 17 cents a pound. This would be equivalent to 25
per cent of the state's wool crop. Ex-Governor Zenas
F. Moody was a heavy contributor to this volume
with warehouses at The Dalles. Influenced by this
position, the Pacific Northwest Woolgrowers Association held a convention at The Dalles, the first of its
kind in this section of the nation, a most appropriate
choice as the town handled more wool off the sheeps'
back than any other place in the United States. Oregon ranked fifth in wool production and second in
sheep.

The Dalles' reputation as a wool-marketing center
and the success of the Pendleton Wool-Scouring and
Packing Company, were responsible for the appearance in town in January 1895, of James Shaw of Oregon City. His meeting with the business men of the
city promoted the appointment of a committee to investigate the possibilities of a scouring-mill. Shaw
wanted $20,000, a site, and a building, against which
he would pledge the mill and machinery. The com-

mittee's counter proposal was that he establish a scouring mill, drying plant, and a 2-set woolen mill; a site and building would be donated but not the $20,000.

The Shaw deal apparently was never consummated, but on February 27, 1900, J.W. Russell, Grace E. Russell (wife), and J.W. Rountree all of Portland, Oregon, executed articles of incorporation for the The Dalles Scouring-Mills Company, with capital stock of $25,000. E.Y. Judd, nephew of the senior Judd at Pendleton, bought in with the Russells.

A couple of other schemes were attempted later, one, that of Colonel J.M. Patterson who planned a $100,000 integrated textile center comprising a scouring mill, pullery, and a soap factory. And in 1905, an eastern promoter projected a 4-set woolen mill to cost $50,000 which would employ 80 people. But the Russell project was the only one which had any substance.

Prior to its incorporation, Russell had been invited to meet with the directors of the The Dalles Commercial Club to discuss plans for a scouring mill. There was talk of a portage railway and a government-built canal around Celilo Rapids on the Columbia River, and it was feared that with the completion of these projects the interior wools would by-pass the town and go directly to Portland. On the other hand, a scouring mill would divert considerable tonnage to be processed for shipment to the larger textile centers of San Francisco and the East.

Russell, who was a vigorous and aggressive business man, may have cherished a plan to build a scouring

Unloading wool at Wasco Warehouse, The Dalles.

Theron E. Fell, one of the founders of the Pendleton Wool-Scouring and Packing Company. *[Melvin Fell collection]*

mill in Portland, as it was alleged that he was sus-
pected of being partial to Oregon's metropolis while
discussing the proposed The Dalles project. Portland
wool dealers favored a scouring plant there, and it
was perhaps their importunities which stirred The
Dalles to action. "Unless The Dalles Commercial Club
acts promptly it (the scouring mill) may go to Portland which has water transportation and other marketing facilities" reported the *Oregonian* on February
13, 1900. Fortified in this position, Russell agreed to
promote and establish a wool-scouring plant if he
could be assured of financial assistance from the
townspeople. A Commercial Club committee was appointed to investigate Russell's proposition and raise
the necessary funds.

The outcome of the meeting was that $25,000 was
to be raised locally through the sale of preferred
stock. The scouring-mill company on its part agreed
to erect a $30,000-$40,000 plant with a daily capacity
of 20,000 pounds of raw wool. Such a plant would be
sufficiently large enough to intercept the flow of the
interior wool clip from as far east as Idaho where
some of the heavier scouring wools were produced.
The promoters estimated that 10,000,000 pounds of
grease wool would be warehoused annually at The
Dalles.

The site selected was about four blocks east of the
Umatilla House on the railroad near the Pease and
Mays department store. Dimensions of the three-story
frame building were 100 feet by 100 feet. When the
plant opened on June 14, 1901, 25 people were on the

payroll including woolgraders whose daily wage was $3.50-$4.00; scourers were paid $4.00.

Operating supplies like soap were essential. This commodity could be bought ready for use, but the The Dalles mill preferred to make its own soap from a mixture of caustic soda and tallow, the former ingredient purchased from the English international trading firm of Balfour, Guthrie and Company which had a branch office in Portland.

In 1901, the The Dalles Scouring-Mills Company exhibited its product at the Buffalo International Exposition and was awarded a gold medal for having the finest grades of scoured wool.

J.M. Russell, when a young man, had come from Canada to San Francisco where he learned the wool business. From there he went into the Rocky Mountain sheep country at Ogden, Utah, thence to Portland in 1889 where he opened an office in the Sherlock Building to conduct his wool, hide, and hops business. Here he represented Brown, Steese, and Clark, wool merchants.

Upon organizing the The Dalles Scouring-Mill Company of which he was president, he and his family moved to that Wasco County town where they lived four years before returning to Portland. Russell, who retained his office as head of the company, kept close supervision over the mill's affairs even after he returned to Portland, and made the round trip to The Dalles every week.

It was during this sojourn in The Dalles that Russell made the rounds of the sheep ranches on horseback during the spring and summer months of the wool-buying season. It was a common practice during those automobileless days to get up early in the morning, ride to some ranch, close a deal and proceed to another before a competitor got there first. It was at The Dalles, too, that Mrs. Russell kept open house for her husband's wool-buying friends. Hotel accommodations in Oregon's ranch country were very inadequate, and the easterners found the hospitable Russell home a delightful retreat from the rigors of the road and saddle.[1]

Although most of the raw wool processed in The Dalles originated in the Central Oregon hinterland, especially Shaniko, considerable tonnage came from the Yakima country via Wallula, Washington, at that time an important railway junction point. The first clips came from the Columbia River ranges and were the early season scouring wools sought by dealers for that purpose only, compared to later season Washington and Idaho wools which were shipped both in the grease and scoured. Some of these were designated "heavy shrinkage" and sold for 10 cents per pound at the stations, while the lighter shrinkage clips brought 13 cents. The raw wool would show from 65 per cent to 75 per cent weight loss after scouring out the sand, burrs, and ordure.

In addition to the wool held in its own warehouse, the scouring mill drew upon the grease wools in the Wasco Warehouse & Milling Company's warehouse, and in Moody's. During the height of the season from thirty to forty wagons would line up at the ware-

---

(1) Interview with Mrs. Russell

houses waiting their turn to discharge the heavy wool bags.

A stirring description of these vehicles and their great loads is recorded for Grade, Wheeler County. This was a natural stopping place for the freighters. The Van Bibbers who operated both the post office and a smithy, also served meals to the drivers for twenty-five cents:[2]

> The toll was twenty-five cents for each horse, regardless of the number of wagons or their weight. We could not charge Indians or preachers, and naturally there was no charge for the neighbors.
>
> In good weather there were often ten, twelve, or even twenty freighters camping along the road from the house far up past the blacksmith shop. It was a sight to remember to see the Grade at starting time, lined with freight teams pulling out toward The Dalles, loaded with huge sacks of wool. Not a few outfits had as many as three wagons and ten or twelve horses.
>
> Some horses were sleek and strong, well harnessed, others were pitiable creatures, victims of cruelty and ignorance. You could almost read a man's character by his team and wagon. One of the best outfits on the road belonged to Jack McCauley who had a family of ten children on a little homestead near the town of John Day.

It was reported that sometimes the drivers would unload their cargoes and dump the wool bags in the many chuckholes on the unimproved roadways leading to The Dalles.

Wool sales were conducted at the various warehouses, usually on a sealed bid basis, but again by direct sale. On June 6, 1903 the opening wool sale disposed of 125,000 pounds at 9-1/2 to 13-1/8 cents per

---

(2)   Oregon Historical Quarterly, December 1947, page 325

pound. Among the buyers who frequented such sales held also at Pendleton, Arlington, Heppner, Baker, Elgin and Shaniko, were Denny, Rice and Company and A. Livingston, of Boston; J.J. Schapelle, C.S. Moses and Company, and T.H. Smith of San Francisco; S. Koshland, Portland; and H.C. Judd and Root of Hartford, Connecticut. Willamette woolen mills also sent their buyers to these sales.

Mr. Russell bought wool at these sales for his own account as well as for the scouring mill, washed it and either sold it locally or shipped it east or to San Francisco. By 1904 choice Oregon wools were being sought in the grease by eastern buyers, as the eastern mills preferred to grade and scour their own wool to suit their requirements as scoured wool was not segregated as to grades. For this reason it was reported that The Dalles began to lose its reputation as a primary wool market and scouring center.

The rail freight to eastern points on grease wool was approximately $1.00 per hundred pounds, and on scoured wool $1.50-$1.80. Scoured wool at the plant was worth 40-50 cents a pound as compared to 10-18 cents in the grease. About 8,000,000 pounds of wool were passing through The Dalles annually in the early years of the century.

Marketing of the wool clips was facilitated by numerous short-line railroads, the northern termini of which were attached securely to one of the transcontinental lines, while the other end figuratively dangled out in the limitless spaces of the ranch country, sensitive to the vast tonnages of grease wool available at interior shipping points. Among the stub

lines was the Columbia Southern which terminated at
Shaniko.

The importance of the town as a woolgrowers' local
market cannot be underestimated in its relationship to
the The Dalles scouring mill. Here the five- and
six-horse teams drew up to the warehouses to discharge their cumbersome loads of bulging wool bags,
later to be transported by the Columbia Southern
Railroad to its northern terminus. The railroad was
headed deep into Central Oregon in 1901 when it
reached Shaniko, but it got no further. It nevertheless
brought temporary prosperity and contact with the
outside world. Livestock pens were constructed to accommodate 5,000 sheep; buildings and store buildings were erected and included a fine hotel, residences, saloons and livery stables. With the decline in
livestock production and changing transportation
conditions, Columbia Southern rails were torn up a
few years ago, population moved elsewhere, so that
today Shaniko remains an interesting place for tourists
to view the remains of what was once the metropolis
of Central Oregon.

There were a number of stub railroad lines serving
the sheep country. Some of them were controlled by
the main line railroads to which they were attached at
the junction points. Construction of such lines eliminated the picturesque, cumbersome, horse-drawn
freight vehicles and aided in the growth of the interior towns like Shaniko and Dayton.

The The Dalles scouring mill continued to operate
until about World War I period, perhaps to 1916-17.
During its lifetime the successful scouring of millions

of pounds of grease wool, The Dalles maintained its reputation as a foremost primary wool marketing center.

Refer to Chapter 17 for the history of the Pendleton Wool-Scouring and Packing Company

PART IV

Southern Oregon Woolen Mills

Chapter XII

THE ASHLAND WOOLEN
MANUFACTURING COMPANY

"No shoddy, nothing but genuine wool"

SUNDAY, January 21, 1900 was a sad day for the little Southern Oregon town of Ashland nestled at the base of the rugged Siskiyou Mountains. The population had been rudely awakened by the screeching whistle of the Southern Pacific's northbound local at 2:15 a.m. when the engineer sighted the dull, red glow of fire in the woolen mill.

The clamorous clanging of the City Hall bell roused two volunteer hose companies which soon had their hoses coupled to the hydrants. Their valiant efforts to subdue the "enormous white heat which puffed forth in the hum of destruction" were of no avail, and within the hour the building was a mass of smoldering embers and useless machinery.

The original Rogue River Valley Manufacturing Company[1] was incorporated on March 8, 1867 and had begun operation on October 8, 1868. The site was on the block bounded by the Old Stage Road (North Main Street), Water and Pine Streets.[2] The

---

(1) Alfred L. Lomax, *Pioneer Woolen Mills in Oregon*, Binfords & Mort, Portland, 1941

(2) Copy of old city map of Ashland courtesy of Ashland Public Library. The reincorporated Ashland Woolen Manufacturing Company continued operations in the old building. The Cascade M-D Products Company occupied the site until that building burned on July 1, 1970

factory ran at a loss until it was sold to G.N. Marshall and Charles Goodchild in 1872. The latter had been operating a one-set carding machine for processing rolls of wool in Eugene.

About 1875, James Thornton, one of the incorporators of the pioneer Ashland mill, bought out some of his associates. In 1878 he bought the entire stock of the concern, and at the same time Jacob Wagner, Eli K. Anderson, and W.H. Atkinson, all of Ashland became associated with him to form a company which they called the Ashland Woolen Manufacturing Company.

On April 12, 1878 the following advertisement appeared in the *Ashland Tidings:*

> Having purchased the entire interests of my late partners, the Ashland woolen mills are now running . . . making blankets, flannels, doeskins, cassimeres and hosery(sic).
>
> In becoming sole proprietor, I assume the company indebtedness and all accounts and notes due the company south of Canyonville are payable to me or my order.
>
> W.H. Atkinson is authorized agent for me and has full power to transact any and all business connected with the Ashland woolen mills.
>
> James Thornton

In the same issue appeared this notice:

> All persons in debt to the Ashland woolen mills are notified to call and settle either in cash or note within 30 days from this date, April 5, 1878.
>
> W.H. Atkinson, agent

The officers of the company were aware of the value of promoting their products in the limited market and ran the following stuffy advertisement in the *Tidings* during the latter part of 1877 and the first months of 1878:

THE ASHLAND WOOLEN MILLS

We take pleasure in announcing that this old and substantial institution is in active operation, manufacturing from the very best of native wool, blankets, flannels, cassimeres, doeskins and all other fabrics usually manufactured in a first class woolen factory.

no shoddy
nothing but genuine wool

Also socks and stocking yarn, colored or uncolored, in qualities to suit purchasers.

The highest market price paid for good native wool in money or goods.

Goods at wholesale at the lowest cash rates.

Come Everybody

Patronize home industry and we will see that you are satisfied.

Address, Ashland Woolen Manufacturing Company

This was followed by J.M. McCall and Company's advertisement stating that the store carried a full line of Ashland woolen goods.

The United States Census (1880) recorded a labor force of 20 composed of 13 males and 7 females at an average daily wage of $2.50 for skilled mechanics, and $1.50 for laborers. Sock knitters were paid 75 cents a day with a daily output of four dozen pairs per worker. Annual payroll was $9,000; value of products was $45,000. Forty women and girls of the town found home employment by finishing socks and flannel underwear.

Output for eleven months of 1882 was 7,500 pairs of blankets; 30,000 yards of flannel, 3,000 yards of

cassimere; 2,000 shawls; 6,000 dozen socks; and unnamed amounts of robes, skirts, and other items. Approximately 100,000 pounds of wool were consumed
in making woolen products under the supervision of
J.R. Casey, an eastern woolen mill man who was
hired in 1883.

A three-story, white, frame structure 64 feet by 90
feet housed these operations. The machinery consisted
of one each of the following:

> 48 inch carding machine, wool picker, card grinder, cen-
> trifugal extractor, Crompton fancy loom, spooler, warper,
> shear, gig, fuller, washer, spinning jack of 240 spindles;
> also two knitting machines and six broad looms. A sock
> washer supplemented the knitting operation.

Factory personnel was composed of ten women and
girls, and twenty men and boys. Finishing work on
socks was done in the homes of Ashland women.

A beautifully-toned bell which hung in a small
cupola called the workers to their looms and to announce quitting time. It was reported that the vibrant
tone was caused by the gold and silver used in its
composition.

Waterpower came from Ashland Creek through
flume and wooden pipe after it had serviced the flour
mill near what is now the entrance to Lithia Park.
The creek had a fall of 250 feet per mile and was discharged from a flume into a forebay. From here it
dropped to a 26-inch Leffel turbine waterwheel to
produce 58 horsepower.

The latter was an invention of James Leffel of Ohio
and was widely adopted by the woolen textile
industry. Greater efficiency was obtained as the water

passed through ducts or vanes in contrast to the traditional overshot and undershot wheels. Price was $200-$700. Sometimes there was not enough stream flow to turn the wheel and wash the wool at the same time, so washing was done at night.

Wool was stored in a warehouse near the flour mill except what was needed for immediate use in the factory. Jackson County sheepraisers found a ready market for their fleeces and received cash or goods in payment.

The principal line of goods was blankets as they were for all of the Oregon woolen mills, followed by cassimeres, flannels, doeskins, and shawls. These were sold in the local stores of Baum and McCall and Hargadine's General Merchandise store. San Francisco distributors were also used to reach portions of the western market, Alaska and even China.

The company was geographically handicapped when compared to the flourishing Willamette Valley mills at Salem, Brownsville, and Oregon City in the 1870s and 1880s. Their advantage lay in having rail connections to Portland as a distributing center with steamer connections to San Francisco. Proximity to northern California was not an advantage as all freight south had to be carted over the rugged Siskiyou Mountains by horsedrawn vehicles until the railroad was built. Nevertheless, Ashland products were exhibited at the California State Fair at Sacramento, and in 1879 an eye-filling display of woolen goods was made at the Yreka, California, County Fair. Blankets, plaids, flannels, breakfast shawls, balmoral skirts, cloak goods and stockings compared favorably with similar goods from the northern mills. The mill specialized in red blankets for which there was a consistent demand.

In the spring of 1883 the completion of a new road over the Coast Mountains to the port of Crescent City, California, put San Francisco as a market and supply center within four days from southern Oregon.

Until the Oregon and California Railroad was completed over the Calapoyia Mountains (a spur of the Cascades) from Roseburg to Ashland on May 4, 1884, orders were shipped by freight wagon to Roseburg, there to be reloaded to freight cars. On one occasion an order was dispatched over the O. and C. to Albany where connections were made with the recently built Oregon & Pacific Railroad which ran to the port of Yaquina on the river of the same name. There transshipment was made to the railroad company's steamer for San Francisco.

Connection with California points by rail from Ashland was accomplished on December 17, 1887 by the Southern Pacific Railroad which had acquired the O. and C. After completion of the line to Portland, Fleischner, Mayer and Company, a large wholesale house became the principal distributor for the Ashland mill.

While railroad building improved market conditions, reorganization occurred at the woolen mill. On September 8, 1885 articles of incorporation were filed with the Secretary of State, Salem, for the Ashland Woolen Mills, capitalized for $50,000. Incorporators were James Thornton, W.H. Atkinson, Eli K. Anderson, and J.M. McCall. Offices were rented in the

Masonic Block. Thornton became president, Anderson vice president, and Atkinson secretary-manager.

The possibility of losing the woolen mill to some other town caused considerable apprehension in April 1889 when a representative of the mill visited Eugene. The plant had been idle since December. Lack of working capital and overhead expenses too great for a one-set mill plagued the company with consequent decline of profits. The situation appeared critical as there was at this time strong support being given by Albany, Salem, and Roseburg to payroll producing woolen mills. For Ashland to lose the little factory which had been contributing to its welfare for over a quarter of a century and owned by local people, would have been a severe economic loss. Fortunately for the community the Eugene transaction never materialized and the mill happily rehired the 35 employees before the month ended.

In August, the annual meeting of stockholders was held and the following people elected as directors: James Thornton, J.M. McCall, E.K. Anderson, Thomas Smith, and W.H. Atkinson. Election of officers followed with Thornton, president; Anderson, vice president; Atkinson, secretary-manager; E.V. Carter, treasurer.

A seasonal threat to operation was the low summer level of Ashland Creek, so to assure the mill received its power requirements a man was hired to prevent stealing and leakage.

A temporary closing order was issued in November to extend over the holidays, but unfortunately closure continued until the last week of May 1890. When the silver-toned bell rang out the seven o'clock call to work, all agreed it was the most heartening sound heard in many months.

Intermittent operation continued into 1891 and 1892. A business carnival in February exhibited the products of the woolen mill and provided costumes ornamented with yarns, flannels, and cassimeres.

In July, the local woolgrowers decided to market their 50,000-pound wool pack elsewhere than in Ashland, presumably either because the mill had closed or could not afford to pay the price asked.

In June 1893 the mill secured a contract for National Guard uniform cloth, and one with the United States Indian Department for blankets and other woolen goods.

In 1895 E.K. Anderson and his son George N. Anderson bought the interests of the other stockholders. Casey remained as superintendent.

Four years later the new owners added $5,000 in new spinning frames, looms and dye vats. Then came the aforesaid January fire which threw 32 people out of work, deprived them of a ten per cent wage increase, the town a regular payroll with its economic benefits, and a place where its residents could wash their soiled blankets.

The fire, the worst in Ashland's history, must have been a miniature holocaust judging by press descriptions at the time. In spite of heroic efforts by the two volunteer hose teams and the dependability of the water system, the conflagration raged out of control, and efforts were directed toward saving nearby residences and the Presbyterian church. The dyehouse and woolhouse with $4,000 worth of wool were saved, but blankets and other goods in process worth $6,500 were totally destroyed. The origin of the fire is disputed, but it was thought to have started in the picking room.

Manager George Anderson and superintendent Casey had left the building after the customary closing hour of four-thirty on Saturdays. The night-watchman had inspected the premises about twenty minutes before the fire was noticed and had seen no evidence of either fire or smoke.

The factory had been a good insurance risk, had been inspected the week before by an agent of one of the insurance companies and had complimented the management on its efficiency. The $14,000 coverage was shared by the following companies: Home Insurance Company $5,000; Aachen-Munich $2,000; Home Mutual $1,000; North America $1,000; Pennsylvania $1,000; Hartford $2,000; Hamburg-Bremen $1,000; and London & Lancashire $1,000. These amounts were distributed to cover the building for $5,000; machinery $6,500; work in process and manufactured $2,500. The plant was valued at $65,000.

Equipment at this time consisted of two sets of cards, sixteen looms, two automatic spinning jacks of 240 spindles each, and two full sets of unused knitting machinery.

Early in March a public meeting was held in the City Hall to discuss rebuilding plans. Under the urging of J.W. Collins, the mill's San Francisco agent, a joint stock company was proposed, $25,000 to be

locally subscribed and the balance of $15,000 by the
owners, C.K. Anderson and G.N. Anderson. The
latter would contribute the mill site, their 75 horsepower water rights on Ashland Creek and water from
the city mains. Plant capacity would be doubled to 32
looms in view of the expanding San Francisco,
Hawaii, Alaska and China markets. The usual solicitation committee was composed of J.R. Norris, E.A.
Sherwin, and J.B. Casey.

The factory was never rebuilt. A few months later a
notice appeared in the Ashland papers advertising the
property for sale. In the latter part of February 1901
the Ashland Manufacturing Company (a planing mill)
purchased the woolen mill site. The transfer included
2-1/2 acres of land and water rights valued at $6,000.
George N. Anderson retained one-fourth interest and
became a member of the company.

Ashland residents spoke feelingly and regretfully of
southern Oregon's foremost industrial enterprise
which had provided a fairly stable payroll for months
at a time. Unlike some of the contemporary Oregon
woolen mills which suffered heavy fire losses, the Ashland mill had survived this menace until its unhappy
extinction.

The original building had housed the operations of
the pioneer Rogue River Valley Woolen Manufacturing Company, the Ashland Woolen Manufacturing
Company, and the Ashland Woolen Mills, all owned
and operated by Ashland citizens, who, by their
astute entrepreneurship brought economic benefits to
their friends and neighbors for a span of thirty-three

years. All the gold was not found in the Jackson County hills.[3]

---

(3)   Interviews with the late S.F. Thornton, former loom boss, and C.E. Lane who worked in the factory, are incorporated in this chapter

Chapter XIII

THE ROSEBURG WOOLEN MILL

"Parts of a loom were found on a sandbar"

ROSEBURG, county seat of Douglas County, unlike the Willamette Valley towns and Ashland, which supported successful woolen mills, lacked the promotional vigor which characterized the northern communities. The ample waterpower of the coursing South Umpqua River stimulated little industrial incentive for disinterested Roseburgers. Exceptions were Aaron Rose, founder of the town, and Joseph G. Flook, who constructed a dam for the New Era Flour Mills on the southern edge of the town in 1870.

A more substantial interest in woolen cloth manufacturing appeared in 1881 when Sol Abraham, merchant, took the lead in offering to subscribe $10,000 toward a projected woolen mill to cost $75,000. Six years later, Aaron Rose, founder of the town, offered free perpetual power to anyone who would erect a woolen factory at the proffered site.

The prerequisites for a woolen mill were evident. Douglas County sheep produced the much sought-after Umpqua fleeces. Mineral-free water for scouring and dyeing was available in the many streams which flowed off the surrounding mountains, and cordwood for fuel was economically available in the nearby forest.

There were no immediate takers of Rose's gratuitous offer, but in 1888, two Scotchmen, James Denholm and James Rentoul invested $15,000 of their own money supplemented by a bonus (amount unknown) and started construction of a factory building. The site was on the east side of the South Umpqua River about a quarter of a mile below the old flour mill dam. By February 1889, a millrace and a building had been constructed. Upon completion of the latter structure, three carloads of machinery were installed preparatory to working the spring wool clip. By April, the promised bonus had been subscribed, and in May the factory was in full operation. Keeping company with the new enterprise were two flour mills, an iron foundry, two sash and door factories, a brewery, and marble mill for cutting and finishing the natural rock, all supported by a population of 2,500. Statistics are not available describing the mill properties, the number of employees, annual production and value of output. The usual blankets, tweeds, and hosiery yarns were produced.

Unlike many of the Oregon woolen mills which suffered disastrous fires which either wholly or partly destroyed them, the Roseburg factory was completely demolished in February 1890 by a flood which swept down the South Umpqua River. Although the building was sturdily constructed it could not withstand the force of the rushing flood water and most of the main building was carried along and deposited with other debris downstream; parts of a loom were found later on a sandbar. The remaining buildings were dismantled and the lumber used for houses which were built near the railroad tracks and are still in use.[1]

The catastrophe took the heart out of any ambition Roseburg citizens had for woolen mill promotion. The cement blocks of the foundation remain as mute reminders of a small community's thwarted industrial hopes.

---

(1) George Abdill, Curator, Douglas County Museum

PART V

Mill Ends

Chapter XIV

GORDON FALLS

"A Woolen Mill Utopia"

MANY years before the system of gigantic hydro-electric dams was built on the Columbia River, industrial promoters visualized factory sites along its banks and power sites at the many waterfalls which poured over the fringing basalt cliffs. In 1908 a group of Portland businessmen planned a woolen mill as the core of an ideal textile town replete with mill buildings, employee houses, stores, and a hotel. The site was an 840-acre tract fronting the Columbia River lying between Gordon Falls (Wahkeena) and Bridal Veil Falls, 28 miles east of Portland.

Principal promoters were Charles Coopey, a merchant tailor, and George L. Peaslee, a printer, who incorporated the Gordon Falls Electric and Manufacturing Company with $225,000 capitalization. An elaborate stock and bond sale was launched from headquarters in the Commercial Club building (later the Oregon Building), corner 5th and Oak Streets, Portland. Bonds of $100 each bearing 6% interest were to be issued secured by a first mortgage on the 840-acre tract and redeemable in ten years. Each purchaser of a bond would be given $50 in common stock when it was fully paid up.

A previous incorporation known as the Gordon Falls City Manufacturing Power and Light Company, also by Portlanders, never was operative.

A woolen mill to cost $39,192 and an excelsior plant to shred the abundant cottonwood trees which fringed the river bank, were to be the first mill buildings erected. The project was on a large scale with the main building constructed of either stone or concrete. Overhead shafting, a common feature in most manufacturing establishments, was to be eliminated in favor of individual motors for the cards, looms, and spinning frames. A boot and shoe factory would augment the other manufacturing activities.

Each employee was to have an interest in the company and a cozy home and garden. A nearby park, recreation area, and gymnasium would promote relaxation after a hard day's work at the looms and dye vats. Guests at the hotel would be treated to an eye-filling vista of great lava cliffs and leaping water falls. Alcoholic beverages were strictly prohibited, even the solacing after-work glass of beer.

Coopey was an Englishman born in the Stroud Valley, a woolen textile area. As a youth he had served a full merchant tailor apprenticeship. In 1892, two years after his arrival in Portland, Oregon, he opened a first-class tailor shop where he catered not only to the town's more affluent business and professional men, but made uniforms for the National Guard, firemen, and policemen.

The potentialities for woolen cloth manufacturing in Oregon made a deep impression on him. The availability of raw wool, pure water, and the damp climate were reminiscent of the Stroud Valley and stimulated Coopey to become an enthusiastic booster for woolen mills, home industry, and on the side, the Columbia River Highway. He later became president of the unsuccessful Bannockburn Manufacturing Company, an Albany woolen mill. His friends admired him for his zeal; his opponents called him a crank. Portland's need was for twenty woolen mills he said, instead of just the one at St. Johns.

Townsite surveys began the third week of July 1908 after which the deed for the gorge tract was recorded in the Multnomah County Clerk's office on October 26, 1908. It showed Charles Coopey, grantor, and the Gordon Falls Electric and Manufacturing Company, grantee.

As the promotion progressed, names of interested parties were revealed. E.Y. Judd, a well-known wool buyer of Hartford, Connecticut and part owner of the Pendleton Wool-Scouring and Packing Company, was prevailed upon to move that factory in its entirety to Gordon Falls. But the transaction never materialized as the Bishop family became owners in 1909.

Both the *Gordon Falls Gazette*, a promotion sheet, and the Portland *Oregonian* listed the following officers:

> E.Y. Judd, president
> Charles Coopey, vice president
> George L. Peaslee, treasurer
> George Sault, superintendent
> J.H. Cunningham, engineer
> J.O. Wren, architect
> A.T. Lewis, attorney

The prospectus written with a Coopey flair: "It will be a great thing when the man of fashion who wants a good thing demands his clothes made from Coopey Tweed, made with Oregon fleeces, scoured and manufactured in an Oregon mill at Gordon Falls City, on the banks of the mighty Columbia in the good state of Oregon. The curtains have been brushed aside and the world may now look through the gates of the newly-born Utopia and behold each heart happy, each countenance suffused with smiles."

There were no happy hearts and suffused smiling faces. Utopia never got off the ground.

Chapter XV

THE BEND WOOLEN MILL [*]

"Thousands of sheep graze on the nearby rangelands"

IN November 1902, Bend citizens were alerted to news that the Columbia Southern Railroad was laying rails from a Columbia River point to Shaniko, eastern Oregon's important wool collecting depot, with a projection to Bend as a terminus. To the transportation-starved little community at Farewell Bend on the Deschutes River this meant contact with the outside world. As a preparatory step for the important event, a Board of Trade was organized on November 2, 1902 to promote irrigation, agriculture, and industry.[1] In February 1903, a circular letter was dispatched to Oregon lumber and woolen mills calling their attention to the nearby vast stands of yellow pine and the availability of raw wool from the thousands of sheep which grazed on the contiguous range lands as far south as Silver Lake.

At the time, the Corvallis and Eastern Railroad was pushing surveys over the Cascade hump to Bend and an eastern Oregon junction with a transcontinental railroad. Less realistic was the rumor that a southern approach to Bend was to be made by the Salt Lake

(*) Phil F. Brogan, former associate editor of the *Bend Bulletin*; Keith Clark on the faculty of the Bend Community College; and Steve Steidl sent data as the basis for this chapter
(1) The *Deschutes Echo*, November 15, 1902

and Coos Bay Railroad via Silver Lake, and by an unnamed electric line from Sacramento. The reported 250,000 sheep on the outlying ranges would contribute revenue producing fleeces for shipment to Willamette Valley and California woolen mills.

Enthusiasm was shortlived; not until 1911 did the costly Deschutes Canyon rail lines make Bend their terminus. Mostly lumber, filled the Union Pacific and Northern Pacific freight cars.

A definite interest in the manufacture of wool textiles was manifested by the incorporation of the Bend Woolen Mills for $40,000 on June 25, 1923 with approximately one-half of the capital stock subscribed by Bend people. The Providence Knitting Mills Company of Providence, Utah was the sponsor. Local capital interests were represented by A.H. Horn, president; C.P. Niswonger, vice president; John Steidl, treasurer; O. Borken, secretary. A 40 by 60-foot factory building was erected costing $20,000 which housed 16 knitting machines and the same number of finishing machines, costing $5,000.

Reliance on local wool supplies was manifested when the factory opened with 400,000 pounds of wool; 2,000 rolls of wool yarn from Portland supplemented the raw wool.

The little knitting mill had the usual problems of training its 40-50 inexperienced employees, mostly women, in the operation of the various machines. Harvard Osmund, an expert knitter from the parent plant was instructor, aided by experienced personnel from the Utah factory.

By August, the factory was in full production and a Fall shipment of 250 packages valued at $5,000-$6,000 was delivered to the post office for mailing.

The company's inability to meet its financial obligations caused its closing in 1926, and the property was sold to a private individual for $2,705.32. In the intervening years proprietorship has fluctuated. Today, the original brick portion of the factory building is occupied by a restaurant known as "The Bend Woolen Mill."

Chapter XVI

VISIONARY PROJECTS

"Many projects were still born on paper".

DURING the last twenty-five years of the 19th century and the first decade of the 20th, woolen mill and scouring-mill projects were proposed only to become space-filling news items in the local papers. Others, enthusiastically conceived in smoke-filled chamber of commerce committee rooms were still-born on paper. Almost any Oregon town of importance was affected by local promotion efforts or by visits of eastern woolen mill owners who were impressed with the natural advantages on which the successful Oregon mills had been established. Astoria, Aumsville, Bend, Corvallis, Hood River, La Grande, Lebanon, and Springfield were in this category.

ASTORIA

Astoria, near the mouth of the mighty Columbia River was no different than the other Oregon towns in its eagerness to have a woolen mill with its lucrative payrolls, but a more illogical place for such a factory can hardly be imagined. Its economic interests centered upon its geographic position as a small fresh-water seaport dependent upon coastwise shipping and river boat traffic; a picturesque salmon-fishing fleet whose daily catch fed the numerous canneries; and its sawmills. The town gazed enviously on the great grain ships which, under tow, made their slow way to the Portland wheat docks 112 miles inland on the Willamette River.

In the latter part of 1901, H.D. Wagnon, well-known in Oregon for his promotional schemes, met with a chamber of commerce committee to discuss the idea of a woolen mill. About a week later, G.W. Hirst, former superintendent of the Brownsville woolen mill, proposed that a bonus of $25,000 be raised by a 10-year, 5% bond issue, and if successful, he would transfer his 4-set Wisconsin woolen mill machinery to the Pacific Coast. Again, a chamber of commerce committee heard the proposal, but as usual it failed to stimulate action. Astorians evidently preferred the odor of fresh fish and waterfront noises to those of steaming scouring vats and the clank of shuttles and looms.

THE THOMAS ROSS
WOOL-SCOURING COMPANY

Sellwood, at the beginning of the century, was a quiet but aggressive little suburb on the southern outskirts of a fast-growing Portland. During the first five years of the 1900s it was the center of industrial interest for a number of projects allied to wool and woolen textile manufacturing. The most pretentious of these were the Portland Woolen Mills Company, and the Thomas Ross and Associates wool-scouring promotion in which J.M. Nickum of Nickum and

Kelly, sand and gravel contractors, and A.C. Mowrey of the East Side Lumber Company were interested.

Mr. Ross came to Portland from Las Vegas, New Mexico in the spring of 1905 with the idea of investigating sites for a wool-scouring plant. After spending six weeks traveling up and down the Pacific Coast, he finally settled on Portland. Pendleton and The Dalles each had scouring mills; a reasonable assumption was that another one in the great wool-growing state of Oregon could do equally well in a metropolitan center under competent management. Ross had thirty-five years experience back of him: fifteen years in Rhode Island, ten years with the Las Vegas Woolpulling and Scouring Company, and at the time of his visit to Portland was president of the Ross and Brown Wool-Scouring Company.

On April 19, 1905, the *Morning Oregonian* carried a news account describing a proposed $100,000 wool-scouring plant to be built in the state's largest city. It was to cover three acres of ground on the site of the former Portland Woolen Mill Company factory which had burned down the year before. Excellent transportation facilities were afforded by the Southern Pacific Railroad and the Oregon Waterpower and Railway Company, as compared to a proposed site in St. Johns, a north Portland suburb where the Portland Woolen Mill had located after the disastrous Sellwood site fire.

The daily capacity of the proposed mill was 50,000 pounds of grease wool, or greater than the combined capacities of the Pendleton and The Dalles plants. The vats would handle 5,000,000 pounds of wool annually. There was talk of a woolen mill and a knitting factory as part of the project. There was every indication that Portland was going to achieve one of its cherished ambitions, that of becoming a great textile center.

In September 1905 Ross arrived and concluded his deal with the woolen mill owners for their old Sellwood site of ten acres for $9,000. Machinery and equipment would be moved north from Las Vegas and Denver in time to scour the 1906 Pacific Northwest clip. In the meantime, riparian rights for 25 horsepower had been acquired on Johnson Creek, whose clear, soft waters were excellent for scouring. Construction was set for the middle of October.

On November 27 the foundation was started with completion scheduled for January 1906. The plans showed an L-shaped building 208 by 155 feet and 173 by 45 feet. A standby flume brought water from Johnson Creek for washing and scouring. A feature was a concrete pit 95 by 45 feet for scouring. The boiler and engine houses were set apart from the main building as a fire prevention measure. Altogether $50,000 was invested in the property.

The foundation and the scouring-room were completed in December, but the opening date had been postponed to May 1st of what was announced as the largest scouring-plant west of the Mississippi River.

This was as far as the well-meant promotion was carried; although machinery arrived it was never installed. When the Multnomah Mohair Company subsequently acquired the property, the machinery was

stored in a nearby warehouse and was still there when
the Oregon Worsted Company took over in 1918.
Whether the mill actually operated is not clearly reported, although a news story in a Portland paper
stated that Ross was manager of the Sellwood woolen
mills, probably meaning the scouring-mill.

THE WOOLGROWERS' SCOURING COMPANY

After the failure of the Sellwood project, Ross, on
December 30, 1908 organized with Robert N. Stanfield and Dan P. Smythe, both of Umatilla County,
the Woolgrowers' Scouring Company with the principal office at Echo. The capital stock of $50,000 was
divided into 5,000 shares of par value $10.00 each.
The Stanfield brothers were among the largest sheep
raisers in Oregon.

There was some question as to whether the plant
should be built at Pendleton or Echo. The growers
eventually decided in favor of the latter place and
Ross was prevailed upon to ship some of his stored
machinery to the new eastern Oregon location. The
purpose in establishing another scouring operation in
the heart of the wool-growing country was to develop
competition with the Judd-owned Pendleton scouring
mill established in 1893.

The Echo plant consisted of two storage warehouses, one building for scouring, and a boiler house,
which made a plant as large as the one at The Dalles.
The mill specialized in the long staple 3X eastern
Oregon wool which was sent to Boston after scouring.

Operations continued intermittently until about 1918 when the operation ceased. Ross was then employed by Crimmens and Pierce of Boston, a position he held until his death in 1926. The plant was dismantled and the machinery junked. The Oregon Worsted Company, which located on the Sellwood site of the first Ross project, did not install any of the Ross equipment as has been reported.

Technical advancements in the textile industry and that Eastern woolen mills preferred to do their own scouring in order to meet the particular demands of their customers, are reasons advanced for the decline of the Oregon scouring mills.

PART VI

Pendleton Woolen Mills

Chapter XVII

THE PENDLETON WOOL-SCOURING AND PACKING COMPANY

"Scores of woolgrowers will come to your city"

EAST of the Cascade Mountains in Oregon is a vast semi-arid plateau region broken by isolated buttes, hills and mountain spurs. This area was the region of big ranches whose owners counted their flocks and herds by the thousands. Sheep thrived on the short grasses and were raised principally for their wool, although the meat aspect was not overlooked. The animals were driven to convenient shipping pens on the newly-built railroads or were trailed[1] to middlewest shipping points and packing houses at Denver, Kansas City and Chicago.

Wool marketing centers were Heppner, Echo, Shaniko, The Dalles, and Pendleton, Oregon; Yakima, Dayton, and other places in Washington. The roads, so-called, were dusty and rutty under the trampling feet of thousands of sheep as they moved from the ranches to the shearing and shipping pens and the almost constant friction of the wheels of the heavily loaded freight wagons. Millions of pounds of the crinkly fiber moved by wagon and rail to the scouring mills at Pendleton and The Dalles.

---

(1) American Sheep Trails, Edward N. Wentworth, Iowa State College Press, Ames, Iowa, 1948

Everyone talked wool and sheep, feed, water, markets, freight rates and the tariff. Wool prices were quoted daily in the Portland *Oregonian*, the Pendleton *East Oregonian*, and other local papers. With these local ingredients at hand, the importance of home industry promotion was emphasized in both news and editorials, especially scouring mills and woolen mills.

The Pendleton plant was the first of these to set the pattern for those to follow at The Dalles, Echo, and Sellwood (a Portland suburb). They scoured wool on contract for large eastern wool buyers whose headquarters were in Boston, and Hartford, Connecticut. Representatives of these eastern middlemen as well as buyers from California and Oregon woolen mills made the interior sheep towns, Pendleton and The Dalles, during the spring and summer wool-buying seasons.

In 1888, Pendleton was stirred by the offer of a German capitalist who offered to erect a $30,000 scouring mill. Three years later a representative of eastern capitalists proposed a large scale industrial development on acreage two miles from town to include a $60,000 woolen mill, scouring mill, warehouse, and other enterprises. He proposed that a $75,000 fund be raised and an eighteen months option be taken on the acreage. But, like so many promotion-inflated projects, this one never materialized.

But the spark of interest never quite flickered out, for in December 1893 the Commercial Association invited Theron E. Fell, a former sheep rancher and wool handler of Heppner and recently manager-receiver of the defunct Tacoma, Washington woolen mill, and E.Y. Judd of H.C. Judd & Root, wool buyers of Hartford, Connecticut, to discuss plans for a scouring mill. On December 20, 1893 the Pendleton Wool-Scouring and Packing Company was incorporated with capital stock of $12,000 in $50.00 shares. Incorporators were R. Alexander, T.B. Wells, and Theron E. Fell.

The Commercial Club and the Umatilla County Woolgrowers' Association began a successful solicitation of stock subscriptions. Sold immediately was $6,000 of the preferred stock with its guarantee of ten per cent annual dividends. But responses to solicitation lagged. For a number of weeks the local newspaper appealed to woolgrowers and townspeople to support the budding enterprise. They were reminded that a stock subscription was not a bonus or a gift but an investment with a guaranteed return. Specific economic benefits would accrue, foremost of which was that Pendleton would become an outstanding wool market and commercial center of the region. Roads from ranches, shearing pens, and feeding grounds led directly to Pendleton.

Prominent business men of the town were on the solicitation committee including C.S. Jackson, editor of the *East Oregonian*, whose vigorous editorials and news items were influential in making the campaign a success. Said he:

> "Now it is your duty and to your interest Mr. Woolgrower, Mr. Business Man, Mr. Property Owner, on whom there are no strings of individuals and corporations profiting

from present conditions, to take one or more shares in the enterprise! Choose ye! Ye pays ye money, and ye takes ye choice."

Before the deadline arrived sixty-one stockholders had subscribed.

The promotion at Pendleton had stirred up friendly rivalry in the sheep towns, especially Heppner. While Judd, Fell and the Commercial Club were dickering, Heppner people had raised $5,000 for a scouring mill by the second week of January 1894, and Arlington on the Columbia River, was also in the mood for scouring wool, but the promotion was ineffective at both places.

By February, 1894 the foundation piers for the main building were in place. Theodore F. Howard's plans called for a two-story structure, 120 feet by 40 feet, with an adjoining sorting room and warehouses on nearby lots. Loading platforms were constructed around the main building. Corrugated iron was the roof covering.

Three Sargent woolwashers and a four-section dryer sixty feet long costing $5,000 were housed on the upper floor. Presses built by Give of San Francisco cost $2,700 delivered to Pendleton. Water for the boiler and the scouring vats came from the Umatilla River. When completed, the value of the property was estimated at $15,000.

On the morning of March 3, E.Y. Judd arrived from San Francisco to attend the stockholders' meeting held in Colonel J.H. Fraley's office. E.D. Boyd was elected chairman, T.E. Fell, secretary. The Board of Directors was E.Y. Judd, E.D. Boyd, H.

Shulthis, R. Alexander, T.E. Fell, C.S. Jackson, W.F. Matlock, W.D. Hansford, T.B. Wells. Judd was elected president; Boyd, vice-president; Shulthis, secretary-treasurer; Fell, general manager; Fred Judd, office manager. An engineer was hired, also two boss wool sorters, a wool grader, a boss scourer, a dry-room supervisor (W.P. Fell), a scoured wool press operator, and a grease wool operator.

As though to confirm his and the other stockholders' judgment, Judd cited San Francisco's six scouring mills and the employment of 200 men. Said he:

> Each year at least 30,000,000 pounds of wool come to San Francisco from California ranges alone, which would be shipped directly east were it not that it is all scoured in that city before consigned to eastern markets. From Nevada, Arizona, Washington and Oregon come fully one-half of the total clip, probably more than one-half of that from Oregon . . . This brings to the city buyers, sellers, large numbers of men interested in wool, and increases to a great extent its importance as a money center.

> You will see scores of woolgrowers coming into your city to bring their clips to the mill . . . Supplies must be purchased and the distribution of groceries, clothing and all the articles of general merchandise by your merchants among these sheep men will constitute an item which will be no means inconsiderable.

> I shall expect to see Pendleton the most important wool market in Oregon. The mill to be constructed will be as good as any now in operation in the United States. As the demand increases the capacity will be enlarged . . . The outlook is most flattering. I shall be able to report to my firm that the enterprise is well started and certain to succeed.

The town was in an excellent marketing position. The main line of the Oregon Railroad and Navigation Company passed through with a branch line north and into Idaho. The Washington and Columbia River Railroad (the Hunt Road) terminated here and ran to a junction with the Northern Pacific near Wallula, thence to Dayton 37 miles northeast of Walla Walla.

In March, 1894 Fell was on his way to Billings, Montana to superintend the removal of scouring-mill machinery to Pendleton. New machinery was also on its way from Boston.

Construction of the factory building was delayed when the corrugated sheet roofing did not arrive from St. Louis, but a temporary canvas roof sufficed until the sheets came. Machinery continued to be set in place by a Portland engineer, F.P. McLennon, owner of the largest San Francisco scouring mill, and Walter P. Fell, the manager's brother. The site was on a block extending from Emigrant Street to East Alta (now Dorian).

News of the new enterprise spread quickly throughout the Pacific Northwest, so that when Fell returned from Montana he found a stack of letters from Washington, Idaho and Oregon woolgrowers inquiring about scouring costs and the facilities of the new mill, and from those seeking employment.

By the end of April Judd was buying wool at Heppner and other supply points. The first shipment was 150 bags followed closely by 1,000 more. Everything was in readiness for the opening whistle on May 9, 1894 and for processing the 700,000 pounds of grease wool on hand. A payroll of $2,500 a month was created.

Daily scouring capacity was 15,000 pounds on a daytime shift; a night run would about double the output. The warehouse capacity was 1,000,000 to 1,500,000 pounds of wool.

Within a month twenty-five woolsorters and a night engineer were added. The scouring tubs were kept constantly full as the strings of freight wagons lined up at the unloading platforms to discharge their cumbersome three-ton loads of a dozen to fifteen sacks each. Speed, production, and tonnage seemed to be the order of the day. Workers in all departments caught the spirit of the occasion in a united effort to make the mill a success. Shearing pens were installed with steampower clipping shears.

By mid-July, over 2,000,000 pounds of wool had passed through the warehouse to the washers. The process required 1,500 pounds of soap daily. Some of this was made at the plant by mixing tallow and imported English soda ash. This homemade product was supplemented by purchases in Portland. Other items kept on hand were wool sacks which sold for 32 cents each, and fleece twine at eight cents a pound.

In October, Fell and F.E. Judd went to Tacoma to purchase a 60 horsepower engine and boiler. A new two-story warehouse was erected with a pullery in the basement. A siding from the O. R. & N. facilitated the delivery of grease wool and shipment of the scoured.

The *Oregonian*, always a booster for home industry, editorialized that the woolscouring Pendleton plant had been operating long enough to prove its usefulness to the Inland Empire. Wool growers were the immediate beneficiaries as they could either market their wool in the grease to the mill or have it custom scoured and choose their own market for the clean wool. Furthermore, a saving on freight was made. From 1000 pounds of grease wool 300 pounds of clean wool would result, leaving 700 pounds of extraneous matter on which freight would not be paid. These were rough estimates as shrinkage varied from 63% to 82% depending upon the growing area. For example, the dry ranges of southeastern Washington produced heavy scouring wools with a high percentage of dirt.

Pendleton was now established as an important primary wool market. Buyers from the flourishing Willamette Valley mills came regularly to Pendleton. These were Albany, Brownsville, Thos. Kay at Salem, Oregon City, and Waterloo.

Judd & Root, although heavily interested in the scouring mill, continued to buy grease wool for their own account and for their eastern customers charging three-fourths per cent on consignment shipments. For growers in need of cash, funds were advanced at six per cent interest. S. Koshland & Company of Boston, which maintained Pacific Coast branches, was one of the biggest customers. This company reshipped the scoured wool in large lots to the East and San Francisco. At one time it proposed to decorate with flying banners displaying the firm's name, a twenty-car wool train carrying 500,000 pounds of the product. Other firms operating in Pendleton in its heyday of new-found prosperity were Christy & Wise, Hendley & Gould, W.J. Furnish, Nichols, Dupee & Company of Boston, and Silberman & Company of Chicago.

Some of these eastern buyers preferred Oregon wool in the grease for combing and worsted yarns.

With seven months of successful operation behind it, the mill reported receipts of unscoured wool at 3,623,824 pounds of which 38% came by rail directly from the growers. The most important supply points for this movement were: Echo, 33 cars; Elgin, 28 cars; Heppner, 17 cars; Baker City, 14 cars; Touchet (Wash.), 13 cars, a total of 1,381,731 pounds of wool. Other contributing towns with rail connections were Arlington, Durkee, Nolin, Union, Walla Walla. In addition to the rail movement more than 900,500 pounds arrived on freight wagons and 600,000 pounds were collected from local warehouses.

Against the incoming tonnage more than 2,000,000 pounds of both grease and scoured wool were shipped out of which 630,000 pounds were scoured wool to the East. Baled, grease wool estimated at over 1,000,000 pounds also went to eastern buyers, and smaller amounts to San Francisco and Oregon woolen mills.

In twenty-eight weeks of operation $10,545 went for salaries. The average daily wage of employees was $2.25. Boys, used in the sorting room were paid 50 cents a day for the first two months of work. As the plant expanded, the working force was augmented to include several woolsorters and an expert scourer.

Early in January 1895, the City Council approved a sewer extension to Byer's tail race. March witnessed needed improvement to include new washer-self-feed presses from San Francisco to double the daily capacity to 40,000 pounds of scoured wool. A new boiler and engine room and two warehouses were completed, the latter built on stone foundations surmounted by an asbestos, fireproof framework overlaid by corrugated iron roofs. Freight elevators, Fairbanks, Morse scales and top lights added a modern note. Complete firefighting equipment included a firehose on each floor connected to the city water mains, and a private pump. Underwriters classed the plant as one of the best protected buildings of its kind in the state. With 150 feet of frontage on the railroad it was ready to handle the heavy seasonal tonnage of wool. Plans were made for a May party in the new warehouse.

After the winter shutdown, the woolbags again started piling up in the warehouse and 100 men were hired to keep the sacks moving through the building to the tubs, day and night. With July came the end of the buying season and 3,000,000 pounds in the warehouse.

Impressed with the vast amount of wool available, Fell was now advocating a woolen mill to be run in connection with the scouring plant. Scouring was at best a seasonal operation, whereas a woolen mill would be virtually a continuous operation except for an occasional stoppage for repairs and overhaul. It was estimated that $30,000 would cover the cost of a two-set mill to make blankets, flannels, and low grade hosiery. Also the woolen mill could use the scouring equipment during the latter's slack season for drying, dyeing and finishing. Off-grade wool could be used for Indian blankets, the Alaskan and local trade. The experienced scouring-mill employees would provide a labor force nucleus around which to build an organization for the planned factory. To prove their sincerity, Judd & Fell subscribed $7,500 after incorporation in July 1895.

The year 1896 was uneventful for the mill. The problem of freight rates was always an important item with growers, mills, and railroads. Both the Northern Pacific and the Union Pacific contested for the long haul on scoured wool from Pendleton to eastern points. Of special interest was the opening of Cascade Locks on the Columbia River about 40 miles west of The Dalles on November 5, 1896. These were built by the federal government to divert river traffic around the violent Cascades of the Columbia River. The effect was to facilitate tonnage moving toward Portland on river boats and tended to lower freight rates.

Farther upstream was another navigational obstruction, where the Columbia's volume plunged over a lava-lipped formation near The Dalles. Discussion at this time centered around the construction of a portage railroad to by-pass it by the Columbia Portage and Transportation Company. Later, in 1915 the federal government built the eight-mile long Celilo Canal to facilitate the sternwheel riverboat traffic from Lewiston, Idaho and way points to Portland.

Midsummer witnessed an unprecedented situation for Oregon woolgrowers. Not a bag of krinkly fiber moved and there were 20,000,000 pounds in the warehouses. The press reported no market, no prices, no buyers; business was at a standstill. From the collecting points along the railroads the story was the same, full warehouses and no wool moving. Growers were holding out for higher prices on the strength of William McKinley's election in 1896 on a protective tariff platform. Wool was selling at this time for four to six cents a pound.

After the winter idle period, the scouring mill began its 1897 season with wool pouring in from the ranches to augment that already in the warehouses.

Pendleton was now definitely established as a wool market where the most commonly noted names were Koshland & Company of Boston and Portland; L. Eiseman, Boston; Pierre Nutte, Roubaix, France; E.W. Brigham, Boston. The Furnish warehouse was a focal point for much of this trading most of which was done on a closed bid basis. Scoured baled wool sold for 65 cents a pound f.o.b. Pendleton.

A change in ownership occurred in January 1901 when the Judds purchased the holdings of C.B. Wade and T.E. Fell, thus becoming majority stockholders. E.Y. Judd succeeded Wade as president, and F.E. Judd became manager. Fifty individuals still held $3,000 of the preferred stock which guaranteed ten per cent dividends and they were averse to selling it. This stock never missed a dividend payment.

At the annual stockholders' meeting in April the number of directors was reduced from nine to five. Officers elected were E.Y. Judd, president and F.B. Clofton, secretary. Another stockholders' meeting was held on May 7, 1901 and a board of directors elected: E.Y. Judd, F.E. Judd, C.S. Jackson, R. Alexander, F.B. Clopton, followed by the election of officers which were E.Y. Judd, president; C.S. Jackson, vice president; F.E. Judd, treasurer; F.B. Clopton, secretary. This change in ownership did not affect mill operations and it ran full blast day and night.

The price of raw wool dropped from 14-1/2 to 9-1/2-10 cents per pound and scoured wool from 55 cents to 40 cents. Unsold wool at interior collecting points was estimated at 9,000,000 pounds which would be augmented by the current year's crop to make 25,000,000 to 30,000,000 pounds available. Buyers were in no hurry to purchase.

At this time about one-half the sheep in Umatilla County were owned by twelve men, each with 5,000 head or better. Charles Cunningham had a reported 155,000 head, the largest flock in the county. Twelve others were listed as owners of 2,500-4,600 head or more. Herders received a monthly wage of $30-$35 with board at $10.00.

One of the largest suppliers of raw wool was the Baldwin Sheep & Land Company of Hay Creek, which announced in May, 1901 it had stored 1,000,000 pounds of wool in the Shaniko, Oregon warehouse and it would put the entire lot on the market in June. This announcement may have caused wool prices to be quoted at 7-10-1/2 cents.

A large portion of the sales of Oregon wool were made under the auspices of the Eastern Oregon Woolgrowers' Association. Sealed bids were employed rather than open bidding as at an auction. Another organization was the Oregon Woolbuyers' Association. The weight of fleeces reported at their meetings averaged 8-1/2-9-1/2 pounds with some buck fleeces shearing as high as 27 pounds.

The scouring company came in for some criticism by the Oregon Fish Commission as to alleged pollution of the Umatilla River from scouring-mill wastes. The action was prompted by a proposed fish hatchery on McKay Creek three miles west of town. But after examination of the situation the verdict was that the refuse was not detrimental to fish life on account of the river's velocity.

Two situations developed, one unpleasant, the other a happy one. Thievery, which had been noted for several months came to light during the summer when one of the first employees of the scouring mill was caught sacking stolen wool in an accomplice's barn, and promptly punished.

A happier situation prevailed when the cherished desire of the employees to have a football team was answered wholeheartedly by the management which equipped them with green and orange striped stockings and sweaters.

The following years were the same as the previous ones with tonnage flowing into Pendleton in the usual amounts. One significant item was noted in the change of freight rates from $1.30 to $2.00 per hundredweight for grease wool, and from $1.50 to $2.28-1/2 for scoured wool to Boston.

The 1905 R.L. Polk & Company directory listed E.Y. Judd, President; F.E. Judd, treasurer and manager; F.B. Clopton, secretary. W.M. McDonals of Boston was superintendent; E.J. Burke, secretary in 1909.

The mill continued in operation for the next eight or nine years when it closed permanently.

Chapter XVIII

THE PENDLETON WOOLEN MILLS—
Early History

*"The blue and gold label becomes an
insignia of quality"*

THE Pendleton Woolen Mills was the natural out-
growth of the Pendleton Wool-Scouring and Packing
Company established in 1893. Almost from the plant's
inception Theron E. Fell, the manager, had talked
hopefully of a woolen mill to augment that operation.
The community had all the necessary production factors to attract and hold such a manufactory, namely
raw wool (Pendleton was a primary raw wool market), scoured wool, pure water from the Umatilla
River for washing, fulling, and dyeing, and a labor
force of forty or fifty men and boys who were or had
worked in the scouring mill and knew wool. Immediately available were certain assets of the physical
plant: the warehouse, the boiler, and the engine. An
unfavorable element was the high cost of fuel. That
the scouring mill was a seasonal operation from May
to November gave added impetus to the promotion.

There had been casual interest in a woolen factory
in the later 1880s, and again in 1890 when a James T.
Haswell arrived in Pendleton to select a site for such a
factory, but nothing more is heard of him or other
similar projects until 1895 when the above-titled company was incorporated.

While public sentiment was crystallizing, T.G. Hailey had drawn up the articles of incorporation for the Pendleton Woolen Mills with $20,000 capital stock divided into two hundred shares of $100 par value each. Incorporators were E.Y. Judd, S.P. Sturgis, E.D. Boyd, W.D. Hansford, T.C. Taylor, and T.E. Fell. The papers were filed with the Secretary of State on July 22, 1895. Supplementary articles were filed March 28, 1898 increasing the capital stock to $40,000.

By mid-July, plans were being shown publicly and bids from machinery manufacturers had been received. Stock subscription books were opened, and impetus given to the solicitation by the Judds' and Fell subscription of $7,500 leaving only $7,500 to be pledged by the public, a total of $15,000 which was the minimum amount needed to get the woolen mill under way. Unlike similar promotions, no bonus was required by the organizers, a point which was constantly emphasized by C.S. Jackson, editor of the *East Oregonian* who vigorously urged community support. But like similar canvasses the campaign lagged, so that by the middle of September only $4,700 had been contributed by 38 subscribers. Money-raising was always a difficult task when starting a new woolen mill, but especially so at this time when the country was just emerging from the panic conditions of the early 1890s. The public was nearly always an indifferent contributor to such subscription lists and the present money-raising efforts were no exception. The campaign was finally successfully closed on October 17, 1895 when R. Albee bought the last share.

Notice of the first stockholders' meeting to be held in the scouring-mill office on October 26 followed almost immediately. Directors elected were E.Y. Judd, F.E. Judd, E.D. Boyd, and T.E. Fell. These then moved to Clopton and Boyd's real estate and insurance office and elected the following officers: E.Y. Judd, president; E.D. Boyd, vice-president; F.E. Judd, secretary-treasurer. The selection of Mr. Fell as manager was made at a later meeting.

W.F. Matlock, who had already subscribed, offered to give a free site across the river near the foundry in North Pendleton and $2,500 if the company would locate there. Apparently, the proposed site was not acceptable for the woolen factory was constructed on property adjoining the scouring mill which was located on Emigrant Street to East Alta (Dorian). Mr. Fell left in a few days for the East to purchase machinery and to leave orders for the looms to be built according to specification.

Construction continued through the winter months, and by January 1896, the stone picker house was up, giving assurance that the plant would be completed before spring. By February, machinery was being installed. Weaving and finishing departments were on the first floor, while carding and spooling were on the double-floored second story. Cleaning and dyeing were allocated to the adjoining scouring-mill warehouse. The interior was coated with fireproof asbestos paint.

The early spring opening did not materialize. On September 7, 1896 fourteen months after incorporation, Pendleton papers carried the glad announcement that the woolen mill had started with twenty-five employees on the payroll, most of them brought from the outside. By the middle of October 1896, the first batch of blankets was delivered.

A week before Christmas, white and brightly colored blankets and Indian robes, as well as unwashed and scoured wool, spindles, and yarns were attractively exhibited in the company's display room on Main Street next to the post office. A placard read "From the sheep's back to your back." Pendleton people took a deep pride in this newest of the town's industries (a sentiment which continues to this day), and well they might, for it was financed and operated entirely by business men of the community.

Shortly after the advent of 1897, Fred E. Judd, Theron E. Fell, and Charles (Sam) Jackson, home industry advocate-editor of the *East Oregonian*, appeared on the streets wearing suits from the first cloth manufactured in the mill. So enthused were they over their $20.00 garments that a "Home Industry Suit Club" was proposed. Said the editor:[1]

> The suits are made from wool, grown on Umatilla county bred sheep in Umatilla county, scoured at the mills in Pendleton in Umatilla county, spun into yarn in Umatilla county, woven into cloth in Umatilla county, worn by Umatilla county business men, and they will be thrown finally into the rag heap in Umatilla county by these Umatilla county business men when they have passed the

(1) *East Oregonian*, January 16, 1897

useful stage and been replaced by more clothing made at the same mills. They are Umatilla county home industry products, and their completion marks an epoch in the industrial history of the county.

From the above it would appear that cassimeres and other suiting materials were the principal products; actually, these were of minor importance as it was Fell's idea to center attention on blankets and Indian robes which could be sold on the adjoining Umatilla and other Indian reservations.

Development of this market proceeded immediately. Total Indian population of the United States at this time (1897-98) was estimated about 263,000 with nearly half living in Indian Territory and Arizona.[2] The potential market extended from reservations in the Pacific Coast states to as far east as Wisconsin. Oregon's Indian population was slightly under 4,000; Washington's about 10,000; and California's approximately 12,500. The company took particular pains to weave the correct designs and color demanded by the Indians of the different tribes now living peaceful, sedentary lives as wards of the government.

Robes with colors acceptable to the Crows in the north were unsalable to the Navajos in the southwest. To meet this diversified demand and to assure accuracy in manufacture, a factory representative visited the various reservations throughout the west. A twelve-page beautifully illustrated brochure was printed addressed to Indian traders and other retailers, showing photographs of well-known Umatilla

---

(2) Statistical Abstract of the United States, 1898, House Document Volume 69, 55th Congress, 3rd Session, 1898-99

Indians wearing Pendleton robes, and excellent reproductions of three styles of these garments.

Brief evidence of this expanding trade is found with reference to the Navajos as that tribe relied more and more upon government aid as it gradually grew less dependent upon the ancient and traditional arts for livelihood: [3]

> Grown people, however, could not afford better things. Sometimes, the trader had ready-made trousers and shirts. He also had big straw hats the Mexicans wear, and *fine soft blankets* in brilliant Mexican designs, made by the *Pendleton Mills in Oregon* (italics ours). Women wore these blankets and do still.

Nor was the local and regional market comprising the three Pacific Northwest states overlooked. The Umatilla Reservation adjoined the Pendleton city limits, and not too far away were the Nez Perces in Idaho, sales to which tribe were made through Coffin Brothers who had stores at Lewiston and Lapwai. Another store, located at Yakima, Washington, supplied the Indians of that area. In March, 1897, this company placed an order for 1,000 blankets and estimated that 1,500 more would be needed to supply their customers.

As an example of the lucrativeness of this market, on one occasion in the above year, the Nez Perces received $200,000, divided so that every man, woman and child received $100, whereupon they proceeded to pay up their bills. Whatever cash remained was spent on purchases of blankets, robes, saddles and

(3) *Here Come the Navaho* (author's spelling), Ruth Underhill, United States Indian Service, page 223. No date.

harness. Some merchandise was bought on credit, but never more than what they knew was coming from the next payment.

In Pendleton, the robes had a certain circulatory value among the less disciplined Indians, especially the young bucks, who would steal the highly-colored blankets off the horses of the Indian women while the owners were shopping in the stores; they would then pawn the blankets and buy whiskey. The practice became so bad that it was unsafe to leave the horses unless someone remained to watch.

At the same time, the "paleface" market was not neglected. Orders came from Spokane, Walla Walla, The Dalles, Baker City, Boise, and Portland. Merchants in the latter city responded to the sales efforts of Ben B. Oppenheimer, a salesman for the company, and Mr. Fell, who as manager of the woolen mill also found time to be on the road. Wherever these men went they left samples of the various products of the mill. One of the heavier Portland purchasers was the leading Olds and King Department store. Exhibits of both the woolen and the scouring mills, respectively, were seen at the Portland Exposition in September, 1897.

As the Klondike goldrush fever mounted orders came from Fleischner, Mayer & Company, large Portland wholesale house whose main business was in the Pacific Northwest. Indicative of the size of these orders was one of twenty bales of blankets, twelve to the bale. Presumably to test the Alaska market, John Dodson, Mr. Fell's brother-in-law, was already on the

ground in that land of gold, mackinaws and blankets.[4]

National demand also had been aroused, evidenced
by the large number of letters received stating that
blankets were meeting with favorable reception along
the Atlantic seaboard. In addition, easterners were
ordering as gifts the increasingly popular steamer
rugs, slumber rugs, and couch throws which
indicated the utilitarian aspects of the Pendleton company's robes. Indian robes done in the individual
colors of the school, continued to be popular with
universities and colleges.

The company advertised in the local newspapers,
especially near holiday times. What to buy for Christmas? What could be more appropriate than a Pendleton Indian robe or a fine-textured blanket.

A studied effort was made to capitalize on the
romantic western Indian. This was comparatively
simple as living subjects were available on the Umatilla Reservation. Indian names were employed and
their customs briefly described but always with
appropriate reference to Pendleton designs and quality. A few excerpts will illustrate what was one of the
first concerted advertising efforts to use the western
theme:[5]

> This reservation (the Umatilla) is recognized not only as a
> social center, but as the emporium of Indian fashion.
> What a Paris hat is to a Chicago girl on Easter morning, a
> Pendleton robe is to the debutante of every reservation

---

(4) Later associated with Jantzen Knitting Mills
(5) Miscellaneous advertising material and scrapbook in the Pendleton, Ore-
     gon office.

Pendleton Woolen Mills, Pendleton, Oregon. Original building, 1909.

A Pendleton Indian Blanket.

from Arizona to the Dakotas. The Umatilla buck is a
fashion plate . . .

She (Mrs. Yellow Hawk) is a lady of judgment, she is
willing to pay a good price for a Pendleton robe, knowing
that it will be bright and serviceable long after the cheaper
grades have been thrown aside for saddle blankets . . .

Our pale-face trade is not unlike that with the red man.
We make robes in college colors; crimson and white,
orange and blank, crimson with navy blue, etc., each college town preparing its own colors.

According to the descriptions given on each color
plate, the robes weighed three to three-and-one-
quarter pounds each, were sixty inches wide and
varied in length from seventy to seventy-four inches.
For the Indian trade, a strong flannel double-stitched
with silk was used for bindings; for the white trade,
silk binding was preferred.

A bed blanket line, the best, measured six feet by
seven feet and weighed eight pounds. These were
packed in "cartoons" (sic) either in pairs or uncut,
and bound in singles; some housewives preferred
heavy, single blankets as they were easier to wash.
This all-wool product contrasted with blankets made
in other Oregon mills which used cotton warps. It
was this emphasis on quality which immediately distinguished Pendleton blankets from others.

Designs were woven on square looms running two
shuttles containing the colored yarns, thus in effect
making a double shuttle weave of contrasting colors
on each side. After being thoroughly fulled, it was
claimed no ordinary washing could shrink the robes
and blankets or affect the dyes.

Dealers were invited to send for sample bales containing from twenty-five to thirty robes. "If upon examination you do not find the shipment superior to anything you have had, and at prices which you can handle profitably, they may be returned at our expense for freight both ways, from any railroad point west of the Missouri River."

Coincidental with this early market expansion came changes in plant equipment. A carload of looms, cards, and other machinery arrived late in 1897, and a new 120 horsepower boiler to supplement the inadequate old one was added. New twin 250 horsepower Corliss engines, dynamos and pumps were placed in a recently-constructed boiler and powerhouse separate from the main building.

There is little to record at this point. W.J. Welch, formerly head weaver at Albany, and recently from San Jose, was added to the staff to become superintendent, succeeding R.F. Howard. He was succeeded by W.E. Richardson of Marysville, California, in April 1899. A fire in September, discovered in the dye house, did $3,000 damage to the main building and machinery, wool and finished products. The loss was fully covered by insurance carried with the firm of J.R. Dickson and Lee Moorhouse. About two months later, T.E. Fell's incompleted home was set on fire by an incendiary it was claimed, and suffered a $6,000 loss.

In July, 1901, the Jacquard loom was introduced and Joseph Rounsley, an Englishman, was selected to operate it. He had met George Fell, T.E.'s brother, while attending the Philadelphia Textile School, where both were learning about the new loom techniques. The young men came to Pendleton upon completion of the course whereupon Rounsley was assigned the job of adapting Indian designs to robes and blankets.

Early in 1901, the mill closed down while Mr. Fell was in Portland, which may have been the forerunner of the disclosure that George Fell, his brother, was to become manager in April upon his return from Philadelphia. At a stockholder's meeting held the same month, E.Y. Judd was elected president. These men together with C.S. Jackson were the Board of Directors. No mention is made of Mr. Fell, and it may be assumed this marked the termination of his able administration of both the scouring mill and the woolen mill.

With George Fell in charge of manufacturing, and Joseph Rounsley his assistant, the mill put on the market a new Scotch-plaid steamer rug weighing six pounds. The company moved its sample stock of blankets and robes from the Court Street warehouse to the mill. A small fire, which originated in the dryhouse from spontaneous combustion and caused $500 damage, was promptly extinguished by Mascot Hose Company No. 6.

During 1902 there was a studied effort at more effective advertising. Photographs of well-known Indians of the various tribes dressed in Pendleton robes were reproduced on 3-1/2-6 inch cards captioned with "Compliments of the Pendleton Woolen Mills"; also strip cards size 11-1/4-3-1/2 inches bearing the red Pendleton trademark with photographs of Indians and tepees.

Five form letters were used which carried small, marginal photographs of interior and outdoor scenes of the robe in use; such as an iron bedstead neatly covered by a Pendleton robe; a traveler in a deck chair aboard ship; and a group of college athletes with Pendleton robes draped over their broad shoulders.

Duplicates of these scenes appeared on 4 x 6 inch cards and an eight-page booklet suggested ways to use Pendleton robes. Persistence in producing quality products enabled the management to announce that sales since July 1, 1902 had amounted to more than they did for 1901.

There was only one departure from the firm policy of maintaining high quality merchandise bearing the name "Pendleton", and that was in a lower-priced line called "Umatilla". This line was marketed to accommodate customers who wanted a quality product but at a lower price than the standard "Pendleton" merchandise.

Three lines of shawls were being made by 1903, namely: heavy beaver, light plaids, and a napless shawl in fancy Roman stripes. Automobile rugs are mentioned as well as the usual couch covers, steamer rugs or robes, bathrobes and curtains, in literature distributed that year. Charles J. Ferguson was general manager.

Special attention was directed to the Pendleton red trademark, a circle enclosing an Indian woman sitting cross-legged weaving on a handloom. On each side of the large circle were two smaller ones framing a ram's head each surmounted with the inscription, "Pendleton Goods Are Fleece Wool". *The Delineator* for December 1903 carried an advertisement headed "Pendleton Fleece Wool Blankets Have the Warmth and Softness of Seal Fur" and quoting prices.

About this time it was learned that a party of eastern bankers was to stop off at Pendleton for twenty minutes. They were not only monied men but tourists eager to learn more about the great West through which they were traveling. Why not exhibit Pendleton robes, a true product of the West, at the station. A pile of 100 of these beautifully designed and highly colored garments immediately attracted attention and before train time there was scarcely a blanket left.

The year 1904 provided no news about the mill. Polk's Directory for Pendleton, 1905, lists Charles J. Ferguson as lessee and manager of the Pendleton Woolen Mills located on the west side of Mill Street, between East Alta and East Court (where the General Foods mill is now located). Page one was an advertisement of the usual products of the factory, but included smoking jackets and fancy outing jackets which were making the Pendleton name famous. Buyers were now requested to look for the Pendleton blue label, a distinctive merchandise mark, an adjuration found in the company's advertising today.

In March 1905 it was publicly announced that the company would add rug-weaving to their other lines, using a coarse grade of wool. This may have been an attempted counter move to forestall closing down on account of the high price of the finer wools used in the regular lines. The change was not successful and the mill discharged its weavers, carders, spinners and finishers.

Serious legal trouble marred the company's affairs when H.C. Judd and J. Root, partners in H.C. Judd & Root, proceeded in bankruptcy against the woolen mill in the District Court of the United States in September 1905. Claim was filed for $1,523.02 on account of a loan made by the creditors. Some un-revealed settlement must have been made for on Oc-tober 31, 1905 a motion to dismiss the bankruptcy petition was filed by the petitioners attorney, J.H. Raley, and the final order to dismiss was signed by Charles E. Wolverton, Judge, at Portland on December 6.[6] Somewhat earlier the Baker-Boyer Bank of Walla Walla had filed an attachment. With the conclusion of these legal difficulties the company con-tinued in business with Ferguson's lease still two years to run. Not until June 1908 is there again news of the factory.

In 1905, a Racine, Wisconsin company negotiated for the Pendleton plant, which might be construed as a strong inference that the mill was in trouble. This company proposed to increase the capacity of the factory three times and to employ 200 people, thus making it the largest woolen mill in the West. They would continue to make the high grade robes and blankets upon which the Pendleton company had made its reputation. But the property apparently did

---

(6) District Court of the United States, District of Oregon in the Matter of the Pendleton Woolen Mills, a corporation, bankrupt. District Court Case Case No. 3-966, File No. 749

not appeal to them for nothing more is heard of the proposition.

About the same time a rumor was abroad that the mill would be moved to Gordon Falls. This would link the names of Charles Coopey and Charles L. Peasley, who, in July 1908 planned a woolen mill town and a large factory at a site in the Columbia River gorge about twenty-eight miles east of Portland. The project never materialized.[7]

But the Pendleton Commercial Club, keenly aware of the importance to the community of the woolen mill payroll, did some promoting on its own by inviting J.P. Wilbur, superintendent of the highly successful Union Woolen Mill Company of Union, Oregon, to appraise the property in October 1908. From this the inference is drawn that the mill had been idle for several months following the expiration of Ferguson's lease in 1907. The Union mill had arbitrarily closed down in August of that year due to its owner's retirement, and it was correctly surmised that a reorganization of the Pendleton mill, if made at all, would require the background of an experienced woolen mill executive which Wilbur was. In December, 1908 he visited the idle factory, then used as a warehouse, and reported that it would cost $10,200 to put the property in good working condition: $6,000 value of the machinery, and $4,200 to repair the leaky roof and reconstruct the badly decayed foundation. The mill should be leased for a year and that lessee should have at least $25,000 working capital.

(7) Charles Coopey was a Portland tailor of English descent who was a vigorous advocate of home industries, especially woolen mills.

There were no immediate takers following this report and for historical purposes it marks the conclusion of the story of the woolen mill which grew out of the very successful scouring mill.

Chapter XIX

NEW OWNERS VITALIZE THE WOOLEN MILL[*]

"Emphasis was placed on the blue and gold label"

T.C. TAYLOR, one of the original incorporators of the first mill, was a very influential resident and merchant of Pendleton, Oregon. He was also a member of the Oregon Legislature where he served with his good friend C.P. Bishop of Salem. Taylor recognized the value of the industry to Pendleton. He also was aware of Clarence and Roy, sons of C.P. and Fannie Kay Bishop, who were graduates of the Philadelphia Textile School, with experience in eastern and southern mills in addition to their early training under their grandfather Thomas Kay.

Mr. Taylor approached Mr. C.P. Bishop with the idea that something could be worked out to open the Pendleton mill utilizing the knowledge of Clarence and Roy Bishop. Two months of negotiation with many discussions within the family circle resulted in an agreement. If the people of Pendleton would put up $30,000, the Bishop family would match it with an equal amount and undertake to bring the industry back to Pendleton on a successful basis. The $30,000

(*) Grateful acknowledgement is made to E.W. Haggerty, Controller, for his collaboration in writing this section of the company's history. His many year's association with the Pendleton organization has enabled him to contribute a vital and historically accurate account of the founding, personnel, and company policies.

from the community would be in the form of bonds to be repaid over a period of time (The last bond was paid in 1929). All was agreed and the funds subscribed. On February 16, 1909 the Pendleton Woolen Mills was incorporated under the ownership of the Bishop family. Mr. and Mrs. C.P. Bishop advanced the $30,000 as agreed.

Clarence and Roy Bishop eagerly accepted the challenge of the management of the new company. The machinery was stored in a Pendleton warehouse while plans were discussed for a new building suitable for woolen manufacturing. A three-story concrete building was erected at the corner of Southeast Court and 13th Streets on land purchased adjacent to the Union Pacific Railroad Company's tracks. Construction began on February 1, 1909.

Clarence told later of the extra strength cement mixture used in construction. Both Clarence and Roy worked right alongside the crew. They were aware of every step in the construction, which was characteristic of the management they brought to the Pendleton Woolen Mills both then and later. Automatic fire extinguishers protected the plant from the worst enemy of the early woolen mills, fire; the building is still in use over 60 years later.

1909 was a busy year. By September 1st, the building was ready, and both old and new machinery moved in, which news stirred the *East Oregonian* to announce, "that the wheels are now humming in the new Pendleton Woolen Mills", and ". . . that lot number one is in the cards". The name "Pendleton" had entered upon an illustrious career. It was an auspicious day for the woolen manufacturing industry in Oregon. Under the astute management and leadership of Clarence and Roy Bishop whose antecedents were firmly rooted in the pioneer period of woolen textile manufacturing, the Company was destined to become the outstanding enterprise of its kind in the United States. This relationship began with the pioneer industrialist Thomas Kay,[1] who came to the Brownsville Woolen Mill in 1863 from the woolen textile manufacturing center in Yorkshire, England. Thomas Kay's daughter, Fannie, married Charles P. Bishop who had been active in marketing Thomas Kay Woolen Mill products but who was better known as a pioneer merchant in Salem. Bishop's Clothing and Woolen Mills Store established in 1890 is still a successful menswear store in Salem.

Everything had to be developed from scratch. Clarence and Roy Bishop worked hard, kept long hours, and drew no regular salary but withdrew only what each required for living and necessary business expenses. As trained manufacturers they had to have a knowledge of the cost of wool, supplies and labor. Nor could the importance of an aggressive marketing program be minimized. They knew that the woolen goods they sold must be priced commensurate with the costs and also meet the special inherent demands of the market. This was especially true in regard to the manufacture of blankets for the Indian trade.

To create the designs for the Pendleton Indian blankets, Joe Rounsley, a Philadelphia Textile School

---

(1) Alfred L. Lomax, *Pioneer Woolen Mills in Oregon*, Portland, Binfords & Mort, 1941

graduate, was hired, and Jacquard looms installed. It has been stated that although Joe was difficult to direct at times, his product was pure art, conceived by actually living with the Indians.

Roy would take a sample line of Indian blankets to the Southwest to sell to Indian traders in the Navajo, Hopi and Zuni reservations. Clarence would take bed blankets and lounging robes made from Indian blankets to the Crescent in Spokane, Meier & Frank in Portland, and to the wholesale firms of Fleischner Mayer and Neustadter in Portland. Pendleton stores pridefully displayed the products of the reorganized mill: Alexanders Department Store, Livengoods, Bond Bros., the Boston Store, Hamley-McFatridge, Powers Harness Company, Wessels, and the Peoples Warehouse Company. It was announced at the time that no one particular dealer would have the exclusive representation in the distribution of the company's merchandise. Displays at county fairs also received attention. Emphasis was placed in all market promotions on the blue and gold label which appeared on every Pendleton product, a guarantee to every purchaser that only virgin wool was used in the manufacture of this quality merchandise. The company has never deviated from this ethical standard in their long and successful business existence. Volume in the first year was $65,000 which was produced at a break-even figure. This volume was to increase steadily through 1910 and 1911.

In 1912 the Union Woolen Mills which had been moved to Washougal, Washington from Union, Oregon, ceased operation. Clarence Bishop learned that a

Vancouver, Washington bank had foreclosed a mortgage on the Washougal mill and that it was interested in finding someone to take over the property. Clarence saw opportunity in its acquisition for product specialization in a location nearer to the market than the Pendleton site, but there was not unanimous agreement in the Bishop family. C.P. and Roy were opposed to the move, but Chauncey, the third brother who had continued with his father in the retail field, supported Clarence. With a loan of $4,000 from his mother, the Washougal mill was acquired by Clarence in August 1912. This, he felt, would dovetail with the Pendleton operation which took the inventory of raw wool and unfinished goods for processing while the Washougal mill was being renovated. The 60 feet by 120 feet three-story frame building was enlarged and the Washougal Woolen Mill was reopened with George Sault as superintendent, and 50 employees.

World War I broke out in 1914 and there was little opportunity for expansion, although orders for army blankets absorbed most of the Washougal production as was true also at Pendleton, except Pendleton retained its colorful Indian blanket trade and supplemented its production through Washougal. In the meantime, on December 24, 1915 the Washougal Woolen Mills was incorporated with Clarence, Chauncey and their father as incorporators. Roy continued to be disinterested in the Washougal operation.

Clarence Bishop had plans, anticipating the war's end, for greater product diversification. In addition to blankets the mill would produce virgin wool flannels.

There was also the famous Washougal Cassimere known throughout the clothing trade, patterned after the popular old-time cassimeres that had been a staple of the Oregon pioneer woolen mills and an ideal suiting and topcoating. Other lines were shawls and robes. Womens coating and suitings were also products of the Washougal mill.

In 1918 Roy Bishop was contacted by E.B. MacNaughton of Portland with a proposition to take over the defunct Multnomah Mohair Mills. Roy was interested and saw this as an opportunity to build something for his own family. He moved to Portland and transformed the Multnomah Mohair Mills into the Oregon Worsted Company, a very successful operation. The original combination of Clarence and Roy Bishop was thus divided for the first time, leaving Clarence with the full responsibility for Pendleton as well as Washougal.

Early in May 1918 as an adjunct to the Washougal Mill, Clarence Bishop had started an operation in Vancouver, Washington. The second floor of the Slocum Building located at 213 Main Street was rented. By the third week of July six persons were employed to operate one carding machine, two spinning mules, and three spoolers. The original plan had been to make woolen shirts and heavy woolen knit socks, but government demands for woolen goods during World War I diverted production exclusively into khaki and gray yarns for blankets on order at Washougal and Pendleton. When the war ended peace time production schedules were resumed. While the Pendleton mill had made bathrobes out of the heavy Indian blanket material, the Vancouver Woolen Mills, as it was called, was the very first step toward garment manufacturing. Woolen shirts had been a utilitarian garment made of solid color flannels in greys, blues and reds, but Clarence envisioned men's shirts of colorful flannel and plaids which the Washougal mill could weave very skillfully. The Vancouver Woolen Mills was the pilot plant with Mr. Weise the production man, Lou Steelhammer sales manager, and a Mr. Delbert as superintendent.

Following the war the opportunity was finally at hand to diversify product lines, to develop high quality virgin wool products and identify them with a name that would be known to the consumer. Other mills sold their fabrics to garment manufacturers whose names were carried on to the consumer with no identity given to the woolen mill. Pendleton had already established a reputation in its trade area for consistent high quality of blankets and related products, all of which carried the embryo Blue and Gold Pendleton label. Not related, but of interest, Pendleton was the first woolen mill to advertise nationally, which occurred before the Bishops took over the Pendleton Mill. This is covered earlier in the chapter which mentions the 1903 ads in the *"Delineator"*. If shirts and other garments could also be marketed under the label, it would add to the consumer impact. Thus the vision that started the Vancouver Woolen Mills was the same keen perception that was symbolic of Clarence Bishop's management philosophy.

World War I ended November 11, 1918. With the three plants operating at full capacity it soon became evident to Mr. Bishop that an organization had to be built with management responsibilities allocated to capable subordinates. At Washougal, George Sault was the capable superintendent of production. Elmer White managed the office and the records. At Pendleton, Walter Jackson was the office man and Clarence Bishop planned and managed production.

In 1919 an office was opened in Portland on the first floor of the Oregon Building at Fifth and Oak Streets, which served as a showroom and office. Both were badly needed with two mills to manage at Pendleton and Washougal, together with the small garment operation at Vancouver. Furthermore, Clarence foresaw the need to become established in a more central market place than either Pendleton or Washougal offered. This period after World War I was a building period with all of the burden and problems involved with growth.

Walter Jackson died in 1920. True to the Bishop family tradition, Chauncey who had been with his father in the Salem store, moved to Pendleton to lend support to Clarence. Ruth Gabrielson Bishop, his wife, had died in 1918 leaving two young sons to accompany their father to Pendleton, Robert who finished the fifth grade, and Charles Kay the first grade in that city after the move. Chauncey took an active part in the community in addition to his work at the mill. He was very active in the Round-Up Association and followed Roy Bishop as Director of Indians for the show.

Aerial view of Washougal Woolen Mills, 1973.

Pendleton Woolen Mills
Head Office

Foundation Mill

Columbia Wool
Scouring Mill

Pendleton Mill

Sellwood Men's
Garment
Factory

Milwaukie Men's Garment Factory

Portland Shipping Facility

Nebraska City Women's
Garment Factory

Omaha Women's
Garment Factory

Fremont Women's
Garment Factory

Composite—Pendleton Woolen Mills Plants, 1973.

In the period from the end of World War I to 1921, prices that had been inflated by the war suddenly fell and many fortunes were lost. This is mentioned primarily to show the vicissitudes endured by this young business and to indicate the strength of management that guided it on proper balance at all times for the present but with a foresight for the potentials of the future.

On September 20, 1922, in Dayton, Washington, Clarence Bishop married Harriet Broughton, daughter of C.J. Broughton, banker, merchant and landowner in that city. Previous to the marriage, Pendleton had been the base of operation with frequent trips to Portland and Washougal. From September 20, 1922, however, Portland was the residence of Clarence and his young wife, Harriet. They were among the first tenants of the then new Ambassador Apartments in Portland. The office in the Oregon Building became the headquarters for the management of the branching textile enterprise.

The source of the raw material was very important to the mills. Eastern buyers swarmed through the wool producing sections at shearing time, and if Pendleton did not provide sufficient wool for its own needs during this season, it was likely everything would be shipped to the wool market center of the country, Boston. To cover requirements at a later time of the year would have involved bringing the wool back with freight costs added both ways, plus a dealer's profit. On July 28, 1923, the Coast Mills Wool Company was incorporated, the capital stock of which was subscribed by the woolen mills under

Bishop. This served a dual purpose, namely (1) it divorced the purchasing function as related to raw wool and supplies from fabric production in the mill. It also improved their competitive position with the Boston wool buyers; (2) financing these purchases thus became a separate function with direct hypothecation with the banks to cover current seasonal production needs until the next shearing season.

Bank relations are very important to any business. The First National Bank of Pendleton and the American National Bank at Pendleton had cooperated in supplying funds when needed to cover inventory and receivables. Upon establishing the Portland base of operations, Clarence went to the First National Bank of Portland. Here he was assigned to Mr. Wilde, a vice president and loan officer. Mr. Wilde was a Scotsman and banker of the old school. He set rigid standards which, if followed, made funds available. Clarence Bishop always considered his training under Mr. Wilde the foundation of his banking relations. He felt the one person in whom to confide, and supply reports of the company's financial condition, whether good or bad, is the banker. He deplored the soft reaction of any loan officer. He much preferred criticism because it pointed the way to improved business standards. In retrospect Clarence Bishop himself had a banker's sense of financial balance.

The small operation at Vancouver had outgrown its quarters and the outlook for the plaid and patterned wool flannel shirt showed potential. In 1924 quarters were leased in a building at N.W. 9th Avenue and Flanders. This was a three story and basement

50'x100' building which served as garment factory, warehouse, and shipping center, and provided space for the growing office staff. The Vancouver garment operation was moved to the new quarters and an enlarged showroom provided for presenting the line. This was another forward step in the development of the company, but it involved both production and market risks as well as the assumption of an added lease expense.

Clarence Bishop actively participated in every phase of the business. One of these, and very important, was the purchase of wool direct from the wool growers for the Coast Mills Wool Company. He and Mrs. Bishop were on one of these wool buying trips when word came on March 23, 1924 of a bad fire at the Washougal Mill. They drove all that tense night to reach Washougal the next morning. It was a disheartening sight! It had been a spectacular fire that destroyed the preparation and finishing departments with a loss of $100,000. The fire had been discovered by a night watchman in a bale of smoking wool in the dryroom. When he tried to smother it, the mass literally exploded gutting the whole interior of the main factory building. The fire raged all around a water tank which stood in the center of the property, but was saved when three employees, part of a 12-man night crew, climbed to the top of the structure, and by using chemicals were successful in preserving the vital water supply. The loss was covered by insurance.

Fire causes a greater loss than just the destruction of a factory building. Involved also are temporary production and market losses. Such misfortune sometimes creates ideas for improvement. This was true when decision was made to rebuild the mill on a larger and more efficient basis by installing new machinery with increased productive capacity. To finance this program Clarence went to the Spokane and Eastern Trust Company which proposed floating a $100,000 bond issue. The proceeds of this added to the insurance would achieve the above objectives. Ring spindle frames and automatic looms were installed, allegedly the first woolen mill on the Pacific Coast to operate such equipment. By November the factory was back in operation.

A rather short-lived venture in 1925 was a part interest in the Eureka Woolen Mills of Eureka, California. This operation never worked out as planned.

In 1925, Clarence Morton Bishop, Jr. was born to Clarence and Harriet Bishop and in 1927 he was joined by a brother Broughton Hayward Bishop.

It became evident that the marketing function of the business must be developed to keep apace with the growing distribution of garments and blankets. Policies had been formulated and in this area the advice and experience of C.P. Bishop, the retailer, had been helpful. The Pendleton label would be aligned with the independent merchant exclusively, and would not serve the mail-order house, chain stores, or price cutters. The store must be financially responsible to meet the terms of sale. Pendleton would have only one price and one set of terms to all customers. large and small alike. To promote expanded distribution, Charles C. Wintermute was employed in 1926.

Wintermute had gained his experience under the guidance of Henry Wemme of the Willamette Tent and Awning Company (later to become Hirsch-Weis, and even later White Stag). Charlie claimed the distinction of developing the "tin pant" worn by loggers and outdoorsmen. The tin pant was waterproof and rugged with a canvas fabric and a treatment for waterproofing that would allow them to almost stand by themselves. Charlie took over the small sales force already assembled—George Bartels for the Washington territory, Herb Jacobs in San Francisco, Clyde Peterson covering the northern plains country and Montana, and Cliff Schonacker in Alaska. This was the nucleus from which distribution expanded.

January 15, 1927 Chauncey Bishop died from a hunting accident near Pendleton. Once again Clarence was left alone in the management of the growing business. Later in that year he employed Melvin D. Fell as Superintendent of the Pendleton Mill. Mr. Fell was an experienced wool buyer and in a way completed the circle begun by his father, Theron Fell, who had been involved in the management of the Pendleton Wool Scouring Plant and the original Pendleton Mill.

The garment manufacturing division could take only a small portion of the mill production, so it was the responsibility of Clarence to sell the remainder. This he did, to men's suit and topcoat manufacturers in the East who featured the Washougal cassimeres and flannels. Also, a good volume was developed on the Coast from the women's cloak and suit houses. Smelter houses had also found that filtering the fumes through woolen bags not only improved the environment, but also reclaimed enough product to justify the building of bag houses for that purpose. Washougal enjoyed a near monopoly of this business for many years.

With the growth of the company, modern cost accounting systems were installed at Pendleton and Washougal. To complement this program a graduate in Accounting from Oregon State, J.D. Buchanan, was employed in 1928. He is still active in the Pendleton Mill in the merchandising of blankets and Indian robes. Another addition to the accounting staff in 1929 was E.W. Haggerty, a graduate of accounting from the University of Oregon. Clarence Bishop was conscientiously fair in maintaining accurate cost of production results for the three factories producing merchandise sold under the Pendleton Blue and Gold label—Pendleton, Washougal and the Garment Division. This was among the first assignments to Mr. Haggerty who worked directly under Clarence Bishop. As his experience with the company developed, he assumed more responsibility, becoming involved in various facets of the wool department, office management and personnel, as well as working with Mr. Bishop in the field of company financing and expansion. He ultimately became Corporate Controller of Finances and in 1961 when the Management Committee of officers and directors of the company was formed, Mr. Haggerty was included in its membership.

The building at 9th and Flanders was beginning to be inadequate, so in 1930 arrangements were made to lease the Meier & Frank warehouse at 2nd and Jefferson. Built in 1903 it had served as warehouse, delivery depot and stable. It was a four story 100'x100' building with Pendleton taking the first three floors leasing the fourth to Goldstein & Company, a good customer which used Pendleton yardage in their manufacture of women's suits and coats.

The stock market had taken its first drastic drop in November 1929. It was Black Friday and the beginning of the great depression. There was still confidence though that it would be short lived, and Pendleton could continue to grow. Hence the move to larger quarters just described. However the confidence of the nation and its people continued to drift to a new low. Unemployment grew. Many people lost everything they had, including their jobs and homes. Even those with savings were reluctant to spend them for fear they would be needed. Stores had a hard time keeping solvent and purchases from Pendleton drifted down in the pattern of the times.

In the office no reduction was made in the staff until May 1931 when the situation seemed hopeless. A skeleton force was retained. Production had been curtailed for some time in the garment factory and mill. There was a bank note that had carried all through this period. It was a time conducive to hypertension. The depression was a period of frustration but even so, planning for a hopefully brighter future made it necessary to take advantage of opportunity when it presented itself, and it presented itself in 1932 when Clarence hired Ernest N. Brooke as superintendent and designer. Mr. Brooke was a trained English woolen mill man with a distinguished career in English, Canadian and American woolen mills, including the Oregon City Mill. His association with the Washougal Mill brought national and regional recognition of its production of fancy men's and women's fabrics. He is credited with bringing the Twist fabric to Washougal, a rugged woolen material of pleasant appearance and longer wear.

Several hundred pieces of men's suitings and top coatings had been shipped to an account in New York that was unable to pay for them. Clarence Bishop arranged for them to be shipped back. This was in 1932. Business was stagnant. Finally and reluctantly a decision was made contrary to anything Pendleton had ever done before, and with fear for the reaction of Pendleton's retail customers. The Portland office, garment factory, warehouse and shipping center must be closed to reduce expense and the inventory liquidated to provide working capital. What remained of the operation could be moved to space already owned at Washougal. This was a retrenchment, a partial surrender, a despairing answer to the nagging months of worry. Joseph Van Reet was the Portland garment factory superintendent. He had worked in the factory for Society Brand Men's Clothing. While Clarence was contemplating the closing of the garment factory at the end of the week, Van Reet came into his office. He explained he had and could get the pattern and asked permission to make up some suits and topcoats to demonstrate his ability. It seemed worth the risk. In March 1933, Pendleton opened a clearance sale to the public. Men's suits at $11.75, topcoats at $9.75, shirts, jackets and blankets at correspondingly low prices. The acceptance was terrific. Gold pieces and the old, large size bills came out of their hiding places to be traded for Pendleton merchandise. Coincidentally the bank moratorium was announced. Pendleton accepted checks that had to be held to the end of the moratorium to redeem, but very little loss was taken. The public sale was successful, and as if it were planned, public confidence generally was restored and orders began to come in from the retail customers. The need for the move to Washougal never materialized.

After Chauncey's untimely death in 1927 Clarence had been named in the will as Trustee of the estate. This brought him in as confidant and advisor to Chauncey's two boys, Robert, age 17 at the time, and Charles, age 13. He followed through with their education and in 1933 Robert, fresh from Harvard Graduate Business School, joined the company.

As the company worked out of the depression, it was a time for consolidating the position it had reached in 1929. The period was approached with caution, with no thought of taking on added risks. For a number of years Clarence Bishop watched a statement of realization upon liquidation as closely as the monthly financial statement. The depression left an indelible brand in the minds of all who suffered the experience. The next few years were recovery years and show the progress which was made from 1932, the low point of the depression. Using 1932 business volume as an index of 100, the record of Pendleton was as follows:

1932—100
1933—134
1934—159
1935—198
1936—231
1937—240

and in 1937 the business had reached the dollar sales volume it had enjoyed in 1929, eight years previously. But the capital investment had been preserved.

In August 1936 a young man came into the Portland office from South Dakota, which was suffering at the time from a severe drought. He was an accounting graduate, and the keen perception of Clarence Bishop foresaw potential. He added Earl C. Rogness to the staff to serve originally at Washougal, but later brought him into the Portland office where he has continued and has been a factor in management.

Clarence Bishop had been in close contact with the Los Angeles garment industry through the sale of yardage produced at Washougal. Pendleton had built a creditable business in men's wool shirts and had developed a line that included mackinaws, stag shirts, hunting jackets, lounging robes, waterproof golf jackets and knickers, and heavy 32 ounce Buckaroo pants. Men's wool pants were a good outlet for woolen fabric, but this was a separate field that Pendleton had never entered. A men's pant firm in Los Angeles, Pollok, Schultz & Boyd, became available, and Clarence after due consideration, felt this would be the natural entry into this market. Pendleton purchased Pollok, Schultz & Boyd in 1939, another step toward expansion, the first since the depression.

In 1939 Clarence Bishop, on behalf of his mother Fannie Kay Bishop, negotiated with Aaron Frank of Meier & Frank Company for the purchase of the 40,000 square foot building that had been leased since 1930. Real property was considered a contingent liability in these years that followed the great depression. So many examples of tax sales were still vividly in mind. Finally price was agreed upon. The building was purchased by Mrs. Bishop for $27,500, and Mr. Frank said he would throw in the unimproved quarter block adjoining. Pendleton purchased the building later from Mrs. Bishop's estate.

Charles K. Bishop had finished his education in 1939 and joined the company at Washougal. He had attended Culver Military Academy, University of Oregon and the Philadelphia Textile School, following in the footsteps of his uncles Clarence and Roy.

A modest advertising budget had been established in 1926 or 1927 consisting principally of a well prepared catalog in color to go out to Pendleton customers. The first advertising agency was Kirkpatrick & Company. The advertising expense was closely controlled and not until 1939 did the company enter into a serious advertising campaign. Expense continued to be controlled but modest ads were run in Life, Esquire, Outdoor Life, Field and Stream and Sports Afield, with a coupon cut-out to be returned requesting the names of dealers in the area. This evoked considerable interest, but World War II came along in 1942 to again suppress civilian merchandise at the expense of defense production of blankets, shirts and sleeping bags. At the end of the war in 1945 there were only 11 shirt patterns instead of the normal 50 to 60 numbers in the line, but the demand was so great that these had to be allocated to Pendleton customers on the basis of their prior volume.

In 1945 Mr. Brooke was in failing health. Clarence remembered a young man he had interviewed in Chicago with another position in mind. He wrote to James C. Aitchison and told him the Washougal Mill was in need of a superintendent and asked him to come out and look over the mill if he was interested. Aitchison was operating a 30-set mill at Mishiwaka, Indiana for the U. S. Rubber Company and was skeptical as to the prospects at a smaller mill in Washougal, Washington. He did come out, looked over the mill, made the acquaintaince of Pendleton products, but most of all was impressed with the earnest confidence of Clarence Bishop. He accepted the position and brought a new touch of textile professionalism to Washougal products insuring top quality to add to the Blue and Gold label. He has become production manager for all three woolen mills.

With the end of the war there was a great vacuum of civilian merchandise. Demand was much greater than production.

Pendleton needed to increase the output of its garment factory. To do this more equipment was required. There was none available because all garment factories were in the same position. Finally Robert Bishop located a garment factory for sale in Omaha, Nebraska by the estate of the former owner. An inventory was taken and a successful bid made for the equipment and supplies. This was in 1946. The intention was to move the equipment to Portland as soon as space was available, but in the meantime existing garment factory personnel in Omaha were utilized to manufacture garments from the Washougal fabric. The labor market was favorable in Omaha as were the tax climate and labor rates. The equipment was never moved to Portland, thus becoming the beginning of an operation in the Nebraska area that was to grow in the future.

Clarence Morton Bishop, Jr., son of Clarence M. and Harriet B. Bishop, had served in the United States Marines during World War II, participating in the Pacific Theater after prep school at Lincoln High School in Portland and Phillips Academy, Andover, Massachusetts. When the war was over he finished his education at Yale and returned to Portland in 1949 to join the staff of the Pendleton Woolen Mills.

By 1949 Pendleton volume had grown eightfold from the dismal year 1932. Confidence in the future was restored. New products were sought to add to Pendleton sales. Clarence and Robert Bishop working closely together, turned to womenswear. So far, with minor exceptions, all garment production had been in the menswear field. Frank King, who was familiar with retail womenswear, was employed to put together a womenswear line. A modest line of light-weight jackets and skirts formed the nucleus of the new products, a pilot effort to test the market. One jacket caught the fancy of the consumer and Pendleton named it the "49'er" for the year of its inception. It was a fortunate beginning because the famous

Pendleton "49'er" made from colorful Washougal flannel in plaids and patterns was a sell-out from 1949 until 1957, an unheard of record in womenswear where consumer tastes change by the season. Thus Pendleton became firmly entrenched in both menswear and womenswear.

The organization was saddened by Roy Bishop's death in 1950.

Broughton Hayward Bishop, second son of Clarence M. and Harriet B. Bishop, had also served his stint in the United States Marines after graduation from Phillips Academy, Andover, Massachusetts. He finished his education at Yale and Philadelphia Textile School, returning to Portland to join the Pendleton organization in 1951.

In 1951 the Korean war, although brief, added its problems with soaring wool prices. However, civilian business was not interrupted as it had been in the World War II period.

"Pendleton" no longer referred to just the mill at Pendleton, Oregon. It was an organization made up of the mill at Pendleton, garment factories in Portland and Omaha, and the headquarter office, warehouse and shipping center in Portland.

In 1953 an agreement was reached for the merger of the Washougal Woolen Mills into the Pendleton Woolen Mills by the stockholders of the two corporations.

This merger brought together a natural combination. Washougal had been producing the fabrics that Portland and Omaha manufactured into garments bearing the Pendleton label. The Blue and Gold label of Pendleton was demanding more and more of the Washougal capacity with less yardage available for sale to other garment manufacturers. Looking to the future it seemed likely that Pendleton would be taking all that Washougal could produce, except the smelter bags which continued to be a special product, exclusive to Washougal. Smelter bag production could be made without disruption of the yardage for the Pendleton label. The 40 to 50 looms of the '30s had been increased to 80 by 1952. New buildings had been added at Washougal for auxiliary departments of carding, spinning and mixing and even with this expansion in the 50's the volume of Pendleton sales was limited by the production capacity of Washougal. Pendleton sales in 1953 were 25% more than in 1952. 1954 increased another 20%.

Pendleton men's slacks had been moved from Los Angeles to Omaha at the end of 1950. But Omaha was becoming more important for the manufacture of womenswear. The production plan began to jell. Menswear would be manufactured in and shipped from Portland, and womenswear would be made in Omaha and shipped from there.

In 1954 negotiations were started to purchase the last manufacturing unit of the Oregon City Woolen Mills which was a garment factory concentrating principally in men's slacks. Arrangements were completed and the manufacture of men's slacks was moved from Omaha to the Oregon City plant. This was not adequate so in 1955 a lease was negotiated for the original manufacturing plant of the Oregon Saw Chain Company in Portland, which had moved

to a much larger facility. This completed the shifting
of production to accommodate the plan of segregation
between menswear and womenswear.

The dream of Disneyland was being put together in
1954 and 1955. Pendleton was approached to become
a tenant in Frontierland where a pioneer store could
exhibit Pendleton products in their entirety. Walt
Disney did not want a dead exhibit. He wanted a
store that would actually sell merchandise on display.
Many meetings were held which involved much
discussion and negotiation with Disneyland executives. Los Angeles was a good market for Pendleton
merchandise. What would the merchants of the area
think of Pendleton making retail sales in Disneyland?
And for that matter, what would be the reaction of
the Pendleton dealers in other parts of the country?
Finally an idea developed—why not send the
Pendleton dealer in the city or town from which the
purchaser came, a check for half of the profit margin
together with a letter of appreciation and the names
of the customers. This was adopted and was a real
success. In September, 1955 the store was opened
under the painted sign:

C.M. BISHOP, PROP.

Blankets	PENDLETON WOOLEN MILLS	Sportswear
Robes	Virgin Wool	Shirts
		Dry Goods

Since that time over one million people each year
have visited the store, seeing the full Pendleton line,
purchasing what they wanted, feeling the quality,
and many becoming acquainted with Pendleton for

the first time. In addition to the consumer impact, it provided excellent dealer relations which resulted from the monthly checks to dealers, which totalled almost a half million dollars by 1969. The store is still a popular exhibit.

Both mill and garment capacity were under pressure. Even though the garment factory in Portland had taken over the fourth floor which had previously been leased to Goldstein & Company, the 20,000 square feet of manufacturing space was inadequate. In 1956 the company purchased 8-1/3 acres along Johnson Creek in Milwaukie, and a 45,000 square foot garment plant was constructed for the manufacture of woolen shirts and light woolen jackets. In the same year the 80,000 square foot plant of the Foundation Worsted Mills on McLoughlin Boulevard was leased from the Oregon Worsted Company for the installation of a small woolen mill in Portland to augment the capacity of Washougal and Pendleton. And 60,000 square feet of space was leased in Omaha to permit expansion of the Omaha operation.

With all of the expansion in 1956, the next few years were devoted to consolidating the company's position. Increased sales brought increased profits, but required more funds to finance inventories and receivables, so the attentive management by Clarence Bishop could not be relaxed. It was true that the banks would now loan 25 times as much as the $400,000 that worried Clarence through the depression, but maintaining the proper relation between the various assets and liabilities still required his financial experience and the same principle of financial balance existed now as it did in the 1929-33 years.

In 1960 the Roy Bishop family withdrew from their partial ownership of the Pendleton Woolen Mills by the liquidation of their capital stock.

The 60's was a decade of continued growth. Facilities were inadequate for warehousing and shipping in both Portland and Omaha. In 1962 a 20 years lease with an option to buy in 10 years was negotiated for a new 50,000 square foot shipping facility to be constructed at Milwaukie according to specifications to feature efficiency in handling, while in Omaha additional floors were added to the original four floors leased. In 1963 an existing garment factory was purchased in Nebraska City to augment required production of womens wear. Garments produced in this plant would be trucked to Omaha for warehousing and shipping. Growing space requirements in the Nebraska womenswear operation led to the purchase in 1964 of the 8 floor and basement building that was originally leased in 1956. This provided 144,000 square feet of space. It should be kept in mind that all fabric for the Nebraska garment operations was shipped from Washougal.

Keeping a careful balance between yardage production, garment production and customer orders required enlarged and more efficient weaving facilities at Washougal. A new humidity controlled weave room with space for yarn storage and pre-loom preparatory operations containing 60,000 square feet to permit more efficient operation of the 120 looms was constructed in 1965. In 1968 another womenswear garment plant was located in Fremont, Nebraska. Nebraska City and Fremont are 40 and 50 miles from Omaha respectively.

Clarence Bishop died July 11, 1969, sixty years after he and Roy took over the Pendleton Woolen Mills. At the time of his death, the company was building a 42,000 square foot addition adjoining the existing shipping facility under lease. The plans for this building in Milwaukie were unique in providing for three levels of storage. Two were added at the time, and another 42,000 square feet was available for expansion when needed. In effect, this building provided 126,000 square feet of warehousing space.

Those who knew Clarence Bishop considered him a very conservative man. How could the willingness to take the steps of added risk and responsibility be explained? Anyone who knew him well could answer this. His ability for deep concentration and thought had worked out the plan of operation in detail. The Pendleton Woolen Mills stand today in tribute to his tireless efforts in the management and guidance of this nationally renowned business.

It is interesting to look back on the steps of progress:

1909—Established the Pendleton Woolen Mills

1912—Took over the Washougal Woolen Mills

1918—Started the Vancouver garment factory

1923—Incorporated the Coast Mills Wool Company later named the Columbia Wool Scouring Mills

1924—Moved the Vancouver operation to larger quarters in Portland

1930—Moved to the present Portland location for additional space

1923-33—Endured the great depression

1939—Purchased a men's slack factory in Los Angeles

1946—Expanded into the Nebraska area

1949—Developed a line of womenswear

1953—Merged the Pendleton and Washougal corporations

1955—Purchased the Oregon City garment factory

1955—Opened the store in Disneyland

1956—Built the Milwaukie, Oregon garment factory

1956—Moved the Oregon City garment factory to Sellwood

1956—Leased larger quarters in Omaha

1956—Started the woolen mill in Portland (Foundation mill)

1960—Took over the Roy Bishop interest

1962—Established a new Portland shipping facility

1963—Purchased a garment factory in Nebraska City

1964—Purchased the building in Omaha

1965—Built a new building in Washougal for weaving and yarn processing

1968—Started a new garment factory in Fremont, Nebraska

1969—Built an addition to the Portland shipping facility

A stimulating record, not to mention such related facets as serving 5500 retail outlets with an organization that covers the entire United States. This translates into millions of items of apparel worn by consumers all over America with confidence in the Blue and Gold Pendleton label.

This story intends to give credit to Clarence Bishop who was one of the founders, and the guiding head of the Company during his lifetime. His policies, formulated years earlier, were followed by all involved with the success of Pendleton Woolen Mills. The Company itself and its history are tributes to Clarence Morton Bishop.